*

NOTHING IS QUITE ENOUGH

*

Other Books by Gary MacEoin:

CERVANTES

THE COMMUNIST WAR ON RELIGION

Gary MacEoin

Nothing Is Quite Enough

Henry Holt and Company
NEW YORK

First Edition

Library of Congress Catalog Card Number: 53-5268

Printed in the United States of America

* * *

Contents

NOTHING IS QUITE ENOUGH

*

CHAPTER 1

The Great Sacrifice

I don't suppose you were ever down in French Guiana. Don't think you missed much, at that. It's not the hell they say it was when the *bagnes* were sardined with convicts, but it's still the last place I know to pick for the comforts of life.

I write these lines in French Guiana. Yesterday I took my life in my hands and ventured a few miles in a jeep into the hills near Cayenne. My host runs the place and he swells with pride as he talks about the new look his countrymen and he are about to give their penal colony. Far be it from me to offend him by yawning at the unfinished water supply, still farther to observe that everything that is not worn out, as well as many of the things that are, is unfinished.

A truckload of workers careering downward nearly pushed us off the rutted dirt track into the ravine. Only a little remnant of a man aged about sixty, bareheaded under the equatorial sun, barefooted, in tattered shirt and dirty ragged khaki shorts, remained. Pleased as a pup with a bone, he dashed hither and thither to see we overlooked none of his exhibits.

"Funny little fellow," my French-speaking host said to me as we followed him along a narrow jungle path to the lakes higher in the hills that fed the waterworks. "I can't place his accent."

"What I thought strangest," I said, "is to find a white man in a place and a job like this. That you don't find anywhere I've been in the West Indies. You didn't ask him where he's from?"

"Not likely," he shot back. "They come here from Devil's Island, not Ellis Island; and they keep their own secrets."

"Let me try," I said. "I shan't ask him. But I'll let him talk."

And he did. We began in French but soon with more realism than flattery he shifted to English.

"You know London?" The question marked a change from the previous conventional remarks, a change no less in tone than in subject.

I admitted I had been there.

"There is a Liverpool Street and in Liverpool Street the Waterloo Station."

"I know it," I said.

"My sister lives across the road." He looked at me with a little gleam in his eyes. It was a tenuous thread but it was a thread, a bond, at least a contact. I knew Waterloo Station in London and his sister lived in Liverpool Street. Now I could ask guarded questions and perhaps get behind the barrier.

"But you don't come from England?"

He did not seem to hear my question. He walked along swinging the short stick he carried to clear the path. He kept looking straight ahead. Then he spoke.

"No," he said deliberately, "I don't come from England. I was born at Yalta, in the spring. In the Crimea it is always spring. I was a soldier, an officer of the Tsar, then an exile—in Scandinavia, in Belgium, in France, in the United States, six years in the United States.

"But I tired of the subway and the time clock. I was a soldier. I wanted to fight. I joined the French Foreign Legion."

His voice trailed off as he made a swing with the stick at a cluster of vines blocking the path. Here the forest was not too tall nor was the head foliage dense, and consequently at the lower levels the growth was riotously disordered. Countless parasitic plants, some so tiny that they looked like little blotches of discolorment on the tree trunks, others bloated and stretched out so that their individual leaves were taller than a man, fought for living space around the bases of the trees, on the ground, on the tumbled rocks, on the trunks and branches and even on the leaves of the trees.

There was something frightening in the silent violence of this struggle to survive. The confusion of trees was no less than that of their parasites. There were acacias with foliage like yellow fans and others with foliage like green ostrich feathers. There were palms of every shape and arrangement; trees with small, round, shiny leaves, trees with long, thin, apple-green leaves, and trees with silvery-blue, furry leaves. Everywhere we had to push our way through vines, disclosing as we advanced great natural baskets of orchids. Enormous butterflies came flapping down the arched tunnel of green filagree, their iridescent blue wings flickering like fireworks. Green parrots with flaming chests and yellow-streaked backs shrieked overhead.

We went on for a bit in silence, always climbing. My guide made a couple of vicious swings at some clumps of *balisiers* and tanias, then gestured with his hands to indicate a resumption of the interrupted conversation.

"You know how it is—a quick temper." His forefinger closed on an imaginary trigger. His eyes smiled mournfully at the memory of a thing long gone. "They gave me ten years."

He gestured again to suggest that was that. So it seemed to me, too. There wasn't much more one could say. We watched the sun sink in the northwest. Shrieking and chattering monkeys swung from hundred-foot-long bush ropes overhead. The rays of light glinted gorgeously on the plumage of parrots flying from the darkness of the forest to the opening whose edge we had reached. A tiger cat growled far away. The Russian's half-grown pet wolf played with our pants and let us feel his razor-edged teeth.

Bak-jak ants were at work. Each carried a green parasol over his head, dashing along to add his quota to the fermenting pile of vegetation on which they grow the fungus that feeds their young.

The sun was still broiling and vapor rose sickeningly from the undergrowth. But those feverish ants induced in me a sudden mental chill. All of us were bak-jaks, our ex-convict barefoot guide, officer of the Imperial Army, who clung to life by deluding himself he would one of these days join his sister across the road from Waterloo Station; my host who eked out the worthless francs he earned as a

French functionary by obscure and petty transactions with American dollars; his wife who ate out her heart for Paris the while she struggled to translate the captions of six-month-old copies of *Life*; myself . . .

Myself. Down here I was the lucky one. I had no daily struggle with convict servants who had nothing to lose because they had nothing to gain. I did not have to look forward to a staple diet of bananas and ray fish. It worried me little that the ice factory broke down three days a week or that the decrepit electric plant seldom gave light from dusk to nine-thirty as it was supposed to do.

I had a return booking for Tuesday morning on the Catalina. That creaking seaplane was a form of suicide. But who wouldn't take the risk to get out of Cayenne?

"You are preoccupied," my host said to me later as we sipped his magnificient Chartreuse (for even Cayenne has compensations for being French) while his wife went to get a kerosene lamp to replace the electric light that had again given up.

"Yes," I said, picking up a candle to light me to my bedroom. "I am thinking of that man out there alone on the mountain, and the bak-jaks, and . . . ourselves."

Still preoccupied I dropped off to sleep. And I dreamt troubled dreams through which as a leitmotiv ran a curious noise. It crashed and thundered in my ears. At last it wakened me.

The night was supremely silent. As I lay sweltering in a century-old fourposter bed, I could see the century-old palm trees silhouetted against the moon. But that internal noise must have some basis. I went to the window. Not even a couple of lovers in the square and not a sound in the ghost town beyond. A century ago it must have been one of the finest cities in South America, I thought. Ghosts and moonlight mix well.

But Cayenne is no place to sentimentalize in the moonlight. Mosquitoes mean not only malaria but filariasis. And the room was buzzing with them. I hastily withdrew under my net and set myself to identify this noise I could not get out of my mind.

It was familiar, very familiar. That I knew. But where had I heard it? It was not the rat-tat-tat of machine guns that made us as children born to guerrilla warfare dive under school desks by day and under beds at night. Not regular enough for the creaking of the blades of the old autogiro in which once I risked my life for six mad weeks as a press photographer. Or was it that blood-chilling crash one dawn on the old *Maaskerk* in mid-Atlantic that could be nothing but a torpedo—but turned out a broken crankshaft? It was like that, but not just it. It wasn't an isolated crash but an erratic series, connected yet without formal pattern.

Irritated, I gave it up and tried to doze. But the sound image would no more leave me alone than would the mosquito who was determined to sup on my fresh red blood. I cursed myself for lack of foresight in traveling without a DDT bomb. Not so much as a Flitgun in this place.

Then I forgot the mosquito. For I had placed the noise. Yes, that was it, no doubt in the world. Come to think of it even the room was similar.

What was it Davy had said when he showed me to it the first night, more than twenty years and four thousand miles away?

"Everything you'll need for the next twelve months," he said, "a bed, a washbasin and ewer, a table, a chair, a kneeling stool, hooks behind that curtain to hang your clothes, a shelf for your linen."

Then he walked over and shut the window. "Better try to sleep with it closed the first few nights," he said, "until you get used to the trains."

"The trains?"

"Yes," he said with a casualness I often afterward thought a trifle overdone. "On the other side of the garden wall is a marshaling yard where they assemble freight trains during the night. But you'll get used to it. After a few nights you wouldn't sleep without."

My mood is at last explained. That barefoot life approaching its inglorious night out there on the hillside has set me thinking of my own morning and its unfulfilled promise. Reverberating across thousands of miles and twenty-odd years, the crash of freight cars being loose-shunted through the night had come to form a single picture in my imagination and a single impression in my memory with the barefoot Imperial guide and the fungus-feeding bak-jaks and the drunken doctor who tomorrow was heading upstream to map the jungles of the Inini. Now I could visualize each detail, the loco's sharp whistle blast, four or five businesslike puffs to start the wagon to its appropriate siding, a moment's silence, a crash as it joined its fellows and the yardman flung its coupling over the hook before it could recoil, and the final querulous series of protesting bumps and rattles as the shunted cars settled again to dream.

It was the beginning of my life, was that sound, not of physical life but of manhood. When I first heard it, I was lying on a straw paillasse in a room as bare as this and free of comforts, in a small Irish town. An unpolished wooden floor, a table with a dozen books, one chair, a washstand, a clothesrack covered with a curtain. That was all, and even that was not mine, for I owned nothing. Yet nothing was quite enough. I was happy lying on that straw paillasse listening to the crash of the freight cars in the marshaling yards just beyond my uncurtained window, a crashing that went on all night and every night as the freight trains assembled to go north and south and west on the morrow. Even the noise itself, speaking as it did of organized purposeful activity, added to my general sense of well-being.

True I didn't approve of it without limitation, but that was mainly because the banging of those wagons all night ate seriously into the seven too-short hours set apart for sleep in a life that was regulated to the minute and the second from month-end to month-end. Perhaps, too, I felt there was something offensive, even indecent, about a noise so blatant during the Great Silence, as the period was called from nine-thirty at night to breakfast at eight next day. It was not just silence, for silence was perpetual save one hour after lunch and another after supper. It had a special solemnity, no word to be breathed unless for an overwhelmingly urgent necessity.

Before dawn on a July morning in 1927 I had left my home on the all-day rail journey whose end was the novice house of an extremely strict religious order. My mother, who wept easily, shed copious tears at the happy development of her life's ambition.

"You can always count on a welcome if you decide to come back," whispered my father, out of earshot of my mother who would have thought so human a sentiment a temptation and a weakness at this point. Under an unruffled exterior my father hid much emotion.

I knew a little about the life I was approaching. The previous five years I had spent at a boarding school conducted by the same monks and consequently had seen them in action at close quarters.

Some weeks earlier, too, I had visited the novice house and talked for a couple of hours with four or five of my schoolfellows now nearing the end of their trial year. They had not changed much, or had they? It was not easy to decide. Certainly they seemed quite proud of themselves. But the gaiety was subdued. And was there something sinister about their lack of enthusiasm when I told them about the latest rag (for we were in the ragtime era) and did not even respond to my assurance that there was no suspicion of impropriety about "Show Me the Way to Go Home." It was not possible that noviceship and such essential human activities as rags did not mix. Or was it?

"But how do you keep silent all the time," I asked. They had been explaining to me that, apart from two afternoons a week when they went walking in the country for a couple of hours, the only time they might talk was an hour after lunch and an hour after dinner each day, while on Fridays there was no break at all.

"It's nothing," somebody said. "Often it's harder to make conversation. The Novice Master is with you nearly all the time and sees to it there is no frivolity or the like. You're glad when it's Friday and you don't have to make the effort."

That was rather disconcerting, but there was no way of carrying it further. If only I could have a chat with Davy or Tom or Ed separately. But I was to learn in due course that was one of the things completely out of the question. If not your thoughts themselves, all expression of them was henceforth to be in common. Private conversation was out. There must be at least three people in every discussion. A fell blow, indeed, which quickly drove one back into the recesses of one's own soul. But I am anticipating.

"One good thing about it," said Tom who felt a change of subject was in order, "is that you won't have to worry about examinations while you're here."

"Nothing wrong with that," I agreed. "But you must do some studying to pass the time, don't you?"

"Absolutely none," said Tom triumphantly. Lessons were not his strength. "You get a copy of the Bible, a copy of the Rule of the Order, the *Imitation of Christ*, the life of a saint, and a book on the spiritual life. They will keep you going for a long time. And when you finish the saint's life, there are lots of other saints I'll engage you never heard of."

"Besides," added Ed, "You won't suffer from time on your hands. Come and look at the timetable."

As they opened the door of the recreation room a solemnity seemed to fall on them. Even then I wondered at the sudden change. Was the manner something that went on and off like a dress? How deep was the real impression? It was a question I was often to ask myself later about myself and my companions. I asked it but did not answer it. Even today I don't fully know.

Outside the recreation room, as I was later to learn, one never spoke at all within the house. But Dave must have felt there was a limit to what could be crammed into one lesson, so he took a chance with his soul and explained the timetable in his lowest whisper.

"It starts at five-twenty-five as you see," he said. "Ten or twelve minutes get you washed, shaved, and dressed, and you are down to the chapel for private devotions till six, when meditation in common starts for half an hour. Then you have chanting of Office for half an hour, followed by Mass and then spiritual reading till eight."

"I'm beginning to get hungry," I cut in.

"That's all right," he said. "Breakfast comes at eight, but on Fridays, when you have a full day's retreat or silence, it's half an hour later. But breakfast doesn't take long. You get through the coffee and rolls in a few minutes, make your bed, sweep your room, empty the slops, and dust around, and you have ten or fifteen minutes in the garden before the next exercise.

"But there's no point going through the whole of it," he interrupted. "You'll learn it soon enough. What I have shown you will satisfy you there won't be much time on your hands."

And in due course I found out from the best of teachers that in fact there was not a moment on my hands from the first boom of the bell which shot you blear-eyed with sleep from your bed at five-twenty-five A.M. to the welcome clang which at ten-thirty P.M. announced lights out and blessed rest.

It was a hard, austere life. But young people don't have much trouble in getting used to any routine. It is little hardship for them to clean their shoes and scrub their bare wooden floors. They have no stomach ulcers and thrive on plain monotonous fare. And if they have an ideal they can take whatever comes and love it.

But the silence did not come easy. It was not a joke to walk about the garden after breakfast, hands tucked in the ample sleeves of your all-covering gown, and try to think of nothing in particular (for this was a time for relaxation) yet resist the opportunity of a word to your pals wandering about aimlessly like yourself with downcast eyes.

And when at eleven-thirty we put on wooden shoes and tucked the skirt of our gowns under our belts to spend half an hour with spade and fork in the garden, how could I but think of the joyous days I used to spend forking the hay or binding the oat sheaves or even digging the bright potatoes laboriously out of the black peaty soil? How hard it was not to share my exaltation with another who was surely thinking the same thoughts by my side?

But there it was. Silence was the keynote of the system, and only an overwhelmingly urgent necessity authorized even the exchange of a single word. Somehow nobody ever questioned this or any of the rules. They existed and one kept them. Young people are logical. We were there of our own free will for a certain purpose. If we didn't like it, we could clear out any day. What that purpose was we took for granted rather than defined. Yet we knew it well enough and were not ashamed of it. It was to find God by detaching ourselves from the world. That was the end, these the means.

I can tell you man clings hard to the world. He is a creature of much ingenuity and has a most uncanny collection of secondary reactions and evasive measures. One got rid of the big attachments. But the small ones automatically not only took their place but assumed their proportions, just as a gas occupies the whole of the space in which it is confined. Wisely the philosopher said that nature abhors a vacuum.

Inspirer and director of every activity, the Novice Master was a thin, gray, ascetic man of sixty. His was the triumph of mind over matter. Though lightly built, he did not look the wiry, athletic type full of energy and physical enthusiasm, but rather a man never keen on exercise, always a victim of a difficult liver. Overcoming such handicaps, he had learned to control his body's slightest movement. His impulses were inhumanly in hand. Undoubtedly he was a spiritual man, but rather than the warm, generous spirituality of Saint Francis it was a cold intellectual version which came near postulating that everything human was wicked and to be suppressed. Still, he compelled admiration even if he rejected love. His stomach was as bad as his sallow face indicated, and dangerous attacks often imposed hospitalization. Yet the morning after return from hospital, he would drag himself by sheer will power from his bed at five-twenty-five and be in his place on the corridor to give the signal to march us to morning prayers. And at the three daily meals he picked at the same frugal fare as the rest of us, eating barely enough to maintain life. On this he placed great reliance, feeling no doubt that high-spirited youth was best curbed by self-inflicted punishment, self-inflicted with a strong dose of example and encouragement from him.

"Mortification, penance, self-punishment are but means to an end," he would say. "But under guidance they are very valuable means." And he supplied the guidance. He had an unholy range of ingenuity from the direct methods associated with the Fathers of the Desert (who could take as much as a fakir) to the subtlest mental stings.

The physical variety assumed many forms, though the precise forms were unimportant once one accepted the principle of the thing. Each new type was terrifying in prospect but sillily simple in application. Twice weekly came a ten-minute communal self-scourging before bed. Assembled in a long corridor spaced at arm's length and in total darkness, we recited introductory prayers while unrobing sufficiently to apply a many-tailed whip to the bare flesh, a performance carried out in unison to a rhythmic movement accompanied by the chanting of psalms in a monotone. It was a calm, detached, impersonal operation. It should have caused considerable pain, for one got the rhythm and did not pull one's punches. Yet the pain was scarce noticed. The effect was more subtle, a firming of the soul and the forming of a bond of fellowship as through a companionship in secret rites.

Then there were the individual performances, governed by one inflexible rule. The Master's permission had to be secured for each act of self-denial or self-punishment. It was a sensible rule, forestalling the hasty excesses of enthusiastic inexperience and removing a fertile motive for spiritual pride. For youth is quick to pride itself on its physical achievements, and to look on the difference between yesterday in the world and today in the monastery made it almost unnecessary to call in the devil. Human nature was waiting to bestow on itself the credit for overcoming itself. But within this rule the Master was slow to restrain, and quick to spur the reluctant. His first mechanism was our nightly game of chance, the only game of chance and indeed only game we played. Toward the end of recreation his little red flannel bag appeared. Each numbered counter in the bag corresponded to a penance inscribed on a card. The choices were many, and all choice. There were scourgings in the privacy of one's room. There were ingenious little instruments made up of wire spikes forming a belt about two inches wide and long enough to go round the forearm, upper leg, or waist. The appropriate one was clipped in position when one got up at five-thirty and worn to breakfast at eight-thirty or occasionally to eleven or even to lunch at one-thirty. The spikes were sharp and every movement sank a dozen or two into the shrinking flesh. To bump into a door while wearing the round-the-waist version was a long-remembered experience. But one quickly acquired facility in avoiding every movement that hurt, the flesh built up a resistance, and terror disappeared with novelty.

It was supposed to be a game of chance but it was played with loaded dice. We often examined those counters and could find nothing to distinguish one from another by the feel. Yet the Master would put in his long sensitive fingers and turn to Bob who was shy and quick to blush. "I've got the very one for you, No. 6," he would say. And out would come No. 6 which combined physical pain with far sharper indignity. Next day, as we walked in solemn silence into the dining room for lunch, Bob would be kneeling at the door on his hands. The combination of discomfort and indignity is appreciated only by experience. It is easy to try, palms upward. Another little game calculated to dispose of the last shreds of human respect was to eat one's meal seated on the floor, plate on lap, depending for what one got on the memory and attention of the person at the end of the table; for it was an inflexible rule never to ask for anything. What was not within reach stayed where it was until somebody realized you wanted it.

Then there were various limitations on variety and quantity of food which at best was moderate in quantity and monotonous in preparation, though always of wholesome quality. One did without salt or butter or took only two slices of bread or two potatoes, easy exercises in self-restraint for the dyspeptic or the middle-age spreader but a challenge to the willpower of red-blooded youth. Here again the Master overpowered by example. As with every other act, he ate because he thought it the proper thing to do. There seemed no question of pleasure or displeasure, just a cold dispassionate calculation that so many calories achieved a precise result.

So we lived a cloistered life, cut off from the outside world, from the professed members of the community whom we joined at meals and at certain prayers yet never spoke to except for half an hour on some festive occasion perhaps once a month, even from each other. Every moment of the day had its prescribed activity, prayer, meditation, spiritual reading. One learned to live by a rigid rule, to make one's bed, sweep, dust, polish, scrub, supply all one's daily needs, to dig in the garden for the prescribed daily half-hour, even to switch off one's mind and stop thinking for a half-hour morning and afternoon when one walked silently in the garden for relaxation and fresh air.

Once I had to leave the monastery alone to visit the dentist. He was a nervy, jumpy fellow. I still remember the torture to which he subjected me. The previous day he had been motorcycling and had a smash. I paid for it as the drill danced in his shaking hand. While he worked he talked.

"Difficult people to handle," he muttered more to himself than to me. "You try to prevent a reaction when I hurt. I never know when I'm on a nerve. No cooperation. I suppose you call it virtue." My mouth being full of paraphernalia, I could only listen. Soon he wandered off on another tack.

"Can't get the hang of it at all. Young, active, educated, you throw it all away and bury yourselves from everyone and everything. No life for me."

He removed his trappings and turned directly on me. "Now let me have it. Why do you do it?"

Silence lets you think long thoughts. You look at yourself and analyze your motives. And young or old, they are complicated. I had been thinking and was not completely off guard. So I mustered a few points I thought effective for the man and the place.

"It's not the worst life," I said. "Some ways it ties you down but others it gives you freedom. Take yourself, for example. You're your own boss. But are you? All day long you poke in people's mouths. Do you like it? You worry about the rent, about money to pay for your equipment, to buy clothes. Your wife runs you into debt. The children get sick. You make yourself sick worrying what would happen if you got sick and couldn't work.

"We miss all that. I haven't a penny in my pocket. I shall never have. But I'll never need it. After this year I have six to study to my heart's content, philosophy, history, physics, languages, theology, law. I like study. Then I go on a mission. I like travel. I expect you like travel. But I'll probably see more of the world than you ever will."

"I heard it all before," he said. "You're not the first. But I still like my own sweet will."

"So do I. I don't deny that at all. But life is compromise. You must decide what to sacrifice. If you don't decide, you sacrifice everything. We sacrifice one kind of freedom, which is only such within the crushing limitations imposed by the need to make a living, for another kind which pinches harder in some directions but gives more scope in others."

"You are wise beyond your years, child," he said slowly and with a kind of acid resignation, "if you know what you are saying. Men only find that wisdom after the event, when it is too late to profit by their knowledge."

Perhaps what I said was part rhetoric, for it is hard to know what you never experienced, yet even then I was acquiring the gift I highly prize, though often burdensome, of sharing and feeling as my own the problems of others. And now indeed I know from experience what I then divined. Years later through circumstances to be recounted in their place I severed my bonds with the community of which I was then a member to fight on my own the battle of life, to know the uncertainty of living on one's wits, the jealousy that greets worldly success, the meanness of petty minds, the sickening feeling of being unable through no fault of one's own to stand by people one has in good faith got into a tight spot. But I am forgetting my dentist.

"All I said to you may seem on a very materialistic plane," I said to him as a parting shot. "But these are only the accidental benefits. The essential one is that this life makes it easier to carry out the purpose for which we are alive.

"You and I and most of the people in the world, even many who deny it if challenged, believe there is a God who created us to know, love, and serve him on earth and be happy with him for eternity. Once you accept this, the rest follows. Your life distracts you every day from this essential object. Mine is so organized that it is hard for me to forget it or get away from it."

So I argued with him as I often argued with myself. And twice at this time I had to try my hand with newcomers who shuddered at the first revelation of the life before them.

My first effort was a ghastly failure. To each arrival another was assigned to show him the ropes and initiate him in the routine. The customary silence was dispensed to the extent necessary to do the briefing. My charge was much older than the rest of us, in his middle thirties. As a boy he had crossed the Atlantic to the United States and become a priest there. He felt called to still higher things and after long thought and discussion with people competent to judge, he decided to become a monk. It seemed a small step. He was already pledged to celibacy and a life devoted to others. The additional obligations of the community, the divesting himself of his few simple belongings, and submission to a stricter and more detailed obedience, what real difference did they make?

But they did. He arrived on Saturday. I undertook my task of initiation with more enthusiasm than discretion, only to realize unbelievingly within half a day that his nerve was shattered. Probably he wanted a cigarette more than anything else. Perhaps a glass of whisky would have pulled him together. But how was a boy who had never really acquired the habit of the one and never tasted the other to suspect the shock to him of learning casually that both were out for the rest of his days? A knock at my door. He had been studying the timetable. Did he have to dig in the garden for half an hour each morning? Every day but Sunday. Another knock. What was this "discipline" after night prayers on Wednesdays and Fridays? I showed him the scourge hanging on the back of the door and explained briefly. He fled. Another knock. Who cleaned his shoes?

I led him to the press where the brushes and polish were kept, together with the broom to sweep his floor each morning, the bucket and scrubber to wash it weekly on his knees.

He came on Saturday. He left on Monday. I never saw him again. Even his name I have long forgotten.

With Norman I was more successful, or perhaps it turned out in the end I wasn't. He was a different problem. We had been schoolfellows. He had gone on to the university but after one year decided he must take the step now or not at all. When he came he was like the drunkard who decides suddenly to cut, and this time I recognized it. I was learning. The second or third day I went into his room to give him some item of instruction. He did not answer my knock and I opened his door to find his head out through the dormer window—his was a fifth-floor attic—watching a tennis game on the courts just outside the wall. I was horrified. All my time I had never raised my eyes to see those tennis courts. There were two big windows looking over them on a corridor along which I walked fifty times a day. But it wasn't done. There was wickedness and the world and temptation. Not to mention Lot's wife.

What should I do? Here was something heinous which only the Novice Master could handle. I had to think quick, think hard, to decide for the first time that circumstances make the spirit of a law more important than the letter. I went into Norman's room and sat on his bed. If the Master were to come along, I had no explanation. I took that chance. I didn't talk, at least not much. I let Norman talk. Several times in the following days I let him talk. He was adjusting himself, getting over his fright, his claustrophobia. Soon he was the perfect novice, exemplar of devotion, radiating a mystic fervor. But it didn't last. It burned out. A psychoanalyst could explain the process beautifully. It's a way they have. Personally I'm not convinced that he'd explain it well. Psychoanalysts have their place and their function but often they don't know them. In any case, it carried him through his noviceship and some years further. But it burned out. And the day came when he didn't fit in any more. He left (as I was later to leave) and went back to the impossible task of becoming once more one of the crowd, of explaining away to others, but mainly to himself, the gap of formative years.

Leaving was about the toughest thing you could do and in fact few left during the year of noviceship. Everything was new. The break was complete. Fervor carried one forward. It was later when one got back to study and, through reading of subjects intended for the subsequent missionary life, into some albeit remote contact with the world, that the crisis usually occurred. This problem of permanence or continuity was obviously one for the community no less than the member. It had to maintain itself or die. A member took a lot of making, and it was a bad break if he wandered off after the trouble and expense. Not that the expense was the primary consideration. Nevertheless, costs of operating an organization that had to invest so much time and money in the training of members were necessarily heavy, while income was what the missionary members raised by appeals to their public and in gifts from well-wishers, uncertain sources of revenue. While the members lived in security, the community lived precariously. So continuity had at all costs to be kept, and as there was neither physical nor legal hold, insofar as the civil law was concerned, there had to be the firmest moral bond. It was the deepest of all traditions, the thing to be done no matter what the circumstances. At the end of the noviceship one gave a solemn vow or promise, first for three years, then for one's life. This was backed by the highest sanctions. Perseverance to death was a guarantee of eternal life. Abandonment of vocation was the rejection of the call to perfection and sent one sliding down the slippery slope to perdition.

The first formal solemn step of integration was the exchange of one's own dress for the community habit, an all-covering garb of rough woolen cloth which reached to the ground and with a substantial wrap-over in front was held in place by a cloth girdle that encircled the waist three times. This ceremony marked the official start of the noviceship year and was preceded by fifteen days of recollection, of which the final three were spent in unbroken silence. One incident characterizes the day for me. It was five to six weeks after my arrival in the novice house, eve of the feast of the Nativity of Our Lady. I had left everything behind, my bicycle and my stamp album, my boyhood romances, my anticipated university course, my occasional cigarette, and my mother. As I said good-by, I thought of my mother as being in a category distinct from my other loves and attachments. Separated, we could still remain together. She would think of me every night, she told me in her tears, and say good-by afresh before she went to sleep.

Each night I had remembered this pact and performed my part. As I lay on my unyielding straw paillasse with modestly folded arms (for so far went the regulation of life) I thought of her a hundred miles away. This gesture to human sentiment had, however, begun to trouble me as I listened during the long days of silent recollection to the retreat master's repeated urging to give all in order to find all. The cutting-off had to be without reservation. Physical separation was but a prelude to willing renunciation. So in those days I interpreted or misinterpreted the build-up. And the crisis came the day I received the habit. That night I turned to the wall with a blank mind. I had made the great sacrifice.

CHAPTER 2

As the Twig Is Bent . . .

I recall a BBC broadcast back in 1940 or early 1941. It was before organized brutality had so surfeited our senses that we grew to forget men and women were involved. This radio talk described an indoctrination course for the recently created commandos, the British equivalent of the rangers. The details of the rigid physical training, the familiarization with novel weapons and guerrilla tactics, the techniques of infiltration, deception, and sabotage have all long faded from my memory. But I haven't forgotten the description of the methods used to condition the minds of the teen-age commandos.

If he had been talking about the aeration of a compost heap, the BBC commentator couldn't have been more detachedly refined in making his report. As they dodged booby traps, stumbled choking through burning buildings, fell on their faces to escape the blast of land mines, and stuck Bowie knives in dummy figures from whose bellies blood squirted into their panting mouths, concealed loudspeakers repeated insistently, commandingly, the single word "Hate!"—repeated it till it became a white oxygen flame that seared their minds and filled them with a single simple lust to kill.

It was revolting, as revolting as war. It was so revolting that a lot of old dowagers, living on the spoils of earlier, less uncivilized wars, wrote letters to the BBC and the London *Times*. The BBC said it was very sorry it had told over the unpolluted air waves such a nasty, uncalled-for story about what was being done to clean-bodied, clean-minded young Englishmen who had answered the call to save Christianity and civilization. It would not do it again.

And it didn't. But the courses, of course, went on, just as they went on in Germany and in Russia and in the United States and in Japan, because young men, naturally fickle and unstable and volatile, had to be conditioned to react in a given way to given stimuli.

The Communists, as mostly everybody now realizes, have made a fine art of the art of indoctrination. Whether you listen to Malik's double-talk at the Security Council or Eugene Dennis' in a Manhattan courthouse or that of the local tub-thumper in a Midwestern town or a French village or a Nigerian kraal, it takes no effort to recognize the mental conditioning which makes all of them dance to one tune and change step effortlessly no matter how amazing the piper's change of tempo.

But it's an old technique, this technique of indoctrination. The Catholic Church has been using it for centuries to train its leaders for the exacting life it exacts from them. How else maintain unity of faith and practice among all races and temperaments in all lands through all the changing conditions of the ages?

And here I was on September 7, 1927, dressed in the habit of the Congregation of the Most Holy Redeemer and started on the first stage in that complicated process. It wasn't for me entirely the first stage, for I had spent the preceding five years in a boarding school conducted by the same Congregation. It was a small school, averaging a total enrollment of about forty boys during the years I was there. We did the usual five-year high school course and took the public examinations, specializing in Latin and Greek. Our life was more secluded than that of most boys of our age, and we had practically no contacts with outsiders except during the two months in summer and two weeks at Christmas we spent with our families. Even that period of vacation with our families, as we were frequently reminded, was an experimental innovation that might at any moment be withdrawn. Those who were seniors in my first year had as juniors experienced the traditional arrangement which provided for only one month annually at home. Though two of my cousins were members of the Congregation, I had never met a member before my arrival at the high school. But from that moment I had ample opportunity to observe them and their ways. Attached to the school was a monastery where about twenty priest-members of the Congregation lived, serving a large public church and giving missions in the surrounding area. In addition, all our full-time teachers were members. Apart from a couple of special grinds in mathematics, the subject in which the school was always notoriously weak, the only outsider to contribute to our cultural evolution was an army sergeant major who once or twice a week put us through our paces in the gymnasium.

The school was not only small but extremely exclusive. I say exclusive, because it was open only to boys who intended to join the Congregation. How a child of twelve or thirteen could properly be said to intend to join a particular religious order I leave to more ingenious minds to explain. If every youngster had to pick his avocation in life at that age, there would be a wondrous glut of space cadets in the labor market. But there it was in black and white in the prospectus, and you had to affirm your intention in order to be enrolled. And if any day you decided to the contrary, or the superiors decided you weren't the material they wanted, that same hour you went packing, even though the end of term was only weeks or days away. I saw that happen several times, and even as a boy I felt hurt at the harsh disregard for the individual in the devotion to a system. But such was the system under which I had lived, a system which for centuries had proved its value in fostering vocations to the religious life, and whether it was good or bad, it had given me a general impression of what life would be like as an actual member of this Congregation.

I felt quite happy about it all when I made the formal start in September, 1927. I saw myself a privileged person, selected from thousands by a special dispensation of Providence to lead a life of perfection. Trifles make perfection, I had been told often and was to be told many times more. I was prepared to accept that dictum and treat as important every trifle of the busy day that started when the great bell clanged each morning and that had a task and a purpose for every minute until the same bell tolled twice seventeen hours later to announce lights out. Nor is it really accurate to say it ended then. For the short hours of sleep were as much a part of the divine plan and as much a dedication to the Lord as the long waking hours. Sleep was no longer an escape or a pleasure but a necessary conservation of physical energies without which the designs of Providence could not be carried into effect by and in me. It was for a young man a terrifying thought, this idea of perpetual, lifelong application, with never a break, never a letup. It was depressing when one felt depressed. Then the only thing to do was to concentrate on the task of the moment, to scorn the temptation of the devil.

During the first months of the noviceship I did not see much of a pattern other than the rigidity of the life and the separation from the world. But I was not looking for patterns. I was just eighteen years old and had scarcely begun to think in universal terms. Yet bit by bit I was becoming aware that I had an organic function in the life of the Church and of humanity. The daubs of paint and clashes of color were assuming perspective and proportion as I lived with them and lived them.

I had plenty of time for thinking. The day's detailed organization provided every so often a short break, ten minutes, fifteen minutes, perhaps twenty minutes, when one might sit at one's table or walk along the high, long corridors and figure things out. And I had plenty of food for thought. The Master of Novices lectured us every day. We read spiritual books at stated times morning and afternoon. Even during our meals each novice in turn read aloud a chapter from the life of a saint or some similar work. The first exercise of the day was a half-hour of formal meditation kneeling in the chapel, and there was a similar period in mid-afternoon and again before supper in the evening. Unobtrusively, unconsciously, this steady rhythm of activity reflected itself not only in external demeanor but in a new mental rhythm. No longer fed by daily contact nor even by conversation or reading of newspapers or magazines, the old set of images of football and movies and dances faded from the imagination to be replaced by others more in keeping with the new life.

The indoctrination of the novices was directed mainly to the emotions and the will. Later, during the years of study, they would take courses on the intellectual justification of their faith, comparative religion, and the mechanisms of prayer, and those who felt so inclined might dig and investigate and analyze to their heart's content. But in the noviceship these things were taken as much for granted as is the justice of his cause by the recruit preparing for battle. We were encouraged to accept without question the new scale of values which made the denials and rigors of our life seem unimportant when weighed against its benefits. At the same time, there was a certain necessary minimum of theory to accompany and support the practice. This was provided by the Master of Novices in his daily conferences in which he explained that the separation from the world and the self-abnegation required of us were not ends in themselves but only means to facilitate union with God. Our task was both negative and positive. The vows of poverty, chastity, and obedience which every member of a religious order had to take and observe were designed mainly to insure the negative. The devotional exercises were directed to effect the positive. They occupied more than nine hours each day, the principal ones being meditation, Mass, recital of the divine office in common, reading of spiritual books, and such traditional devotions as the rosary, way of the cross, visits to the Blessed Sacrament, and examination of conscience.

Most of us were already familiar with the outline of the story of the order of which we now formed a part. During the three to five years we had spent in the high school conducted by its members, we had listened each evening at supper to a chapter from the biography of the founder. It was a young order, as they go. Just two hundred years earlier its founder had been a lawyer in Naples, a very brilliant young lawyer who in several years of practice never lost a case. Then one day he overlooked an important point in a brief and went down in inglorious defeat. "World, I know you now," he muttered in his disillusioned chagrin and strode from the court vowing never again to seek the approval of men. Tossing aside his gown and his honors, he pledged himself to spend his life in bringing the knowledge of God to the abandoned goatherds of the Abruzzi. He enlisted a band of helpers and soon was putting his legal talents to work in writing a rule of life designed to secure for those who followed it the rigors of Carthusian contemplation combined with the simple, direct style of teaching and preaching which characterized the apostolate of Christ himself and that of his immediate followers.

When Alfonso de Ligorio, whose name was later entered in the exclusive listing of canonized saints because of the holiness of his personal life and the still more exclusive lists of Doctors of the Church because of his contributions to the literature of theology, looked around him in Naples, he found no shortage of clergy to minister to the spiritual needs of the upper and middle classes, while the peasants on the mountain sides were as neglected as their goats. Not only did he decide that his companions and he should concentrate on this abandoned group, but he wrote into his rule stringent provisions to insure that the same singleness of purpose should continue in later times. His viewpoint was that a vocation humanly so unattractive could be maintained only on the basis of extreme personal holiness combined with strong central control and the exclusion of other activities. The rule accordingly laid down that the members should pass more than half of each year within the monastery concentrating on spiritual exercises, and that when they went outside, they did so only to preach missions and retreats as requested by the diocesan clergy, giving preference always to requests from country places. The rule prohibited the establishment of schools (except those maintained exclusively for the education of candidates for admission to the Congregation), the care of orphanages or other social institutions, and the direction of parishes.

The Father General, residing in Rome, had immediate and complete control over everyone and everything; and this over-all control insured ultimately the maintenance of a uniform interpretation of the rule in all monasteries throughout the world and was at the same time a guarantee to each that the resources of the whole order were at its disposal as it might need them. Whereas in most religious orders the members have a substantial voice in the selection of their superiors, the monks in each monastery in many cases electing their own superior, our rule provided that the Father General appoint all provincial and local superiors. They held office for three-year periods. He himself was elected for life by delegates from all provinces assembled in General Chapter, the majority of the delegates being superiors who had been nominated by the previous Father General, the others chosen by a complicated process within each province. Only a General Chapter could change the rules of the Congregation.

Groups of monasteries formed the provinces, each province being normally coterminous with a national state. Each province had a novitiate and a house for students, to the maintenance of which each monastery contributed a quota. Revenue of the order came mainly from contributions of the faithful who attended the churches attached to each monastery and from stipends given members for preaching missions and other spiritual exercises up and down the country. One monk in each monastery handled its finances. Candidates for membership did not have to contribute. If they had property, they did not have to surrender it, but they had to get an administrator to look after it. They could no longer use either the property or the revenue coming from it, nor could they even transfer their property once they took the vows. Before profession, they had to make a will disposing of it in case of death, and that was the last exercise of property rights they might make. Only if they left the Congregation did the property revert fully to them. Surplus revenues and personnel of the Congregation were channeled into overseas missions in underdeveloped parts of the world, each province being allotted its mission field by the Father General.

All this and much more about the history, the organization, and spirit of the Congregation I learned or relearned as a novice. All of it was extremely important to me as an introduction and background to the religious life I was aspiring to lead as one of some six thousand men physically scattered in all parts of the world but spiritually united into a single close-knit family by reason of their common sharing in that history, organization, and spirit. I did not think of it as an odd or exotic life. I knew this kind of community life went back uninterruptedly to the early days of Christianity and based itself on such precepts of Christ as his advice to the young man who asked what he should do to be perfect, that he should sell what he had, give to the poor, and follow Christ. I did not think my life was going to be wasted or useless. I knew it was the same kind of life which had been led by many who had made valuable contributions to the progress of mankind, that religious orders had been largely responsible for the creation and extension of Western civilization, and that they were still centers of learning as well as of work for the benefit of humanity.

One of the things that did surprise me, when I got round to thinking about it, was the great number of religious orders that had sprung up through the centuries, and the amazingly different ways in which they interpreted the counsel of Christ. It was also a shock to discover that my brethren had quite a feeling of superiority about themselves. Members of other religious orders were all good people, well motivated no doubt, but they didn't really have the same spirit as we had, and of course the work they did was nothing like so apostolic and important. The attitude was seldom expressed in so many words, but there was that story about the Jesuit whose theological views were so lax that when a penitent confessed he had killed a man, said, "You know, my child, you are bound to confess only your grave sins." And another one about the Franciscan whose rule forbade him to touch money but who never tired of pointing out that he didn't have to touch it if it was dropped direct into the copious hood that more than supplied for the lack of pockets in his dress. It was true the Passionists got up at one A.M. to recite the divine office, but that didn't amount to a thing when you got used to it. And besides they had an allowance of pocket money. They could spend five shillings (it then came to a fraction over a dollar) a week almost without restriction. Such practices took all the meaning out of a vow of poverty.

There was both smugness and self-complacency in this attitude. But it was also in large part an expression of the natural tendency of every living body to preserve itself. And the more uncongenial the milieu in which it has to live, the harder it fights for life. Human nature being what it is, any organization which demands of men the sacrifices involved in the religious state has to struggle all the time to hold them together. It didn't take me long to absorb the general attitude, to learn to preen my spiritual self and instinctively to balance our perfections against the human frailties of the other orders.

All religious orders in the Catholic Church are alike in that their primary purpose is to facilitate and encourage the spiritual perfection of their members. Catholic spiritual writers agree that while people in every walk of life, coal miners, soda jerks, lawyers, can lead and have led lives of heroic holiness, the religious state (as they technically describe the life led in a community bound by vows) is in itself more perfect than the lay state. Even within the religious state they make further distinctions of perfection, teaching that the purely contemplative life, such as that led by Carthusians and by Carmelite nuns of strict observance, is more perfect than the active life in which the monk or nun interrupts contemplation in order to minister to the needs of others. And Saint Thomas Aquinas carried the analysis a step further. While agreeing with his predecessors that the contemplative life is in itself more perfect than the active, he said that in certain circumstances the mixed life may be the most perfect of all, namely, if the monk can achieve such a degree of contemplation that he can engage from time to time in activities calculated to spread to others the superabundance of the spiritual fruits of his contemplation.

Application of these rules to the specific needs of varying circumstances of time and place has brought about the establishment of the thousands of religious orders and congregations of men and women which today exist. The founders of each either believed they had discovered a better way to achieve the primary object or decided to devote themselves to a distinct secondary object. The number of strictly contemplative orders whose members do not normally engage in any active work of direct benefit to outsiders is small, while each of the others specializes in a particular type or types of external work, teaching, caring for the sick, the spread of the gospel in non-Christian lands.

During the centuries Christians fought to prevent militant Mohammedanism from overrunning Europe, several orders were founded with the specific object of ransoming Christian captives held by the Moors. Still earlier, when Europe was primarily a pastoral society tending by reason of population pressures and the desire for higher living standards toward a system of mixed tillage farming, various orders took the lead in discovering and applying the techniques of the new agriculture. Building in solitary places all across western and central Europe, the Irish monks hewed from the wilderness model farms and established patterns of land use which still survive. They were harsh, austere men living by a rule that was merciless to human weakness —"Let a man go to bed when he sleeps on his feet before reaching it"—yet they loved the fields they created and were attuned to nature around them. When the monks of Luxeuil paused in their tremendous task of reclaiming the Vosges, the squirrels would come and rest on the shoulder of their founder, Columbanus, and run in and out of his cowl. And when Valery the gardener came into the classroom, bringing the scent of roses on his robes, Columbanus would stop in his lecture to cry, "Nay then, it is thou, beloved, who art lord and abbot of this monastery." And further south at the same time, the sons of St. Benedict were pursuing the similar yet more subtle objective of showing people how to live with moderation, laying the foundations of a new civilization amid the ruins piled up by the Barbaric Invasions, teaching even more by example than by word how to till the land, how to build, how to read and write, how to behave.

Each century had more complex social and religious needs, and for each there arose some further specialization of the religious life. Each new order went its own way, developed its own methods and techniques, developed its own peculiar brand of spirituality, adapted itself to its particular environments.

Some twelve hundred years ago, in one of those centralizing and streamlining efforts that hit the world every so often, somebody got the idea that the most efficient way to run the religious state was to have just one big order with one rule and one supreme command. Amalgamation became popular for a time. But the Church in its secular wisdom and its genius for molding human material in superhuman forms quickly veered away from this policy. With its unique ability to maintain the essential controls while interfering as little as possible with local autonomies, it renewed the former trend to a multiplicity of orders and congregations, each left to follow its own devices and to set its own standards within the framework of the three vows and the general principles laid down in Canon Law. But for all of them the external activities are secondary, subordinated to the primary purpose of achieving the personal perfection of their members by following the evangelical counsels. The armchair efficiency expert who wants to streamline their organization, to amalgamate, to redefine functions, to increase social effectiveness, or to raise the personal living standards of the members is way off beam so long as he thinks of the religious life as designed to cater to the religious or social or educational needs of others. That is the job of the bishops and the parochial clergy. The religious orders help them only insofar as such help doesn't conflict with their real work.

Though the legal structure is accordingly well defined, there always remain the application and observance of principles. Even in a monastery, life is normally a series of compromises between man's aspirations and his frailities. While intransigent in its definition of the goal of the religious life as the subjection of one's lower to one's higher faculties, the rule of the Congregation recognized there are limits to human endurance, that there must be variety and adjustment of pressure, now less, now more, if mind or body or both are not to break under the strain. Each Tuesday afternoon the normal routine was accordingly relaxed to allow the novices go walking for a couple of hours in the country; and on Thursdays there were still more important concessions, of which the principal were an hour's common recreation in mid-morning, a walk in the country in the afternoon, and permission to talk during the midday and evening meals. To readjust the balance, Friday was a day of complete silence and intensified spiritual and penitential exercises.

Each of these variations in the routine was trivial in itself, but for us they assumed importance because in a mountainless country a hillock is a landmark. And the Master of Novices made use of all of them, of the relaxations no less than of the rigidities, to help him form in each novice the particular kind of character he desired, to develop in each the spiritual forces to the point where they could normally and almost effortlessly exercise a reasoned control over instincts and senses. Nobody gives what he doesn't have, the Father Master frequently told us, repeating a commonplace of philosophy. Our first task, our only task as novices, was to put our own house in order.

I learned this lesson early in my noviceship. Young idealists inevitably think of themselves as world reformers, and I was no exception. The Master of Novices soon disillusioned me. He was a man of strong personality and strong views. Many members of the community disapproved of the rigidity of his interpretation of the rules and his inflexible regime. But that didn't worry him. What anyone thought never cost him a thought. Indeed, he was so impersonal in everything as to be almost inhuman, so that his methods produced with certain temperaments an external conformity without full inward conviction, a veneer of spirituality that wore off when conditions changed. But as far as I was concerned, I had no complaint. He was so utterly sincere, and his own life conformed so fully to his austere theory, that I was ready to take his word for almost anything. And so I didn't challenge his ruling when he told me confine my enthusiasms to myself.

"Put aside any idea you are going to reform anyone or anything, until you have first reformed yourself," he told me after he had read a few of my enthusiastic letters telling different friends what I thought they should and shouldn't do. It was part of his duty to read all letters, outgoing and incoming. "As a novice, confine yourself to one letter weekly to your parents. That's all. Let them know you are well and happy—you are happy, aren't you?—and leave it at that."

One of the notions I found most difficult to absorb was the exact concept of religious poverty, far harder than it was to swallow its practical effects. We hadn't been used to any kind of elaborate living. We were all sons of middle-class and lower middle-class families, of farmers, artisans, civil servants, storekeepers. That is the social and economic section that provides the bulk of the members of religious orders as well as of the parochial clergy practically the world over, certainly in countries where the Catholic Church flourishes. Catholic countries like those of South America which lack a solid middle class suffer from a perennial shortage of vocations. We were adequately housed, clothed, and fed. There were no frills and fancies in the monastery, none of the niceties or delicacies or small comforts which reflect the presence of the woman's hand in the middle-class home, but the essentials were there. And it was easy enough to understand that in the community all shared alike, that practical effect was given to the Communist formula that each gave according to his ability and received according to his need.

But it took much explaining and many practical lessons to make me realize that religious poverty is not so much a formula as a frame of mind. It does not mean doing without things so much as using them without being attached to them. And people grow attached to the most ridiculous things, tiny things that become symbols of pleasure, of comfort, or just of preferential treatment. One of the most elementary of human desires is to be a shade higher than the other fellow.

Many of us at one time or another developed all kinds of frivolous neurotic ailments or peculiarities for the satisfaction of having an individual diet or an exemption from some exercise or a piece of equipment or furniture that everybody else didn't have. The process was complicated by the fact that you first had to persuade yourself of the reality of your problem before you could do anything about it. Nobody would practice deliberate deception. You just couldn't live that kind of life unless your minimum standards of conduct excluded any idea of wrongdoing. You would be so out of tune and besides have so little to gain that you'd quickly find your way out. But human nature driven back from one line of defense rallies on another. It's always easy to persuade yourself, when it's your own case, that there is a justifying cause for the special treatment. I remember at one point having the frames changed on a pair of glasses four or five times. The plain steel frames which alone we were supposed to use kept irritating my skin, or so I persuaded myself. Only when the oculist ruled that the solution was to give me tortoise-shell frames with a gold bridge did the fancied irritation disappear.

But the superiors worked hard to see that kind of technique didn't succeed too often. As novices we weren't allowed to use gloves when we went walking in the country, but we knew that professed students might have one pair of woolen gloves. I thought maybe I could do a little better. I had heard of somebody who had. And when my sister, during the single visit of his family allowed each novice during the year, asked if she might make me a present of something for my forthcoming religious profession at the end of the noviceship, I suggested a pair of leather gloves. But it didn't work out. I duly arrived at the house of studies with the gift. But then I discovered one had to report every gift to the superior, and he followed the standard procedure of directing me to place the gift in the common store. If I needed gloves, I might ask the brother in charge of the store give me another pair.

The principle behind the practice was clear. One used things because one needed them, not because one liked them or had sentimental attachments to them. But it was a tough fight to reach the degree of detachment needed to avoid ensnarement by innocent human bonds. Admittedly it is perfectly silly to be concerned about such trifles. But rationality is not a characteristic of one's reactions when one's interests are affected. And the less remains to fight for, the more determinedly one fights. One of my companions went through what was probably the crisis of his religious life over a fountain pen. He was the only son of moderately wealthy parents to whom he was the sun in the firmament. He had given up the comforts and prospects of his home without a thought. It is easy to do something big, heroic. But one day, a considerable time after he had settled down to the routine of the noviceship, he learned that the fountain pen he had brought with him should be surrendered because of a narrow band of gold on the cap. He worried and worried for days. His impulse was to say nothing. Soon the concealment began to upset his peace of mind, became an obstacle to recollection and mental prayer. He had to face it. He had made a bargain with God and with the Congregation. And one day he marched up to the Master of Novices' room, handed him the pen.

That was about the size of our normal problem. But any problem is big or small in relation to the others with which it competes for attention. The mind is at peace only when it divests itself of all attachments, small as well as big.

Perhaps it would be much simpler if one could live without anything at all, but neither Saint Francis of Assisi nor Ghandi got so far. Even the simplest life commits a person to dependence on many objects, and the decision as to what is a necessity and what a superfluity must always be made in terms of time, place, habit, age, condition of health, and a dozen other factors. The rules and practices of each particular order, as modified from country to country and from century to century, establish the norms for the members of that order. We as novices and students, living within earshot of the bell, didn't need a watch, for example. Only the bell ringer had one. I remember it well, for I carried it for two or three months. It had a case of black gunmetal and must have weighed at least three ounces. The most peculiar thing about it was that it incorporated an alarm device in addition to the normal works of a watch, and this served to arouse the bell ringer in time to make the rounds each morning with the utilitarian object of seeing that each novice hopped out of bed when the big bell clanged the reveille and with the spiritual one of having him start a new day by answering "*Deo gratias*" ("Thanks be to God") when the bell ringer opened his door and in sepulchral tones summoned him to action with a phrase from Complin, the aptness of which to the occasion always eluded me, "*Tu autem, Domine, miserere nobis*" ("But thou, O Lord, have mercy on us"). That one watch supplied the timekeeping needs of all the novices. But the priest-members of the Congregation, who had occasion to travel far from the monastery when giving retreats and missions, each needed a watch as a normal part of his equipment.

The application of the principle thus varied, but for all the principle was the same in that the vow of poverty taken by the religious pledged him not to use or dispose of anything of value as though he owned it. Whatever he might acquire, he acquired on behalf of his order and consequently might deal with it only as authorized by the superiors who administered the affairs of the order. The superiors in turn might allow him to keep in his possession only what he required for his normal current needs.

And that is where you get down to interpretation of the law to fit in with the different traditions of each order and the varying requirements of place and time. I have met a Benedictine monk who carried a gold watch and told me this was normal with his community. Many orders allow their members a dollar or two weekly to spend on cigarettes, bus fares, and similar requirements. We had a particularly strict interpretation of religious poverty. Smoking was forbidden, not only to novices and students but to the priests. Obviously, therefore, no cigarette allowance figured. Our needs were so few and simple that we seldom needed anything that had to be bought. Then we had to ask the superior's permission, even if it was only a razor blade, to get the item from the common store or have the brother in charge of stores order something he didn't stock. I believe

I never touched money during my noviceship and hardly a dozen times during the six following years. My entire wardrobe consisted of two habits of coarse black serge, a black suit, and an overcoat of clerical gray for use when we went walking in the country or visited a doctor or a dentist. Each year the sleeves got a little shorter and the legs of the pants climbed a little higher about my ankles. One of the habits was still sufficiently preserved after I had finished with it to provide a couple of years' wear for somebody else, but the other was such a collection of darns and repairs that the tailor could only salvage a few pieces to add to his store of patching material.

People of this generation, for all their scramble for money and comfort, are nevertheless to some extent attuned to the values inherent in voluntary poverty embraced with the idea of making a man strong by freeing him from all ties to material things. The asceticism of Ghandi, like that of Saint Francis of Assisi, has been an inspiration not only to his followers but to good men everywhere. But no corresponding enthusiasm is aroused by the second of the voluntary renunciations of the religious state, the vow of chastity or continence. Yet it is a logical development of the idea underlying voluntary poverty and justified by precisely the same arguments. To marry and bring up a family is a normal activity of the average person. No more consistent and enthusiastic defender of the family, which she proclaims the fundamental and primary unit of society, exists than the Catholic Church. It is good to marry, she has always taught, but it is better not to marry provided one is prepared to live a life of continence. And accordingly she imposes this obligation on those who elect the priestly state and on those who join religious orders.

There is also a practical reason for the law of celibacy. It enables the priest to have an undivided loyalty to the ministry. The married man has a natural and necessary loyalty to his wife and children, a loyalty that demands lifelong devotion and unrelaxing vigilance. The priesthood likewise demands a single devotion to the offices and requirements of the ministry. Like the other, it is a dedication until death and permits of no division. While these two loyalties are not by nature mutually exclusive, in practice each would constantly clash with the other so as to make it extremely difficult to give to either the attention to which it is entitled. This practical argument has added force in the case of monks living in a community. If they were married, it would be impossible for them to observe the prescribed silences and carry out the monastic observances and duties.

Absurd, unnatural, impossible, say the critics, Kinsey report in hand. Not so, says the Church, if one takes the means and in addition relies on God's grace which is never refused to one who asks for it with the proper dispositions. The means are exacting and the road one to be traversed only by the determined. Constant vigilance is required over one's senses, control of the eyes, of the ears, of the touch, of one's reading, of one's company, of one's thoughts. Eating and drinking must be in moderation, and interests and activities must be developed to work off one's surplus energies. Psychologists call it sublimation. I rather like the term, for it emphasizes the positive purposes of continence. But it can be done. In the intimate association in which we lived in the monastery, nobody could long carry on undiscovered any misconduct or misbehavior. When you know people that well, they don't have to tell you what they are thinking. And of all the hundreds of members of religious orders with whom I have lived or whom I have known, I have known only one of whom I could say with certainty he had been unfaithful to his vow of chastity.

Of course there are others. From time to time a monk leaves his monastery against obedience, as Luther did, and lives in concubinage. But the number is amazingly small. I was able to study from the inside and over a long period the level of sexual morality among members of religious orders. As a witness, I am absolutely of no help to the Maria Monk school. My entire contribution is one person, and his lapses occurred outside the monastery to which he was attached, and in circumstances that facilitated misconduct. I knew him very well, a very abnormal person in many respects and admirable in not a few. I believe that his problems were pathological rather than moral, that the sentence will not be too heavy in the only judgment that counts.

The vow of religious obedience is the third universal characteristic of the religious state. It of itself covers the essential ground in that it binds the person who takes it to obey every lawful order of his superiors, to abdicate his own will and to a large extent his own judgment in favor of the will and judgment of others. Ascetic writers speak constantly of the duty of religious to practice blind obedience, but the expression is exact only within clearly defined limits. Neither a member of a religious order nor anybody else is justified in doing what his conscience tells him is wrong, no matter who orders him to do it. Some of the defendants at the Nürnberg trials discovered to their cost that this principle is valid even in a criminal court. A man must always in the last analysis use his own judgment to decide whether a particular command is morally wrong, and if he is satisfied it is, he is bound to disobey it. But in every other situation, the member of a religious order is bound to do what his superiors tell him. If a given order seems unreasonable, he is entitled to appeal it from his immediate superior to the higher superior, and so on until it finally reaches the Pope for final decision, just in the same way and with much the same formality with which one can in civilian life go through the courts right up to the Supreme Court to appeal what one considers an unreasonable judgment. Of course, the scales are heavily weighted in favor of the administration as against the individual, as I was to discover for myself some years later. But the administration has to prove its point. Precise limitations on the discretion of the superiors are imposed by Canon Law and the rules of each order. The religious state is not a slavery under arbitrary bosses. On the contrary it represents a highly developed rule of law. A superior, for example, cannot order his subject to ask for a dispensation from his vows. Nor can he expel him except for proven misbehavior repeated in contravention of warnings given as provided by Canon Law.

Another and in practice equally efficient restriction on the whims of superiors results from the temporariness of their tenure of office. The constitution of all religious orders is democratic to a greater or lesser degree. Some communities elect their superiors by direct vote of all the members. In others, the election for all communities in a given territory, technically called a "province," is made by the Provincial Chapter to which each community sends delegates. The congregation to which I belonged had less popular influence on the selection of superiors than most. The Superior General appointed the principal superiors for three-year terms, but a provision of Canon Law operated to prevent automatic reappointments. The superior of a community might not remain in office for more than six years without interruption. When his term ended, he went back into the ranks without any privileges. The anticipation of this inevitable denouement undoubtedly helped to condition the attitudes and methods of many superiors who might otherwise have given freer rein to their ideas.

The nature of the duties he was called on to perform naturally dictated the type of person chosen as superior. A certain minimum of diplomacy was required, but the essential quality was stolidity and determination never to depart from the beaten track. Anybody who showed any tendency to innovate or to take a chance could be dismissed without further thought from a discussion as to who might figure on the next list. The Superior General, though he lived in Rome, kept in close touch by reports from the Provincial and periodic visits of himself and his advisers.

Our Master of Novices was strict, remote, and conscientious, but he was also highly spiritual and he devoted himself assiduously to making us understand that the external controls which he manipulated were valueless unless we for our part set up equally strict internal controls. He never let us forget that the observance of the rules and of specific commands would get us nowhere in the spiritual life unless we acted to please God and not merely to avoid being found out. He was there not to make us do things we didn't want to do, but to see that we did what we wanted in circumstances that might tempt us to forget our ideals. Once you accept the basic fact of original sin, you cannot challenge the idea of having somebody else stand beside you to remind you which is the way you want to go.

One of the distinctive institutions designed to maintain this delicate balance between internal and external controls on the actions of each member of the community was the *zelator*. The English *zeal* comes from the same root, and it was the *zelator's* job to see that zeal was maintained. The rule directed the superior to select a particularly zealous member of the community for this important post, and I must have qualified, for I had the thankless distinction for several months during my noviceship. As *zelator*, I had no right to correct anybody. But I had to keep my eyes wide open (yet discretely downcast) all the time, and when I saw anybody transgress, I had to note mentally and at an appropriate moment transfer to paper the time, place, and circumstances.

The *zelator* had to keep constantly on the move, using all his ingenuity short of actual cheating. He might enter any novice's room, and if the novice was there, he was supposed to continue whatever he happened to be doing, just as though he hadn't noticed. A considerable part of each day was spent in exercises to be performed privately in our rooms, a half-hour of spiritual reading before breakfast, a half-hour of spiritual reading and a like period of mental prayer during the afternoon, and so on. At any moment he might open a door noiselessly to see what was happening inside.

I can't say I ever found anything very alarming. Occasionally somebody would be asleep at his table, his head sunk on the book he had been reading. Sometimes a novice had not heard the bell and consequently was reading when he should be praying or praying when he should be reading. A common thing was to find somebody standing when he might have been sitting at his table. We all found our sleep ration extremely meager, and the standard method of keeping awake was to stand erect, well away from any support.

No matter where you were, if you found yourself nodding, you had immediately to get to your feet and remain standing until you were sure the danger was passed. Often, by the end of a lecture or reading period in the common room, everybody would be standing in a semicircle behind the row of chairs. Mental prayer periods had to be passed on one's knees, and not infrequently when I opened a door, I found the novice kneeling bolt upright with arms extended in the form of a cross. Even if he heard the door, he would make no move, immersed in his devotions. At other times, I would visit the rooms while the occupants were absent, turn down the bedclothes to see the bed had been properly made, look in the small locker for soiled linen that should have been sent to the laundry, rub my fingers on washbasin, ewer, picture frames, tabletop, and window frames for dust, and lift the cotton curtain behind which hung a suit of clothes and an overcoat to see that all was in place and in order.

Friday mornings came the hour of reckoning. We assembled in a semicircle in the common room. The Master of Novices gave an exhortation. Then each in turn knelt and publicly accused himself of all his breaches of the rule during the previous week. As he ended, the *zelator* also dropped on his knees and repeated from his list whatever items he had noted that had not been included by the other. The Master of Novices then imposed an appropriate penance, to recite certain prayers, to eat bitter herbs, to scourge oneself while reciting the *Miserere* psalm. And last of all came the turn of the *zelator*. He recited his own breaches, and then the others were invited to add whatever they might have noticed. Always there were a couple of volunteers.

This institution operated very strongly to prevent any kind of prank or joint operation, no matter how simple. There was always the risk that one of the parties in a mood of fervor or self-recrimination would confess his part in an escapade or a moment of originality, and a subsequent inquiry by the Master of Novices would reveal the others. Later on, during the course of studies, when we had settled down to some sense of perspective, it was possible within narrow limits to carry off a practical joke. But during the noviceship there was only one single deviation from unimaginative normality, an operation so original in its conception, subtle in its execution, and strategically timed that no retribution ever overtook the virtuoso who staged it.

The setting was as follows. Two afternoons a week we spent a couple of hours walking in the country. A frequent route included a shortcut by a narrow footpath joining two roads, and at one point this meant squeezing between two upright posts not designed to pass anyone weighing over one hundred and fifty pounds. One afternoon we were overtaken at this point by a shower of rain and took shelter under some bushes. Just then the superior and another priest member of the community came along. Both were protected from the rain by an umbrella the superior was carrying. He managed to wriggle through the gap but his companion couldn't make it. The superior thought it a good joke. Standing well away under the umbrella, he expressed his deep concern for his companion's plight, finally suggesting it might do the trick if he stripped down a little. The priest took off his overcoat, but it was no good. Then he took off his coat. Still he couldn't squeeze through. The waistcoat made the difference. Soaked through with rain and disconcerted by the indignity, he rejoined his companion and they went their way.

We laughed a little at the incident and then most of us forgot about it. But the novice whose turn it was to read at supper that night had a brilliant idea. The book was a very dull life of Blessed Anthony Baldinucci, about whom all I now remember is that he was an Italian Jesuit. But that night the story was enlivened. At an appropriate point the reader inserted a footnote in which he recounted, as an illustration of the simple obedience of Blessed Anthony, the humiliation to which he was once subjected by his superior in a park in Naples, repeating in exact detail the incident that had occurred that afternoon. We had the greatest difficulty in keeping our faces straight, lest the Master of Novices smell a rat, while the community superior and the victim of the double joke laughed uproariously, to the mystification of all the others who couldn't see anything particularly hilarious about the holy man's mortification.

CHAPTER 3

Beginning of Self-knowledge

Often in later life I've visited monasteries, four or five times stayed in one, but nowhere found so elaborate an organization of isolation of the members as we practiced. It is normal for monks to live cut off fairly strictly from outside contacts, especially as novices, but we went further. The members of the Congregation were split into distinct units, the relationships between them fixed by elaborate rules and still more elaborate conventions.

Among my first surprises was the discovery that we novices were completely isolated from the professed members of the community. In the novitiate house lived about a dozen priests whose principal activities were to go about the country preaching missions and retreats and, while at home, to conduct the services of the public church attached to the monastery. We joined them for various religious exercises each day and took our meals—at a separate table—in the same dining room. But we might speak to nobody other than the Master of Novices and his assistant. The superior of the house, the Father Rector, had the right to speak to the novices, but by convention he left them severely alone. Our rooms were in a part of the garden reserved for ourselves. Only on very important feasts was the rule relaxed to allow a half-hour of common recreation of the novices and priests, and even then convention forbade them retail to us news of outside events they might have read in the papers or discuss any subject calculated to distract our thoughts from the pursuit of interior recollection.

During the six years of studies of philosophy and theology that followed the novitiate the students were in like manner isolated from the rest of the community, though there was in their case somewhat greater liaison because the professors were free to talk to the students outside as well as inside class, and at the same time remained members of the general community. But even this liberty was limited by convention which forbade familiarity or fraternization.

In addition to the priests, the average community included five to ten lay brothers. They maintained the buildings and the garden, prepared the meals, served in the kitchen and dining room. One was a tailor, another a carpenter, another a gardener, another a cook. The community had no servants. Each member looked after his room, made his bed, swept, dusted, and polished. We novices also swept, dusted, scrubbed, and polished the other rooms in our own part of the monastery, our separate oratory, common room, bathroom, toilet, and corridors. The lay brothers performed these chores in the rest of the monastery and in the public church. Theirs was a particularly thankless life. They took the same vows of poverty, chastity, and obedience as the other members. Normally a candidate for membership elected to become a lay brother because he didn't have the education or the inclination to take the training in philosophy and theology required for the priesthood. The lay brothers, consequently, had few of the intellectual interests and relaxations within the reach of the priest members. Nor were they encouraged to spend their free time in theoretical studies which might develop tastes and attitudes distinct from those of their companions. Any of them who wanted an outlet for his energies found it in a trade or craft. While not cut off formally from the priests, they constituted a subcommunity of their own, eating at a separate table, walking by themselves in the garden at recreation, and indoors in the same common room as the priests forming a group apart that discussed its own affairs and left them to discuss theirs.

Lay novices constituted yet another distinct group, cut off as completely as the choir novices from all contacts other than with their Master of Novices and his assistant.

Combined with the almost continual silence and the formalism of the relationships even among ourselves, this isolation of the novices served to concentrate all energies on the work in hand and to change our behavior in ways I could notice in my companions before I became conscious of them in myself. By narrowing to the vanishing point the opportunity to know or hear anything other than what came to us through the Master of Novices, we absorbed more rapidly his philosophy of life. And as he was almost always with us at recreation, we had little opportunity to develop an independent common life of our own even within the tiny group we constituted. The only chance we had to exchange ideas, other than the afternoon walks in the country twice weekly, was the hour of common recreation each day except Friday (on which the silence was unbroken) after dinner and again after supper. The first half was spent walking in the garden, two leading with the Master of Novices, the others following in threes, the second half in the common room sitting round a table, all joining in general conversation led by the Master of Novices. This meant nobody might ever exchange confidences. There was at least one witness to every conversation.

What one mightn't talk about was well established. The taboos extended to practically the entire range of our previous lives, our families, our friends. All those things lay behind. The quicker we forgot them the better. That left little more than the weather, the progress of vegetative and flower life in the garden (on which subject we were particularly informed because we dug, weeded, and planted in silence for half an hour each morning), the saint's life being read at the moment during meals, plans for the celebration of whatever religious celebration happened to be approaching, a sermon we had recently heard. Relations among ourselves accordingly became extremely tenuous, the two hours' recreation the dullest part of the day. It was hard going, with all the good will in the world, to talk about nothing to a stranger. And that was what we were turning into. Of the nine or ten novices of my year, all but two or three had been my classmates for the previous three to five years. We had had the normal friendships and enmities, the common interests and temperamental clashes. We had played football and endured examinations together, had shouted and gossiped for all we were worth. We knew one another's kinks and fads. But the new atmosphere and relationship changed all that. Each began a concentrated effort to establish a uniform attitude toward all, hiding likes and dislikes behind a wall of artificial affability. Even friends gradually lost a sense of common understanding, developing their separate islands of isolation, islands within which built up pressures and tensions that in other circumstances would have discharged unobserved in the exchanges of ordinary give and take.

The two or three novices who had come from other high schools and were accordingly strangers both to us and to each other were even a greater problem to themselves and to us. We never really got to know them, at least not during the novitiate year. The contacts remained superficial, the best-intentioned actions were wrongly interpreted. Silly little incidents could cause acute pain because there was no way to talk them out, and resulting annoyances sometimes assumed momentous proportions.

One such triviality caused me more suffering than many more serious events of my life. And what added salt to the sore was that I had myself started the whole thing with no thought of starting anything. Every morning about nine-thirty we read for half-an-hour a spiritual book, something like Saint Teresa of Avila's *Way of Perfection,* in the common room. Each read aloud ten minutes, then passed the book to the next in line. We sat in a semicircle, in order of seniority. We hadn't been very long novices, and the Master was still actively engaged on what proved one of his most thorough and successful campaigns. He was breaking us of boyhood habits of levity and spontaneous reaction to external stimuli, teaching us to walk—always and everywhere—with composure, to keep eyes modestly downcast, never betray surprise, anger, or other emotion, to behave in a word with the gravity of bearing that becomes the monk.

The new ways were hard to learn or rather the old not

easy to shed. Performance was still spotty. But we were trying hard, aware we should miss no opportunity to practice. And so one morning, as I finished my ten minutes' reading, it occurred to me—half in earnest, half in jest—I should pass my neighbor the book with a little ceremony. Perhaps it was the monotony of the reader's voice, perhaps the dullness of the subject, but whatever the reason, this was one of the most sleep-inducing periods in the day. All started off sitting upright in hard-bottomed straight chairs, but one after another heads began to nod. And as each nodded, it became his duty to rise and stand unsupported behind his chair. One or two even became expert with time in dozing on their feet. But generally speaking the stratagem achieved its end.

Now it happened that on this ill-omened morning, my neighbor and I were standing when the devil inspired me. Instead of handing him the book in the ordinary way, I held it stiffly before me, took one step in his direction, made a formal inclination of head and shoulders, and then delivered over the book with a reserved gesture. The ceremony was not really so extravagant a creation as it may appear, being merely an adaptation of a ritual (with which then we were becoming familiar) occurring in various Church services.

I don't know how I expected him to react, but I'm sure I didn't anticipate what did happen. Without raising a surprised eyebrow, his face expressionless as my own, he completed the ritual, holding the book up and bowing as I had done, then stepping back and turning smartly to his home position. That would have been nothing, but with what seemed to me a "you asked for it" manner, he repeated the ritual the next time the occasion arose, and the next and the next. Each time it rasped more on my nerves. And the maddening thing was there was no way to stop it. If only I could make clear it had been a silly joke not worth repeating. But our life allowed for not even that slight self-revelation. The same performance was repeated two or three times a week right through the novitiate; each time arousing scarcely controllable anger and frustration, each time building higher a wall of resentment and inner estrangement from my fellow novice. I knew I had only myself to blame for starting it and was conscious of the guilt of such uncharitable impulses. But I couldn't help it. The most I could achieve was to hide them within me and use them to remind myself of my own pettiness whenever I might feel inclined to superiority at my fancied progress in spirituality.

Each little idiosyncrasy of one's companions and of oneself could thus assume major proportions because of our artificial social relationships. All the emphasis was on reducing differences, eliminating personal peculiarities, establishing uniformity of action. Yet each instinctively sought to retain individual characteristics, no matter how limited the area the rule and conventions left for them, and at the same time to react against similar attempts at withdrawal on the part of the others. One insisted on carrying his handkerchief tucked in his sleeve instead of in his pocket. Another made a point of always yielding the right-of-way when passing through a door and raised a fuss if anybody else refused to precede him. Another bound the cincture so tightly around his habit that it seemed he must crack his ribs. Only one or two seemed able to sail along in a condition of blessed oblivion to the details that had to me and apparently to most become of transcendental importance. And they were to me the most annoying of all. It seemed indecent they could be so insensitive.

I regarded my inability to rid my soul of uncharitable reactions a serious defect and tried hard to correct it. It came to me as something of a consolation to discover in our studies of the spiritual life under the direction of the Master of Novices that the same problem had been experienced by most of those who through the centuries had aspired to the perfection of detachment demanded by the religious life. As spiritual writers put it, the first step in detachment was represented by the vow of poverty. The notion of religious poverty when first presented to us seemed noonday clear. The monk abdicated the right to exercise independent use of any object of value. Whatever he needed to maintain life and perform the duties of his state, he used by authority of the rule or by permission of his superior granted under authority of the rule. Even those things he required continually did not cease to belong to the community, and he had no right to use them for any other object than that for which he had received them. As novices, we carried this principle to the extremes of scrupulosity, considering it wrong even to clean one's razor in a towel provided to dry one's face and hands.

But as we went along, it soon became apparent that religious poverty was something more subtle. Its communism had only the most superficial relationship to that of the Communists. Marx thought of the mathematical distribution of goods as an end desirable in itself, in that it would provide more material satisfaction to more people. The communism of the monastery sought freedom from the cares and burdens of worldly business and ambition, but only as a means to a further end. The getting rid of big things from one's concern and one's affection, when pursued as an end in itself, only meant that the affections and desires seized the more tenaciously on smaller things to take their place and prevent the vacuum which nature in all its forms abhors. Poverty could be no mere formula concerned with the use of objects. It had to be principally of the will, and with a positive purpose, to free the affections for the object for which they were intended, to know, serve, and love God.

This emptying-out of self had to be the constant preoccupation of the novice. On the theoretical level, as he knelt in prayer, pondering on the infinite goodness of God and the amazing proofs God had shown of his love for all men and particularly for himself, it was easy to achieve that poverty of spirit. But when one left the oratory to apply the conclusions in daily life, it quickly became evident that self-love clung stubbornly. The practical measure of one's love of God was the degree of love of and consideration for one's fellows, no abstract notion of an idealized mankind but the individuals with whom one lived. And the daily reactions of annoyance at the ways of my fellow novices, the daily desire to criticize, to consider as superior my own interpretation of what was proper to do in any given circumstances, these provided continuing evidence of the unreality of the protestations made at the hours of prayer.

Such was the beginning of self-knowledge. It is not a pleasant activity, principally because self-knowledge is not conducive to self-esteem. And it is useful only when conducted within the frame of reference I have described, namely, when it is joined with a humility that enables the searcher to recognize his weaknesses less as something of which to be ashamed than something urging him the more earnestly to seek the peace of acceptance of God's guidance and help because the human is inherently weak and self-insufficient. There is thus created in the soul a sense of the need of grace, which the spiritual writers unanimously agree is a first step toward perfection. Our Master of Novices had himself a high degree of the resulting spirit of gentleness. Though rigorous in his interpretation of the rules and almost fanatical in his demands on us to divest ourselves of ourselves, he had the tenderness toward others of one who has experienced much suffering and in particular the suffering of having to recognize one's own infirmity. And as he kept hammering away in conference after conference at a thousand different facets of the meaning of poverty and its relationships with the whole of the spiritual life, it seemed finally to emerge that what one had to strive for was the incorporation of one's individual will in a community will in tune with and expressing the will of God, so that every act of oneself and of one's companions became equally understandable and acceptable as deriving from that common will which has replaced one's own.

Just how near the goal we reached must this side of the grave stay largely a matter of opinion. The simplest human soul remains a substance of near-infinite complexity even to itself. The philosophers describe self-study as reflection, folding back; and each time the soul folds back on itself it finds yet another fold beyond. Even opposites like humility and pride melt into each other, especially in the extreme reaches. To expose those deep thoughts that tell how one works and why to public dissection under the scalpel of the vulgar curious calls for much humility or much pride. But which? Yet I think we novices substantially reached a practical solution in that we learned the wisdom that it didn't much matter which. Acts of public self-humiliation which constituted an integral part of the novice's life became through habit a matter of course, to be done almost without thinking about them.

Progress to this point was in several steps. During the days after one's arrival one saw with mingled horror and amazement acts of abasement performed by the older novices already approaching the end of their year of trial. They dropped on their knees without offering a single word of excuse when publicly corrected by the Master of Novices. They knelt bent over double on the palms of their hands in the corridor as the members of the community filed silently into the dining room. They took their dinner seated on the floor. One's unthinking reaction was to revolt internally at the idea of ever constituting such a public spectacle. But when one's turn came, it proved to be just possible. There was a hot flush of shame, but nobody laughed, nobody in fact took the least notice. Soon, instead of feeling ashamed, one began to experience a sense of complacency at one's virtue and sedulously to search out opportunities of shining as the humblest, the most mortified of all. That was a harder condition to conquer than the other. But by keeping at it, stolidly, matter-of-factly, given stout aid by the Master of Novices who was as careful to prevent any from standing apart by greater performance of public acts of mortification as he was to spur on the laggards, one came to acknowledge with a mature sadness that as far as public opinion went all came out about the same.

Reaching the frame of mind in which one's actions ceased to be influenced by what one thought the other members of the community thought of one was facilitated by the gradual realization that the public acts of self-humiliation the novices performed were as stylized as a game or play, something the priests and lay brothers themselves had gone through as novices and now looked at with good-humored tolerance. It was harder to reach a like indifference to the possibility of public humiliation in the presence of strangers. Of that possibility we were all extremely conscious. It required great effort to walk along the streets of the town, when we went out for walks or on the rare occasion of a visit to doctor or dentist, with eyes downcast, observing the rule that forbade ever to look fixedly into the face of the passer-by. That curious intangible called human respect made us feel every stranger asked himself what sort of creatures behaved so unlike the rest of mortals.

Novitiate folklore, passed on with fanciful details from year to year, told of strange assignments to test the novice's ability to disregard the opinion of the world. There actually existed for all to see a collection of weird hats of various sizes, shapes, and forms, which the novices might any day be ordered to wear when going for a walk. Another horrible possibility, vouched for by credible witnesses as having frequently occurred, was that a novice might be sent into a store with a single penny to buy candies. And at any moment the Master of Novices had only to correct a novice in public for any offense real or imaginary to compel the hapless one to cast himself on his knees wherever they happened to be. None of these things did happen to us, and after the first few months, I think any of us would have taken them in his stride. Yet for a time their possibility constituted a real source of terror, a sort of concretization of the sacrifice of self that had to be made before a person could say he had truly renounced the world.

As we lost relish for the symbols and values that dominate the thoughts and dictate the course of action of people in the world, we simultaneously familiarized ourselves with the pattern of life in the direct service of God which in its broad lines is common to all religious orders and congregations of the Catholic Church. Like any way of life, it is a whole compounded of a multiplicity of details. To the newcomer one of the most striking because one of the least familiar elements is the divine office. Already back in the fourth century, the monks who had left solitary hermitages in the desert to establish monastic cities along the banks of the Nile, were gathering together several times each day and night to sing choral offices based on the Psalms attributed to King David, voicing through that sublime poetry an unending hymn of praise and thanksgiving to the Lord in their own name and that of the mass of faithful they represented and to whom they gave savor.

There was much in the regime of those Egyptian monks one could accept only with reservation. Their excessive asceticism tended to make the domination of the flesh an end to be pursued for its own sake and harden men into self-worship as heroes of physical endurance. When Saint Benedict in the sixth century led the reaction against it, insisting with the Greek and Roman philosophers that virtue stands in the middle, he reduced the choral offices of the Egyptians by about two thirds. But he thought no less than they of the importance of communal acts of praise and thanks to God and approved also of the way they had chosen to express this basic obligation. The Psalms continued to form the nucleus of the divine office, as they do to this day. And so the custom grew up for all priests and monks to assemble at fixed times for common worship. Matins and Lauds sung at the eighth hour of the night (according to the Roman system of reckoning) or about two A.M., Prime at the first hour or sunrise, Tierce at the third hour, Sext at the sixth, None at the ninth. Vespers, most familiar of the canonical hours to the modern layman, followed in the peace of sundown of a day fruitful of prayer and toil. And finally, before the monk hastened to snatch a few hours' sleep to prepare him to resume the cycle shortly after midnight, came Complin, a brief completion in which the Psalms sang of physical and mental tranquility, the reward on earth and in heaven of a life lived in communion with nature and nature's God.

Benedict's scheme underwent many changes through the centuries. Poet after poet labored lovingly on hymns in diamond-hard, deceptively free-flowing medieval Latin rimes to grace the great feasts of Our Lord and the Blessed Virgin and of those saints who happened to be the object of a particular cult in a given time or place. The Gregorian Chant contributed the support of a musical form sufficiently simple to allow all to participate, sufficiently reserved to be appropriate to the liturgy, yet flexible to express and lift beyond the fluted, delicate arches of the choir the vehement soul's eternal longing for the infinite. Gradually the hours grew longer again and more complex, threatening once more to become an end in themselves, to absorb so much of the day as to leave the monk no time for other duties. But by a gradual process of readjustment linked with reforms of monastic orders in the twelfth and thirteenth centuries and the establishment about that time of such new orders as the Dominicans and Franciscans, they were again purged and streamlined, and brought into much the form they today retain. The contemplative orders still chant the hours in choir at approximately the times of the night and day established by tradition. Many of the newer so-called active orders and congregations, whose rule prescribes they devote a substantial part of their time to an outside activity such as preaching missions or teaching, follow a modification that grew up among priests charged with administering parishes. They either read the hours privately at their convenience or simply recite in common in a monotone, instead of chanting, at times that fit in with their other duties.

The rule of our Congregation, reflecting this last practice which itself is typical of the adaptation of the Latin Church to changes in the social and economic order through the centuries, provided that during the mission seasons the priests should read the office in private and at other times should recite it in choir. As novices unconcerned with outside activities, we recited the hours daily in common, and at the times at which the priests recited them in choir when they had to do so. These times had been fixed in accordance with a curious yet apt principle which finds itself reflected in many liturgical offices and ceremonies, the principle of anticipation. This is a tendency to perform an obligation before it falls due and to advance the time of a celebration, a simple, easily intelligible externalization of the eagerness of the children of God to anticipate his commands and participate in his delights. The most obvious of its many applications is in the offices of Holy Saturday morning which already celebrate the Resurrection, being in fact the ceremonies that originally began late in the evening of Holy Saturday to be continued through the night and to terminate with the sunrise of the Risen Christ.

By an application of this principle, when the hours of

the divine office were assembled into groups for the convenience of busy men, they were simultaneously advanced. We accordingly recited the Matins and Lauds of each day's office in mid-afternoon of the previous day, the Prime, Tierce, Sext, and None immediately after morning meditation and before Mass, and Vespers and Complin at midday. Since by a further application of the principle of anticipation earlier incorporated into the office itself, the celebration of more important feasts began with the Vespers of the previous day, this meant that by noon each day we were already conscious of what the liturgy had in store for the day to come. Our lives thus became inevitably, effortlessly, intertwined with the tides and seasons of the Church's spiritual life, as they rose and fell, ebbed and flowed, baring the recesses of the deeps of suffering in the seasons of sorrow and overflowing majestically the upper limits of more than human joy on the spring tides of the great festivals.

This panorama paralleled and complemented the daily celebration of the same liturgical seasons in the Mass, which in the same way as the hours of the office superimposed an ever-changing superstructure of prayers and hymns and readings from the Scriptures and the Fathers of the Church on an unchanging central theme. The very language had a firmness, a definition, and a culture from the polishing and repolishing of scores of generations of the world's best writers. We were brought on conducted tours through the whole of Scripture, both Old and New Testaments, with commentaries and explanations adapted to the subject of the moment by the exegetes of the centuries.

In this way we became attuned to the liturgical significance of each of the big divisions of the ecclesiastical year. Opening this year with Advent, we shared the longing of the Old Testament prophets for the Messiah as they prayed the Lord that he might come and show his face that they be saved. As the artist paints his background in somber colors to intensify the highlights, the Church prepares for its celebrations by appropriate periods of penance. The vigils of the feasts were days of strict fast. The divine office was geared to the spiritual preparation to commemorate a great mystery. The priest at Mass wore purple vestments to signify sobriety and self-restraint, and the flowers were removed from the altars. At Christmas we joined the angels, shepherds, and kings of the East in going over to Bethlehem to fall down and adore the infant wrapped in swaddling clothes and laid in a manger.

Septuagesima reflected a transition, a reluctant parting. It broke the mood of quiet possession that represented the childhood of Jesus spent with Mary His Mother in the home of Joseph the Carpenter, where he was subject to them, sensed the distant rumblings of the conflict and rejection, the terror and self-oblation that were to dominate Lent's seven weeks and culminate in that outpouring of passions, of sordidness and weakness, of treachery and hatreds and redeeming love, that was the Passion and led to the life-giving Death of Holy Week. Then from the darkness of the tomb burst out the light of restored life at Easter, a light and a life repeated by nature as the spring awakened the songbirds and the grass and flowers and treebuds to confirm the reality of the supreme miracle. Pentecost followed with its commemoration of the coming of the Holy Spirit on the first disciples and the notification to them that the time had come to expand their mission to all nations and peoples. And in the long series of weeks that followed till the end of the year we were conscious of the response of the Church to that mission, for the readings developed continuously and methodically the events of the public life and teachings of Christ, sating the senses with a splendor of poetry and music and filling the soul with the spiritual peace of a mission fulfilled and a goal reached.

Such was the theme of the year-long symphony of which each day's office constituted a movement. And like ever-novel variations on the theme came the feasts of the Mother of God and of the saints, each with its appropriate lessons, reflections, and hymns, each illustrating a new facet of the mysteries of the relationships between God and man, of the heights to which mortals like ourselves were capable of rising by attuning themselves to their Creator and losing their nothingness in the allness of the infinite.

Just as in nature the seasons dominate every aspect of the life of the tiller of the soil, dictating the activities to be performed at any given time, and even suggesting the forms in which he expresses his joys and relaxations, so for us the spiritual seasons each day imposed their modifications on the measured rhythm of our regulated life. The subjects allotted for meditations in common, the books selected to be read in the dining room during meals, many of the daily conferences of the Master of Novices, these and other influences on our thought habits were directed to creating ever-greater consciousness of the spirit of each succeeding season. In Advent, for example, the rule prescribed complete abstinence from meat. By custom we performed more exacting works of mortification than normal. On top of this came the three days of fast in the third week of Advent and yet another on the eve of Christmas. This penitential preparation created a sense of the importance of the mystery we were about to celebrate, and highlighted by contrast the gaiety of the subsequent feast solemnized with several days of relative freedom from normal routine, more elaborate meals, and a sense of personal participation in a joyous event. Similarly, more than six weeks of strict observance of the laws of fasting, as well as a variety of special penances and other restrictions of our modest relaxations, prepared for the solemn commemorations of Holy Week.

During Holy Week we parted company with the simplifications and abbreviations of the liturgical ceremonies which during the rest of the year the rule permitted in deference to the partly active character of the life of the Congregation, and carried out the ritual with most of the solemnity proper to a strictly contemplative Order. Starting with the blessing and procession of palms and the chanting of the Passion at High Mass on Palm Sunday, we sought to relive as closely as possible the events of the final days of the life of Christ as recorded in the gospels. We carried out the Tenebrae rituals, chanting David's plaintive psalms and singing the soul-stealing lamentations of Jeremias set to the age-old incomparable music that groaned and wept and humbled itself and soared in confiding faith with the prose poetry of the Prophet.

On Holy Thursday we repeated the ceremony, once practiced by kings and emperors, of the *Mandatum* which gives the day its old English name of Maundy Thursday. It was a ceremony with which we were not unfamiliar, for each Thursday evening it was carried out in a simplified form at the beginning of the evening meal. While all stood in their places at table, the priest to whom it fell to lead public prayers for the week read the corresponding story from the Gospel and then the superior knelt before each and kissed the toe of his shoe. But on Holy Thursday it was more elaborate and imposing. We assembled in the dining room in mid-morning, shortly after the end of the morning hours and solemn Mass. A priest began to sing. His tenor voice was sweet and unforced. The cadences of the Plain Chant gave magnificence and sonorousness and limpidity to the words. He described a scene even like this. A group of men gathered in a dining room, bare and simple as ours. The meal already on the table. The host, the Master, knowing the hour of his death was at hand, knowing that one of those present had resolved to sell him for a little silver, would yet show one more mark of his affection. He got up, tucked back his cloak under his girdle, took a basin of water, and got down on his knees in front of one of his guests. It was Peter the Fisherman, the unpolished Galilean peasant who hadn't even learned to cover up his provincial accent. Never, he protested bluntly, never would he be party to such an indignity. But the Master insisted: it was a gesture of belonging. And Peter shouted agreement with typical abandon: in that case, not only the feet but also the hands and the head. And he washed Peter's feet and those of the others. And he sat again at the head of the table and explained with equal simplicity what it all meant.

"You call me Lord and Master; and you say well, for so I am. If therefore I, your Lord and Master, wash your feet, so you also should wash each other's feet. For I have given you an example, that as I did to you, so also do you."

The voice of the singer rose and fell in the final modulation and was silent. It was a moment to which to cling, and with the consummate skill of simple art, the ceremony continued without breaking the imagery. The cantor intoned and the choir took up the antiphon which repeated with variations the words and theme of the preceding phrase: *Mandatum novum:* "A new commandment I give you, that you love one another . . ." As one floated in the music, one became aware that something new was happening. The community superior had taken off the violet vestment in which he had presided over the ceremony and was tying a white linen apron around his waist. Then he came first to one and then another of the priests, lay brothers, and novices. Kneeling he poured water into a basin over the bare foot of each, wiped it dry in a towel, and then kissed it. He was a man well up in the fifties. If you met him in a railway carriage not wearing a clerical collar, you might categorize him as a middle-class farmer or a cattle jobber. The scant hairs separated by a desert patch on top were steel gray. His face was weather-beaten and deep furrowed. He even stood normally with his feet apart and the shoulders slightly stooped as one must to balance on an unsprung farm cart. In our life as novices he mainly entered as corrector of the mistakes of pronunciation we made when reading at meals. Seated at the head of the table, his ear cocked to catch the sense (for he was slightly deaf), he pounced unmercifully on every error, repeating the offending word in his high-pitched voice harsh as a cracked bell until the hapless novice got it right, the while worrying his dictionary with the doggedness of a tugboat easing a liner into dock.

The chanting of the variations on the theme continued, now the cantors, now the full choir: "I have given you an example . . . Later you will understand . . . In this shall all men know you . . ." As I sat awaiting my turn, it suddenly shot through my mind that the Greeks had a word for it. It seemed irreverent, but then I realized it really wasn't. For them the function of drama was catharsis, purification. And here was indeed great drama that in artless symbols purified and idealized each simple act that went to make up the life record of this man and such men. Even the rasping voice protesting against our inflictions on the King's English ever after came to me enveloped in the catharsis of that spiritual moment.

It was Holy Thursday, anniversary of that supper at which Jesus had taken bread, blessed it, handed it to each, and said: "Take and eat. This is my body . . . Do this in commemoration of me." Though it was a season of penitence, this stupendous event could not pass uncelebrated. The silence, which would continue until after the long ceremonies of Holy Saturday morning, was not interrupted. Nevertheless, at dinner on Holy Thursday, the only full meal of the day since we were still in Lent, we had an extra course and more elaborate dishes than normally. And the priests and lay brothers had two glasses of wine as on feast days. The rule authorized the novices also to take the wine, but the Master of Novices didn't approve. Instead, the lay brother put a bottle of lemonade or ginger ale at each place when wine was served the priests.

It was the night of the vigil in the Garden of Gethsemane, and we took turn with the priests to keep vigil, two by two, all through the night before the tabernacle in the church where lay the host consecrated at that morning's Mass for the Good Friday Mass of the Presanctified. As we watched, we read again and meditated on the gospel accounts of those final hours, pondering on all the human emotions and reactions revealed in that tremendous twenty-four hours in Jerusalem two thousand years ago, the cupidities, spites, hatreds, fears, tendernesses, braveries, and all-conquering love. It was no mere mental gymnastic. It was a meditation leading to self-revelation, revelation of potential for evil and for good, and through self-revelation to self-realization in a firmer, more conscious assumption of position in the perennial conflict within each and among all of good and evil. And in that mood Good Friday was passed, the anguish of the psalmist in the morning office, the bitter self-reproach of the lamentations at the Mass of the Presanctified, the leaden-footed hours of waiting through the soul-darkened afternoon, the calm of confidence that sang through the Tenebrae lessons after evil had done its worst and the shuddering earth was firm once more in its course.

And so we came to Holy Saturday. There were still hours of processions and chants and prostrations before the bells, silenced since Thursday morning, rang joyously, and the muted organ pealed again as the celebrant of the Mass intoned "Glory to God in the highest" and the choir took up ". . . and on earth peace to men of good will . . ." But those hours passed lightly. Though the Church was still officially in mourning, the grieving was really over. Man had been redeemed in and through the oblation of Christ's death. And those who had died with Christ—Paul had said so in express words—would live also with him. All that remained accordingly was the fitting period of symbolic waiting. The farmer does not grieve for the seed he casts in the soil. He waits in confiding calm its germination.

But the man who dies and rises with Christ does not take on again where he left off. He is changed by the tremendous experience. He knows that while he must continue to live in the body, the spirit can and must control.

He knows that while it is fit to rejoice, the expression of joy and of triumph must always reflect this new relationship, that the spiritual forces within must normally, almost effortlessly, exercise a reasoned control over the instincts and senses. Dominated by this new knowledge and new realization, we reached the triumphant celebration of Easter Sunday. We first expressed our joy on the purely spiritual level in the ceremony which constitutes the central act of worship of the Catholic Church, the commemoration and renewal of Christ's sacrifice in the Mass in which we all participated—as was our daily wont—not only by assisting and ministering to the celebrating priest but by partaking of the sacrament of the body and blood of Christ. Today it was celebrated with more solemnity than on any day of the year, with incense and music and hymns of victory and the rich pageantry with which the celebrant and his assistants dressed in vestments of cloth-of-gold moved about the altar.

Then came the celebration on a more material level, for we were still men composed of body and spirit, a single unity entirely in the service of God. Shortly before the hour of dinner we assembled in the dining room for a celebration which I had never before witnessed. I might call it a monastic cocktail party. Tables were laid out buffet-fashion down the center of the room, and all of us, priests, lay brothers and novices, intermingled. Plates of paschal lamb and hard-boiled eggs dyed in bright colors took pride of place among the savories on the tables. We wished each other a happy feast, the novices and brothers kissing the hands of the priests, and those of equal rank embracing in the Italian manner. Glasses of wine were served to the priests and lay brothers. Dinner followed at its regular time, after an interruption to allow the tables to be restored to their normal separated positions, one for the priests, one for the lay brothers, and one for the novices with the Master seated at the head. It was an elaborate meal and, as customary on feast days, after a few minutes the reading was suspended and conversation allowed. At the end, all had recreation in common before the novices went back to their own part of the monastery to resume their life of silence and recollection.

What impressed me most about such periods of relaxation was the relativeness of the freedom they authorized. We had been accustomed to celebrate with the gusto of youth, often found it easier to fast with enthusiasm than to feast with discretion. Yet on nothing did the Master of Novices insist more emphatically. The test of self-control was not to reject but to use temperately, to take a single candy when they were handed round at recreation on a feast day and to look with indifference when the box was returned to its cupboard—an unlocked cupboard guarded by one's own conscience—to await the next occasion for celebrating.

Such devices brought the novice each week and month a little nearer the goal of independence of material things. He lived in his bare cell. He ate with moderation, controlled his eyes, ears, and tongue, slept only enough to maintain health and strength, endured heat and cold with patience, practiced penitential exercises, followed a uniform pattern of activities from morning to night, never idle for a moment; and did all these things from a sense of duty and not through fear or external compulsion. That was the first step. But more important was the spirit according to which he lived. Pleasures and comforts were not rejected as evil in themselves, since according to Catholic teaching all things created by God are good, but only because attachment to them distracted man from higher spiritual pleasure. It was not a rejection of the bad in favor of the good, but of the good in favor of the better. The physical regime was accordingly only the negative part of the novice's conditioning. The positive part consisted in developing, through lectures and conferences, through daily recitation of the divine office and participation in the rites of the Mass, through attunement to the ecclesiastical seasons, through reading of spiritual books, through prayer and meditation, a familiarity with and affection for the things of the soul and a concentration on God, who not only modeled the human soul in his own image and likeness but created it to know, love, and serve him.

With Easter it was again spring and the end of our year as novices was in sight. Once again on the other side of the wall we could hear the thud of tennis ball on racket and the chatter and laughter of young people in the long evenings. But now there was scarcely a temptation to raise one's eyes for a glance at the game as one passed the windows at the end of the corridor overlooking the court, and one's thoughts lingered on the matter only long enough to grieve that the world was still full of people wasting their energies on frivolity. The days seemed to fly more quickly, and more things were happening to interrupt the routine. There were important feasts to celebrate, Ascension, Pentecost, Corpus Christi, the feast of our founder, Saint Alphonsus. Four or five times the Master of Novices took us out for a whole day in a couple of hired cars to Warrenpoint or Bettystown or some other beach where we swam in the surf and ran races on the sand and picnicked among the dunes. Our Tuesday and Thursday walks had now always the same objective, a sheltered inlet on the river estuary. We waded in mud when the tide was low, but we didn't mind. It was good to plunge in the cool water, and besides the time passed more quickly than when one was just marching along having to make conversation. Before we realized, the postulants—the aspirants for the next year—had arrived, and each of us had the task of coaching one of them in the mysteries of a life that to us had become normality. We gasped at the uninhibited way they ran along the corridors when they thought nobody was looking, at the frivolity of their conversation at recreation time about movies they had seen and parties they had attended and boyish escapades in which they had participated during the summer vacation, at the snatches of ragtime hits they hummed softly as they dug in the garden.

And while we watched the rapid transformation that took place in them, a transformation that had occurred in ourselves a year earlier but which we hadn't seen, the day had come to begin the fifteen-day retreat which preceded the taking of the vows and integration into the Congregation. They were days of tremendous intensity. From the moment the bell summoned us to morning prayer at five-twenty-five until it tolled at ten-thirty the end of a tired day, there was no moment not dedicated directly to increasing our realization of the immensity of the step we were about to take.

On both sides it was a serious step. As our Master of Novices had explained day by day throughout the year, and as the old priest who lectured to us four times daily during the retreat now repeated, it was a step that imposed permanent moral obligations. True, the vows were taken for only three years in the first instance, since Canon Law so prescribed in order to provide a longer period of probation in case either party should on closer acquaintance repent of the bargain. But according to the teaching of Saint Alphonsus on the vocation to the religious life, as interpreted in the Congregation, the fact of taking the vows of membership carried with it the moral obligation to persevere to death so that subsequent abandonment, even if legally permissible, meant the rejection of grace. Once again we reviewed the obligations assumed with the vows, the giving-up of the right to use anything as our own and of attachment to worldly possessions involved in the vow of poverty, the obligation of celibacy and the consequent never-ending watch on our senses and passions required by the vow of chastity, and finally the undertaking to observe the rule of life of the Congregation and to carry out all lawful commands of our superiors demanded by the vow of obedience.

The Retreat Master did not hide or minimize any of these obligations. But at the same time he pointed out the benefits we could count on receiving in return. The Congregation undertook to receive us as members, to provide the necessities of life, in old age as in youth, in sickness as in health. It offered us freedom from the preoccupations of the world to permit us to devote ourselves without distraction to the service of God. It guaranteed that if we did what lay in our power, we should not lack grace and strength to persevere until death. As I listened to him speak, and as I turned over in my mind what he had said during the meditation periods in church and during the hours of relaxation when we walked in silence in the garden, it all seemed to make supreme sense. There was nothing wrong with a bargain that offered so much in exchange for so little.

So arrived the final day of the novitiate, September 8,

1928. Never did the first clang of the morning bell announce a day more sweetly. Never did it seem so easy as during the half-hour of common meditation that opened the day to praise and thank the Lord who from all eternity had chosen me not only to accept his true faith but to follow him in the literal fulfillment of his words, shielded from the dangers that beset the common path of men. Never were the verses of the Jewish poet which countless monks and nuns chant daily from the morning watches even until night more brimful of meaning. "I chose to be the least one in the house of my God rather than to live in the tents of sinners . . . Behold how good and how pleasant to live as brothers together . . ." Never did the sacred mystery of the death of Christ renewed on the altar, the uniting of the creator with his creature in Holy Communion, reveal more palpably the inward grace of which the wafer was the outward sign. For on this morning, after these holy preliminaries, the solemn pledging was to follow.

I could not but feel elation and gratitude at having been chosen without merit of my own for a privilege so great. Yet such is mortal's misery that his every mood contains its own undoing. I had to ask myself if the satisfaction I felt was gratitude for a gift received, or self-complacency for the privilege that was mine, or nothing more than relief that the aridity of the novitiate was over and I was about to embark on the great intellectual experience of the house of studies.

It was hard to get to the bottom of one's emotions. When one succeeded in suppressing the cruder forms of pride, their place was taken by subtler forms, and so on apparently ad infinitum. One could find motives for self-complacency in anything and everything, equally in performing a public virtuous act and in not performing it so as to avoid the notoriety. There always remained that ultimate uncertainty about oneself. Was it possible to count on oneself for the strength and determination to continue to death in that narrow course? At the age of nineteen one's life seems to stretch away infinitely into the future. One year, five years, twenty years, one might pledge. But a lifetime . . .

All of these doubts suddenly came to a head as I knelt in line with my companions before the main altar in the public church that morning. The ceremony of profession and taking of vows was about to begin for us. A sudden impulse seized me to rush away before it was too late. Furtively I glanced around for the nearest exit. Then, when I saw how easy it was and how easy it always had been to escape if I really wanted to, I recognized the impulse for what it was. The Master of Novices, the spiritual writers I had been reading for a year, the Retreat Master, had all identified it in turn. No matter what decisions one took in life, each was a plunge in the dark, an act of faith. I was quite right in doubting my own strength and ability. That was a simple act of humility, which—as Saint Teresa never tired of saying—was neither more nor less than the ability to recognize things as they are. But one could not stop there. One had to plunge in the dark, make the act of faith, remembering that God will not deny grace to the man who does what in him lies. I was again at peace. There was no reservation in my mind as with trembling voice I read aloud in turn the solemn pledge which, received by the superior, conferred the rights and imposed the duties of membership of the Congregation.

CHAPTER 4

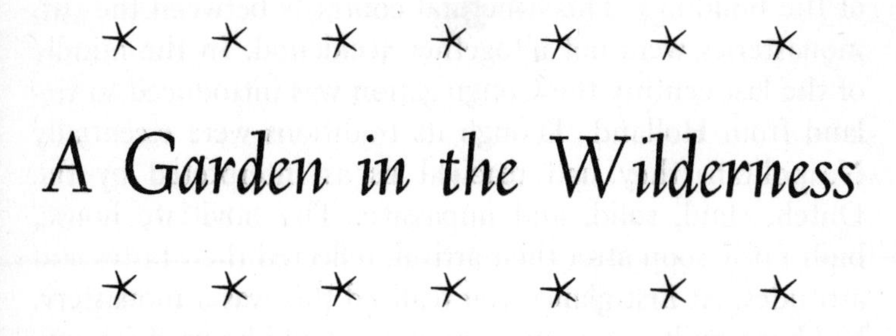

A Garden in the Wilderness

Progress in the form of an automobile had reached the house of studies where we went by train next day. A jaunting car had carried me the three miles from the railway station on previous brief visits. Few other evidences of the twentieth century were, however, observable in the routine of the inhabitants of this uninteresting group of buildings planted in the flat and barren expanses of East Galway. A small electric plant chug-chugged noisily from early morning to bedtime three days a week to charge batteries that lighted dim bulbs over our study tables. But not even a telephone connected us to the outer world. Our life required no mechanical complications, and it was regarded essential to the contemplation of knowledge on which we were to concentrate for six years that every outside distraction be ruthlessly barred. Neither newspaper nor radio would disturb that solitude.

One of the more obvious differences between the student house and the novitiate was the physical appearance of the buildings. The structural contrasts between the two monasteries were not altogether accidental. In the middle of the last century the Congregation was introduced to Ireland from Holland. Though its traditions were essentially Neapolitan, they had reached us as interpreted by the Dutch, staid, solid, and impassive. The novitiate house, built fairly soon after their arrival, reflected their tastes and attitudes. At first glance you realized this was a monastery, had been built as a monastery, never could be used for anything but a monastery. The style was a firm and unimaginative revival Gothic, all buildings faced in cut stone from ground to eaves, and little dormer windows typical of the Low Countries peeping from the high-hipped roof. The main building, five floors high, formed two adjoining sides of a square, the public church a third. The designer had allowed for possible future expansion in the shape of a wing to complete the square. In the meantime, the fourth side was closed by a corridor which gave access from the ground floor of the monastery to the sacristy of the church. The only point at which the original design had not been followed through was in the church tower. Its proportions called for a structure rising a hundred feet or more, but it had been stopped short just a few feet higher than the roof of the church and capped with a squat slate roof. The gardens had been laid out with equal precision and thoroughness, formal terraces and symmetrical walks. The limits of the cloister, within which by Canon Law no woman might ever come, were unquestionably established by ten-foot-high walls topped with broken bottles set in cement.

The house of studies, by contrast, reflected the attitudes of a more recent period. The Irish priests who had replaced the Dutchmen as superiors revealed in their work little indication of any long-term plan. They started off by buying an existing three-story rectangular building without architectural character, and added to it—as the need to expand became acute—first one, then another wing, each with less beauty than its predecessor, fewer architectural pretensions and greater sacrifice of function and efficiency in order to cut costs. The two main structures were at right angles to each other, as in the case of the novitiate, but separated by a one-story room which served as oratory. And while the small public church formed a third side, the nature of the terrain excluded any possibility of completing the square without earth-moving alterations that our amateur architects would never have considered. Instead they had pushed out various substructures at different angles from the back of the principal buildings to form a rambling, disjointed group beyond hope of ever pulling together, short of pulling down and starting again, into an efficient unity.

The grounds around reflected a like haphazard growth. Only a token fence marked the cloister. Instead of the solid, stoutly locked doors of the Dutchmen, the entrances were guarded by ordinary gates secured by a latch. The gardens lacked formality and precise limits. They had expanded gradually outward from the buildings, each generation of students interesting itself in some new project without too much thought of how it fitted into what already existed or how it might affect the next effort to tame a further section of wilderness. Some worked on formal gardens, rock gardens, fruit orchards. Some built roads and paths. Some planted trees on the sand dunes, filling holes with rich soil to nurture the seedlings until they sent tap roots deep in the sand and built up with their neighbors a matting of tangled roots to hold firm in the bitterest storms. Another built a landing stage on a little lake. Yet another tried his hand at a ram to pump water; or a new type of septic tank. There was no such thing as a clearly defined official project or over-all plan. Rather the results came as a sort of by-product of the varied urges of interested and interesting people who enjoyed the creative satisfaction of controlling nature and teaching her to do better than herself.

The atmosphere of informality, almost of sloppiness, which impressed me as characterizing the physical conditions of the house of studies and its surroundings by contrast with the novitiate from which I had just come, seemed to carry over into the conduct and attitudes of the students. The first glimpses shocked me. Had I then been asked, I shouldn't have admitted it, but I was frightened to find the supports suddenly pulled away. For over a year every moment had been organized and accounted for. I followed a timetable in prayer, meditation, eating, relaxation, sleep. It is easy to be a machine. The restoration of discretion was disconcerting. Hours of recreation were considerably longer. A whole day each week had to be allocated according to one's own judgment to prayer, study, and recreation. Substantial parts of the daily study hours were to be occupied as one thought best.

Equally disturbing was the change that seemed to have taken place in the colleagues who had by now finished their first year's studies. As I had watched them during my first and their final month of noviceship, I had wondered how they had altered since they had left secondary school a year previously. They had learned to walk gravely, to keep their eyes downcast, to restrain their voices and their opinions, to exhibit all the outward signs of deep spirituality. Now they seemed more easygoing, slapdash, interested in their food, casual about their prayers, anxious for diversion. Some did not delay to hint that a lot of this noviceship stuff had been overdone, the sooner we learned to be more reasonable the better for everybody. But our Master of Novices had warned us against that. There had to be a variation of activity but no slackening of spirit. Yet I wondered secretly if I had really scaled the heights of sanctity which in the protected silence of the noviceship I had assured myself were planted firmly under my feet. Or was it all just external? The answer I didn't know and feared to learn.

Though my first impression of the student's life was one of substantial relaxation from the rigors of the novitiate, it was actually both highly organized and ascetic. Each morning the great bell clanged at the same unearthly hour as in the novitiate, giving time to shave, dress, and get in fifteen minutes of private devotions before the morning meditation in common began at six. Mass and Holy Communion followed at six-thirty. Making one's bed and dusting one's room took five minutes, which left fifty for study before breakfast at eight. As in the novitiate, this was not a formal meal. Because the Italian founders two centuries earlier regarded coffee and rolls as a normal breakfast, it was still a normal breakfast. We kept silence, of course, but nobody read to us, and each left the dining room as he finished. The tables were not even covered with a cloth as at other meals.

Thirty minutes of walking and chatting in the garden helped to digest breakfast before we started back to study and lectures which occupied the day till seven-thirty in the evening, with a short mid-morning break, a longer break in the early afternoon and another half-hour break at six. The longer break allowed for lunch, one hour's recreation, a half-hour's siesta, and a half-hour's spiritual reading. The siesta again reflected the persistence of tradition, another carry-over of the customs of south Italy. A few actually slept the entire half-hour. Most walked in the garden, reciting the rosary and making the way of the cross. I frequently compromised, devoting twenty minutes to my devotions and sleeping for ten. The half-hour before supper at eight was again devoted to meditation in common, each kneeling in his place in the community oratory. After supper came the final hour of common recreation. The bell ending recreation and summoning us at nine-thirty to night prayers marked the start of the Great Silence. After night prayers, one might go immediately to bed or might stay on in the oratory to pray in private. But all had to be in bed when the bell signaled lights out at ten-thirty.

The principal variations from this routine came on Sunday, Tuesday, and Thursday. Sunday morning till noon was spent in spiritual exercises, including a lecture from the Father Prefect which was followed by the same ritual of self-accusation of one's faults which took place on Fridays in the novitiate. As in the novitiate, here also one of us had the office of *zelator*. He came round our rooms from time to time to see that everything was in order, most frequently dropping in during spiritual reading or at some other period allocated to prayer in our rooms. On Sunday afternoon we either went for a walk for a couple of hours or played football. A similar break occurred on Tuesday afternoon. In both cases, after the game or walk, we spent the rest of the afternoon at study until the hour for evening meditation. But on Thursday the entire day was free from morning Mass till evening meditation, except that all had to show up for dinner in common and the recreation that followed. Some studied the entire day, but others made a real break in the routine, working at their hobbies, chatting in the garden, or playing the piano or phonograph in the common room.

It was immediately obvious to me that this changed routine and tempo would involve adjustments not only in my habits but even in my way of thinking. Though I hadn't yet got to the point of rationalizing my actions and attitudes very much, I reacted instinctively against the idea of having to turn myself right around again. Nevertheless, since the rules said certain things had to be done, they had to be done. And one of the most urgent was to recover the faculty of speech, all but lost during the noviceship. Several daily hours of recreation were now as much an obligation as prayer and study. But I found myself with next to nothing to say to most of my companions. Before I had gone to the novitiate, I had anticipated that the silence would be the hardest thing. If it hadn't started by being easy, it had become part of me to the point that my own company was generally less tedious than that of others. The rules and conventions forbade discussing frivolous matters unbecoming to our state, and in any case our complete isolation from everything that happened outside the monastery left us without the trivia of politics or sport or amusements that keep the tongues of mankind wagging.

My inability to keep up a flow of appropriate conversation within the imposed limits worried me greatly. I realized it was unfair to the companion of the moment and consequently a serious failing. When I could, I avoided the issue by doing manual work instead of walking in the grounds. Often it was possible to work alone, and if there was a companion, the work either itself provided material for comment or reduced the embarrassment of the long intervals of silence.

But certain periods of common recreation were obligatory, nearly half an hour after breakfast, an hour after dinner, and another after supper. We then walked in the garden two by two, or in wet weather in a long, low, corrugated hut—army surplus from the first World War—where the dust rose in clouds from the wooden floor under the tramping feet. One's companion was decided by the chance order in which each two happened to reach the door where we knelt briefly in prayer before opening conversation by the senior of the two saying in Latin: "Praised be Jesus Christ and Mary ever Virgin!" and the other replying: "Now and always." The precise and definite prohibition of the rules against allowing personal preference to influence the choice of one companion or the avoidance of another was strictly observed. That was a straightforward obligation, like white and black, and accordingly simple to fulfill. More complicated was the consequent duty of talking to the companion sent by fate. We did have a few extroverts, people seldom at a loss for frothy, time-passing chatter, and with a few others I could for various reasons of close previous acquaintance or natural attunement relax. But they were exceptions. My normal condition at recreation was one of distasteful struggle during the first years as a student.

The second half of the after-dinner and after-supper recreation was spent in the common room. At the far end of one of the rambling additions to the main buildings, it was about fifty feet by twenty in extension, with a long table down the center and a raised platform at one end that served at Christmas as stage for dramatics and at other times as rostrum or pulpit for practicing preachers and orators. Just as each was individually responsible for cleaning, brushing, and scrubbing his own room, so collectively we had to maintain the common facilities. We kept the classrooms and common room brushed and dusted, and the latter also had generally a creditable gloss on its waxed bare floor. But in other respects it was as drab and unhomely as the dayroom of an army barracks. It was easy to see that no woman had ever set foot within its walls, for it lacked utterly the significant details of comfort and adornment that women seem to achieve by their mere presence. The furniture was not only old and strictly utilitarian but roughly made, and I do not think a single brushful of paint went on walls, woodwork, or window of that room during the years I was there.

At recreation time we sat demurely along two walls. One might unbend a little more than was permissible in the noviceship, but certainly not to the extent of slouching in one's seat, crossing one's knees, or raising one's voice. Conversation was generally easier than while walking outside, especially when one was fortunate enough to get near the angle of the walls where four or five might join in the common discussion.

Other opportunities also presented themselves from time to time to shorten this period. On our way back from the garden to the common room halfway through the after-dinner recreation, three or four students in the leading ranks detached themselves from the main body and went to the kitchen to make coffee, thus enabling the lay brothers (who by then had finished washing and cleaning up after dinner) to take a turn in the garden. The coffee-making ritual was a source of unending friendly disputation, for no two agreed on the correct technique. But that for me would long remain a purely academic problem. As a junior, my standard chore—when I was lucky enough to attach myself to the coffee-makers—was to turn the handle of the old grinding mill while the heady fragrance of the rich brown grains filled the nostrils and stirred in the imagination vivid if far from accurate pictures of steaming jungle, blazing sun, bright-colored birds, and sweating natives in far-off Africa or Brazil. We made coffee not only for the students but also for the fathers of the community who with the professors were simultaneously taking their recreation in their own common room. As with the totality of our communal relations, tradition arranged every detail. When the coffee-makers arrived in the common room, three or four other students took over to pass out the cups, pour the coffee, and hand round hot milk and sugar. Others collected the cups afterward and returned them to the kitchen.

Simultaneously, at the long table in the center of the room yet another set of activities progressed. The principal ones were the stringing of beads to make the outsize fifteen-decade rosaries each wore at his cincture, the plaiting of the many-tailed whips we called disciplines, and the weaving of cilices, the flexible, tooth-studded wire bands likewise used as instruments of self-punishment, and bookbinding. All were precision jobs, calling for a degree of craftsmanship which we had already acquired during the noviceship or gradually picked up from our seniors. Bookbinding in particular demanded a set of specialized skills. Most of the theology, philosophy, and other textbooks, in Latin, came in paper covers from the publishing houses of Italy and France. Our work added little to the history of the noble craft, but we did deliver volumes solidly bound in half- or three-quarter calf that stood up to the handling of generations of hard-thumbing searchers after wisdom.

Occasionally somebody was authorized to take a place at the table for an activity other than those mentioned, but usually only for a limited time. On that basis I started a stamp collection. This was a popular pastime in student houses of our Congregation in many parts of the world. Students frequently wrote us asking for exchanges, and by following up their requests, I quickly amassed an imposing assortment. But I failed to infect any of my companions with my own enthusiasm. Anything that hadn't been done before was to them a novelty and a fad. And when, at the customary half-yearly reallotment of tasks, the stamp album was passed to another who had neither interest nor the sense of obligation created by tradition, it faded from the picture.

Sundays and feast days these manual tasks were suspended. Instead, we sometimes got permission to move the phonograph from the so-called museum where it normally shared a coating of dust with boomerangs, coins, Belleek pottery in various stages of manufacture, and other nondescript bric-a-brac. Standards of musical taste were not high. We were given a solid grounding in the Plain Chant which we sung at the solemn liturgical ceremonies, but otherwise there was little formal effort to develop musical appreciation. Our record collection, from which were rigidly banned the ragtimes that then constituted popular music, consisted mainly of selections from Gilbert and Sullivan and light operas, with some marches, hymns, and the popular concert pieces of John McCormack, Galli-Curci, Tauber, and Gigli. And I mustn't omit a few Chopin nocturnes, the Polonaise, and the haunting Minuet in G, though they weren't exactly what went down at recreation. Paderewski played the Chopin as well as his own Minuet, revealing to me for the first time the excitement and wonder and tart loveliness of music. I wasn't musical. At least I could never sing in tune and had accordingly either been ejected from or reduced to the status of mute observer in every singing class of which I had ever formed part. But I wouldn't admit defeat. I studied the theory and read what I could lay my hands on about the meaning and interpretation of famous pieces. Then I listened to them. They meant nothing the first or the second time. But bit by bit I began to feel the shape and form, the motifs, the tunes, the challenges, the restless searchings, the promises, the fulfillments. It wasn't easy but it was rewarding.

So far I've been describing the things that might interrupt the routine of recreation and obviate conversation. But they left long gaps with no choice but talk. I was conscious it was as much my duty to talk at these times as to keep silent at others, and I was just as anxious to comply. The current subject of study was the standard opening gambit, but it didn't help much when one's companion had lost interest in and familiarity with a topic he had studied without enthusiasm several years earlier. There were such. Some never lost touch, others seemed to vacuum their brains as they returned their books to the library at the end of each course.

For such emergencies I adopted a technique of making notes in advance on items of interest from my reading or other sources. Like the after-dinner speaker I strove mightily after lightness, and with about the same average of success. Our library didn't run to any of the how-to books in this genre, but I rooted out a couple of bound volumes of humorous magazines of about thirty years earlier which had in some never-explained way found a resting place on a shelf devoted to liturgy. As anyone who watches television knows, jokes provide a most telling argument against evolution. And that is a comment I can illustrate by recounting the pick of my bunch of anecdotes suitable for after-dinner monastic consumption:

Adam returned to earth and naturally caused quite a stir. He was interviewed ad nauseam by newspaper and radio reporters. He was inveigled by publicity experts into promoting their wares, got fantastic offers from circuses and music-hall scouts, and was made a guest of honor at innumerable businessmen's lunches and pacifist dinners. He took everything in good part but with an attitude of supreme boredom that gradually irked the welcome committees. They felt he should in all reason show himself a little more enthusiastic about the terrific advances public relations and other arts had made since his day. Left to himself, he wanted to go nowhere and see nothing, and he was accordingly left more and more to himself. Then one day his hosts were electrified by the sound of wild guffaws of laughter coming from his room. They rushed to see what could finally have struck a chord. And there was Adam stretched like a little boy on the floor devouring a newspaper. They crouched over his shoulder to discover the source of the merriment. It was the joke column.

My efforts as a humorist met a mixed reception. Particularly uncooperative was a colleague who one day caught me consulting my little notebook and ever afterward stopped me even if he hadn't heard that one.

In those circumstances I regarded as providential the coming of Father van Haver. He was a Fleming, assigned to a mission on the tiny island of Dominica in the Caribbean and sent to our monastery to learn English. A combination of earlier circumstances had left me with a greater smattering of French than any of the other students. One was the already-mentioned lack of an ear for music. The professor of music in our secondary school, who also happened to be a Fleming, decided one day to eject four or five of us from his classes as musically unfit. The Superior of the moment had just returned from a trip on the Continent, a little heady at his success in making himself understood in French. He decided to indulge his enthusiasm on us nonsingers. Our normal course already included four languages, Latin, Greek, English, Irish, left no room for a further modern tongue. I soon discovered that French carried a premium. Our school rules incredibly permitted no vernacular reading of novels during term, and the nearest I had reached to indulging my passion for light reading had been the fancy-flecked historical meanderings of Tacitus and Thucydides in the original Latin and Greek. But as a student of French I was able to get an occasional novel in that language, very sedate novels indeed as befitted our library, but novels nonetheless. Combining dictionary and imaginative interpretation, I worked my way through one story after another from *Lettres de mon Moulin* to *Quatre-vingt-treize*. There was an epidemic of influenza that winter which put so many of us to bed that classes were suspended for several weeks, leaving those who escaped it endless hours in the study hall. It marked for me the glorious moment when French ceased to be a struggle with blurred words, transfering itself instead into a vehicle of luminous ideas. By the time classes were renewed, I was able to skim off the adventure of a tale with a minimum of dictionary thumbing.

And so I was delegated to teach Father van Haver English. He had apparently studied English as unscientifically as I had studied French. But he was less conscious of the inadequacy of his approach than I, and accordingly far more disillusioned at the discovery that neither could make head or tail of the other. There are moments in every life which stand out significant peaks between the plains of routine existence on either side, not so much for the intrinsic importance of the events that fix them as for the subjective impact of a disappointment, a discovery, or an illumination. For such reasons I recall every slightest detail of time, place, and circumstance of my first effort at conversation with Father van Haver.

It was toward the end of our mid-morning break, a thirty-minute breather between the eighty-minute philosophy class and a following ninety-minute study and minor-class period. It was a sunny fall day. The five-minute warning bell had already rung, and as we returned sedately through the orchard toward the house, rich odors of fullness rising from the apple trees and the ripening grass around their roots filled our nostrils. The chubby, round-faced stranger who came toward us in the company of our superior was dressed in the same habit as we were, and not more than a few years older than ourselves. The superior introduced me to him and broke the news that from now on he was my pupil. We exchanged a few courtesies in both languages, but very soon he produced a word, meant to be an English one, that was unintelligible to me. With great effort I got across to him the idea that he should spell it. And then came the shock. He called the letters by their French names, which I had never before heard. It hit me like the collapse of a first principle. A great new chasm had opened under my unsuspecting feet. I don't think I'd have been more amazed if somebody had arrived from the Antipodes with a third eye in the middle of his forehead like the pictures in medieval maps.

Father van Haver eased considerably my conversational embarrassments in that I spent with him a substantial part of recreation times, as much as a couple of hours daily. But he didn't help very much to learn to talk again. He was, as I see it now, too like myself, engrossed in himself, unconscious of the pleasures and values to be drawn from exchange of ideas and union of minds. But we hit on a way to get on with the joint undertaking. He would read and I would correct his pronunciation. The book he insisted on using as text was the *Imitation of Christ,* an excellent book full of down-to-earth wisdom but far from ideal for the job. The English was stilted, the ideas expressed far removed from the colloquial needs of daily life. But that was how he wanted it. Probably he had some sentimental attachment because the unknown fifteenth-century author was his fellow countryman. And I was too inexperienced to realize how much better something modern would help him, too unsure of myself to insist, even if I had. The *Imitation* it was.

In return for my sacrifice of time, Father van Haver offered to try improve my French. We followed much the same routine as with the English. I believe we even used a French version of the *Imitation of Christ*. He didn't claim to be particularly good at French. Tension between Flemings and Walloons was then considerable, and perhaps he deliberately played down his knowledge of the enemy tongue. For all our straining after objectivity, few of us were perfectly detached. But in any case he carried me a step beyond my all but home-made accent, so that when Father Duerloo replaced him after six months and again when Father Gelaude replaced Father Duerloo, I became as a matter of course official instructor to each in turn.

Fathers van Haver and Duerloo were very much what might be expected from the life they had led as novices and students the previous seven years, identical in every detail to our own. They were silent, serious, undemonstrative, loath to discuss their personal affairs or feelings. But Father Gelaude was different. He had a light, breezy character, firm enough to keep within the rules but resilient enough not to be broken by them. Though he didn't pretend to a word of English when he arrived, in a few months he had gained a far better accent and more freedom of expression than Father van Haver ever achieved with his false foundation and self-satisfaction. He didn't worry about making a mistake. I'm sure he exercised a good influence on me, though possibly it would have been greater if he hadn't been such a contrast to what I considered the norm. At the time I was often shocked by what I thought his laxity of interpretation of rules and conventions. Looking back, I can't recall a thing meriting condemnation. He was a jolly soul and a good religious, with some of the wisdom I later learned constitutes the Benedictine spirit: to live one's life in the middle way, avoiding the abnormal and the extreme. From living with him I learned many things, many of the trivial human things that make living. I learned the Flemish method of taking a nap by resting the closed hands on top of a table with a handkerchief draped over them and leaning forward in a straight chair until the forehead rests on the hands. I didn't think much of it then, for I was impatient at the idea that anyone should ever be tired, but I changed my mind.

As I look back, we were all by way of being linguists. It was the high point of the Irish revival, or so it seemed. Many were idealistic enthusiasts and most of the others recognized a duty, as part of our missionary training, to become proficient in the language the people for whom we would work were trying to restore. Several spoke it fluently, though few with a really good accent. The words and phrases were Irish but the sounds those of English as spoken in Ireland. Not content with the prescribed class lessons, we delved into the literature and worked out abstruse problems of grammar and dialectal variation. While there was no compulsion, there was a seldom-evaded understanding that at the beginning of each recreation period Irish was spoken until we reached the cemetery at the southern end of the far sand dune or esker. The more fluent or more enthusiastic might continue it for the entire period. Modern Irish, deliberately drawn by the writers from peasant sources, was short on scientific terms, raised many points of lexicography and definition in our efforts to discuss our problems of philosophy and theology. The critics of the revival made great play of this lack. We who believed in it worked hard with what material we could draw from the library to establish or extract from early modern sources, sixteenth- and seventeenth-century writers whose diamond-sharp language reflected the thousand facets of the brilliant culture that had subsequently been strangled almost to death, the words and phrases we most frequently needed. That was one of the good features of our attitudes to problems. No task was impossible. We set to work with the tools to hand, and the results sometimes surprised even our sanguine selves.

Latin was another language we all spoke well or badly, not the steely language of Cicero on which we had polished our first teeth but the less artificial, more pliable form developed by churchmen from the vernacular of the later Empire, a language derided by many who never troubled to learn it or who lack the sense of mental discipline to appreciate its functional aptness for the job the Church makes it do, namely, to maintain clear and exact meanings in an idiom easily grasped by peoples of many linguistic and cultural backgrounds. Our philosophy, scripture, and theology textbooks were written in it. Some authors were Italians, some Germans, some French, some Spaniards. An Irishman had written the philosophy text, two Dutchmen the moral theology. The stylistic differences were scarcely perceptible. Each word and phrase carried the same emphasis and connotation throughout, and this without having sacrificed the ability to adapt to the nuances of thought of each new development of the arts and sciences.

This study of languages, though often intensive, was generally haphazard. The official attitude toward activities other than the major studies prescribed by Canon Law, which were principally philosophy, dogmatic and moral theology, church history, scriptural exegesis, and Canon Law itself, was peculiarly negative. The superiors didn't seem to mind how we occupied or amused ourselves within a traditionally defined range of subject, so long as we did occupy ourselves to the extent of the time each had available after getting in the prescribed studies, an amount of time that naturally varied according to the ability and judgment of each. That was in tune with the general method of indoctrination which depended primarily on a traditional system of living that perpetuated itself without explicit analysis of the ideas behind it or the precise object sought, and which consequently tended to intervene to check aberration rather than to whip up enthusiasm or urge the scaling of new heights. The pattern excluded all but the most carefully screened contact with contemporary life and thought, which was presented by clear implication as unimportant where not positively harmful. But the openings into the past were so ample as to exclude any conscious sentiment of imprisonment or stultification.

The present might be closed but the past and the future were open. And while I delved into the past, I soared in spirit toward the future. The most abandoned, they were our mission in life. And the most abandoned within our specific framework were the people of the Philippine Islands to which a considerable proportion of our priests and lay brothers went for a term of five years or longer. It was not for the individual to decide to go or not. He might indicate his wishes, but the selection lay in the absolute discretion of the superiors. Each year they dispatched a group, made up mainly of the young and the active. They had by all accounts a tough life out there, traveling from their monasteries through the islands, preaching in remote jungle parishes in languages of which few ever succeeded in acquiring more than a smattering, trying to bring back to a Christian life people with a Christian background but with little knowledge of the faith they professed and a tradition of lax observance and of ways and customs far different from ours. Living conditions were primitive. The missionaries had to follow almost without modification in the intense, moisture-saturated heat the same strict life they led in Ireland. Yet many of us were not only reconciled to the possibility of but anxious for the coming of the day we might be considered worthy to be chosen. A few even tried to prepare by studying one or other language that would be useful. Such preparation was more or less frowned upon, for some reason I never established, though I suspect it may have been connected with the idea that it betrayed a condemnable desire to anticipate or at least influence the superiors' decision as to what work one should be assigned. If such was indeed the reason, it would have been more intelligent to follow the technique of the Jesuits and make a tentative decision at a relatively early stage, thus giving each individual a chance to direct his surplus energies into the specialized channel of his later career. But it is also not impossible that it was tied up with a general dislike of specialization or unusualness, an emphasis on uniformity. One of the directors, when we were in secondary school, used to pay monotonous lip service to this idea by repeating in his pep talks that he didn't want brilliant boys but only average ones, an attitude that would have impressed us more if his deeds in this respect corresponded to his words. Whatever the motives, the result was an unnecessarily wasteful use of finely tempered instruments with a cavalier disregard of the divinely taught lesson of the Talents.

Notwithstanding such official lack of encouragement, a few of us (as I said) tried to give our interest a practical slant. The most useful language from our viewpoint was Vesayan, spoken in a variety of dialects in Cebu, Ilo-Ilo, and other islands. But it was so removed from the languages we knew and study material in it was so scarce that it was more common to concentrate on Spanish, no longer essential but still widely used by Filipinos. That was how, after a brief and unencouraging encounter with Vesayan, I settled down to absorb the rudiments of Spanish. To take the books from the library, as to take any other books, I had to ask permission. No objection was raised.

It mightn't have built up to more than any other of a score of courses through which I read myself from astronomy through bee-keeping to physiology, were it not for the arrival shortly afterward of Father Enríquez for a stay that lasted two years. He came from Rome where for several years he had been a secretary to the Father General, and the stated reason for his coming was to perfect his English. I never understood why the task of teaching him was unloaded on me. Naturally I didn't expect any notice to be taken of my private enterprises. But I was known to be deeply involved in coaching two backward classmates who had little head for philosophy and in addition I was officially committed to the third of my Flemish students. I wasn't even consulted, and if I had been, I don't imagine I'd have done more than say I was happy to do whatever my superiors wanted. Besides, as a long-term project, I was quite pleased. Only the timing was awkward. I've always tried to take my opportunities as they come, even though I might prefer a different day.

With each of my Flemish students I had established an exchange practice in a ratio of roughly one to three, so that out of an average of nearly two hours' instruction each day, a half-hour went in teaching me French. Father Enríquez was happy to follow a similar pattern. In fact for a time I found myself the subject of an embarrassing squeeze. A rivalry developed between my two pupils. Father Enríquez during his years in Rome had acquired a profound book knowledge of English. He had a set of German-language English grammars, five or six encyclopedic tomes. He studied them incessantly and believed they enshrined the answer to every problem, as indeed with German thoroughness they went as near doing as could any written work. But his accent was little short of atrocious, his expression pedantic and bookish. It hurt him that Father Gelaude, whose knowledge of nothing was profound and whose English dated from only a couple of months back, should be so much more proficient conversationally as to win all the bouquets. One way the rivalry expressed itself was in the eagerness of each to teach me his language. Father Gelaude even tried to persuade me take lessons in Flemish, but there I drew the line. Not that I had any prejudice against Flemish, but I saw no likelihood of its ever being an asset to me in preaching the Gospel, and that was the test I sought to apply in allocating the working hours of a day that was already too short by half for all the things I tried to compress into it.

Father Enríquez was an extraordinary young man. My association with him caused me many a headache and many a heartache. It also taught me a lot about human nature. Within a few months of his arrival, Father Gelaude left us to cross the Atlantic to his poverty-stricken Negroes in the most beautiful and most shamefully neglected of the pearls of the Caribbean. That gave me extra daily hours to devote to Father Enríquez and his problems. I never did know except through vague hints and deductions why he had been sent to our remote and secluded monastery. Officially, he was perfecting his English so he might go back to Rome as English-language secretary to the Father General. Rumors however soon began to float around that it wasn't as simple as that. Father Enríquez was a man who aroused violent feelings and created extreme enmities. I believe a grapevine stretching all the way from Rome had brought some scandal, perhaps nothing more serious than a clash of personalities, to explain the banishment.

But if the facts were known to the members of the community, they never percolated through the barrier to us students. We were cut off from the fathers, though we prayed in common, ate in the same dining room, walked in the same grounds, lived in rooms side by side. To our professors we might talk freely, yet even with them unbreakable custom forbade any intimate association or any discussion other than about the subjects which the students might freely discuss among themselves. Nevertheless, though the obligations of living the common life imposed a rigid observance of the proprieties and a suppression of all manifestations of personal clashes, we could sense a tension in the community created by the presence of Father Enríquez. He had been trained in a very different school of behavior from ours. We had been taught a tradition of life for the priest and the religious which involved an absolute separation from the outside world and a rejection of amenities and creature comforts. Our ideal was a physical toughness to enable us to endure with stoic indifference heat and cold, rough food and clothing, pain and loneliness, a mental toughness to raise us above human sensibilities. And softness was a sign of weakness. The history of monasticism, especially the almost incredible penances of the Fathers of the Desert and of the early Irish monks, offered plenty of support for such an interpretation of the obligations of the religious life. But it had undoubtedly also suffered the influence of French Jansenism carried into Ireland early in the nineteenth century by the abbés who had fled the Revolution and who helped to start Ireland's central seminary at Maynooth. Catholicism in Ireland has not yet recovered from that experience. These abbés were not heretics, but their thinking was infected with the central heresy of the Jansenists, the belief that human nature is not merely weak and prone to evil but evil in itself. Out of this approach had grown a suspicion of everything rooted in man's nature, developing into a philistinism that condemned good grooming, care of one's dress and appearance, elegance of speech, and polished behavior. It is a tradition poles apart from that of Spain, which never lost the Renaissance emphasis on the beauty and magnificence of man at his natural best and who saw the perfection of the works of grace as a superstructure raised on the perfection of the works of nature.

In the eyes of his Irish confrères, Father Enríquez was effeminate and affected. His old-world Spanish courtesy had been further refined by his training as a junior diplomat in the home of diplomacy. Rome had taught him to sparkle, to present his real intellectual qualities in a way that showed up as country clodhoppers even the most brilliant of our professors. He was like a fencer parrying the lunges of half-trained bayoneters. And they didn't like it.

Their leader was a man with a much keener brain than Father Enríquez, a young professor who had the qualities and the defects of Irish education. He had done his secondary studies in a minor seminary which placed exceptional emphasis on study of the classics, but a study directed exclusively to acquiring a knowledge of Latin and Greek as languages, immediately as the means to pass examinations and secondarily as tools to be used later to study philosophy and theology. No effort was made to stir the student's imagination with anything of the epicurean and sensuous spirit of Greece and Rome. On the contrary, he was offered an ideal of roughness: roughness of clothing, of food, of surroundings, of speech, of bearing. Even the naturally refining influences of home and of womenfolk were absent during his teens. Excluded likewise were the polishing pressures of university life, since he went straight from the seminary to the novitiate, unskilled in the ways of men, their interests, urges, and motivations. This young professor had a naturally magnetic personality. Had he half of Father Enríquez's experience, he would have outshone him in his own sphere. And to make things more complicated for me, he had always shown himself particularly well disposed toward me.

I soon found myself in the middle, suspended as uncomfortably as Mohammed's coffin between the invisible tuggings of the opposing forces. My fundamental loyalties remained with Father Enríquez, partly perhaps because he was fighting a lone battle but also because I admired his gameness and felt the radiant influence of his charm. Yet at times he wasn't very helpful. He had a characteristic which in my experience is almost universal among Spaniards. Everything for him was black or white. He could not see the infinite gradation of grays which makes possible the holding of an equal diversity of opinions about most matters. Whatever the subject, he knew it was so. Evidence to the contrary was simply not considered. I once became so exasperated that for four or five days I made notes of statements of fact he alleged in support of different views he put forward. The year was 1931, just before the abdication of King Alfonso of Spain. There had been an abortive antimonarchist rising, during which a group of airforce personnel briefly seized the

Madrid airport, whence the ringleaders fled by plane to France when they realized their cause was lost. The world press gave the incident more importance than Father Enríquez was willing to concede it. Since we students were not allowed to read newspapers, I was dependent for world comment on the secondhand version retailed to us by our professors. We were all fundamentally promonarchist in the Spanish struggle of parties and ideologies, though we had sentimental sympathies with the Basques and Catalans in their separatist efforts, because of the more or less justifiable parallel between their ambitions and our own centuries-long rejection of British efforts to absorb us.

But the anti-Enríquez group was no more interested in facts and principles than was he himself. All each side wanted was a chance to knock the other down. And when Father Enríquez wanted to cover up the weaknesses of his extreme partisanship, he dragged in the then constitutional relationship between Ireland and the British Empire, arguing that the dominion status which Ireland enjoyed and which had recently been defined by the Statute of Westminster as one of absolute equality in all respects existed by virtue of an act of the British Parliament and could accordingly be voided at any time by a further act of the same superior legislature. There was no logical relationship between this issue and that of the Spanish monarchy, but they became inextricably mixed.

It all affected me very deeply, not so much because of the issues at stake, which I regarded as important yet not likely to be affected seriously one way or the other by our views and attitudes, but because of the intellectual irresponsibility it betrayed in these men I admired and looked up to. I could not but ask myself what was defective in the training that had made them and was making me. Our spiritual and ascetic formation had the express object of raising up above petty prejudice, spite, malice. Our intellectual schooling, the long years of philosophy and theology, were supposed to purify and clarify so that we should seek only after truth as the one intellectual object worthy of our efforts and desires. Could it really be, I asked myself, that the ultimate impression was so shallow that the fortifications melted away like the turreted castles built by children in the sand when the tide of passion and jealousy flowed on the beach? It hurt me to find myself being forced to the conclusion that the residual effect remaining only a few years after the studies had been completed was so slight. Admittedly, the novices and students maintained higher standards of action, but if the facts were as this evidence seemed to establish, that had been effected only by reason of the external compulsion of vigilant superiors. When the outside pressure was eased, human nature reasserted itself. I didn't want to accept this conclusion. I tried to persuade myself all the parties were in good faith, that each honestly felt it was his right and duty in the interest of truth as he saw it to push in the direction in which he was pushing. That was only a partial consolation, for it stressed the inadequacy of even these highly developed intellects for finding the truth about an apparently simple and straightforward matter. But it was better than the more obvious explanation.

I couldn't be content just to cherish this consoling theory. Having made me a helmet, I had to put it to the test. And the only person on whom I felt I could make the test was Father Enríquez, with whom I was on terms of greatest intimacy because of our long daily periods of language study, during which I heard over and over again his version of the points at issue. Over several days (as already mentioned) I noted down without being observed by him statements of purported fact, the accuracy of which I doubted. With the aid of dictionaries, encyclopedias, histories, and other reference sources at my disposal, I established five or six significant points of error. Then at what I considered a suitable opportunity I challenged the line of argument in support of which he had adduced the misstatements, quoting chapter and verse for my corrections.

His reaction was a revelation to me of the complexity of human motivation. After an initial outburst of petulant anger, he went off sulkily to his room. About an hour later he came into my room, where I was studying, one of the very few times he ever did so. He was still tense with anger and his short fat fingers trembled as he emphasized his words. Brushing aside as irrelevant what to me had seemed the whole substance of the matter, to wit, the correctness or inaccuracy of his claims, he upbraided me for spying on him, checking upon his statements as unworthy of credence. Unless I wanted to end our association, I must never do anything like that again.

The disillusionment and disappointment were deep, but I could do nothing except drop the matter. Nevertheless, though I didn't realize it until long afterward, I had learned one of the important lessons of life. A man is a saint by the time he shakes off pettiness, and saints are few even in monasteries. It was also an introductory glance at another lesson that took still longer to learn, that friends must be taken with their defects, the greatest wisdom to put those defects in a perspective in which they can be understood, forgiven, perhaps even loved.

Father Enríquez departed as mysteriously as he had come. He never did go back to Rome, nor did I ever have reliable news of him again, though there was a hearsay report that he had left the Congregation and become a pastor in Mexico.

CHAPTER 5

And Heard Great Argument

Philosophy started out as a purely intellectual exercise and, after a fairly short period during which it made no sense at all, proved a pleasant one. There were two main reasons why it made no sense at first. The textbook was in the language usually called Church Latin. Our secondary schooling had familiarized us with Caesar, Cicero, Ovid, Virgil, Horace, and the less lascivious effusions of Catullus, but their sculptural and formalized tongue did not seem to help much in extracting the sense enshrined by Hickey in his compendium of philosophy. It was easy to translate the words, or most of them, but translated they remained as obscure as to meaning, though for a different reason, as Ovid's elaborate mythical allusions. The second reason was that we happened to be beginning in the middle. Philosophy was a two-year course with a single set of lectures. Students of one year began at the beginning and those of the next joined in. We in consequence were thrust into psychology without the benefit of a grounding in logic and metaphysics.

But it straightened itself out, thanks in no small part to the genius of a professor who conceived of his task in the highest traditions of education as being to lead his students into the realm of the spirit and encourage each to build his own workshop and carve his own niche. For him there were no limits to intellectual curiosity, no restrictions on the search for truth but truth itself. His methods were too daring and too disregarding of the rigid conventions by which we were bound. He survived as a professor for only a single year. But in that year he lighted a torch for me, and I believe for others, that still burns.

Young as I was and protected as I had always been from the influences of the age, I had picked up somewhere along the way a prejudice, almost universal among those who pride themselves on freedom from prejudices, against Church Latin, unworthy and degenerate offspring of a noble forebear, a debasement for which the Church was in some never-explained way responsible. The more I got to know Church Latin, the more I divested myself of this prejudice. Classical Latin was without doubt a wonderful vehicle of expression, steel-hard in its precision, concision, and polished unadornment. But it was never more than the formalized idiom of a group of *littérateurs*, scarcely more adapted to the exchanges of practical daily life than sculpture or painting. The Romans themselves seldom succeeded in speaking as Cicero wrote, and the later classical writers reflect the tendency to write in the vernacular, which is what the early Church Fathers did, creating the style which is still that of Church Latin at its best. The Latin Church was always characterized by its practicality, inspired to select from the tools to hand those capable of continuing usefulness in the multiplicity of circumstances to develop in the centuries yet unborn. Church Latin was such a tool for the official expression of its teaching and its legal norms. It retained the precision of classical Latin but with a fluidity of construction and an ability to expand its vocabulary and idiom to meet every new requirement. Speaking of the twentieth century's greatest contribution to the communication arts, television, Pope Pius XIII said in April, 1951: "*Homines . . . electrica vi possunt . . . rerum eventuumque imagines ante oculos relatas, etsi iidem procul commorantur, presentes conspicere.*" Cicero needn't make excuses for that. And this language had another characteristic the Church has always prized highly in its art, its liturgy, its ascetical and mystical concepts, and all its forms of expression and communication. It was not esoteric. It was capable of operation at all intellectual levels. It was not too complicated to be usable by those of average attainments, yet delicate and malleable enough not to restrict the highest flights of the poet, the philosopher, the mystic, or the jurist.

Our textbook of philosophy represented the strictly practical side. The Church makes every candidate for the priesthood complete a basic course of scholastic philosophy and of dogmatic and moral theology. The requirements presuppose a certain minimum level of intellectual ability, but the minimum standard (about that of a primary university degree in each country) cannot be fixed too high if the tens of thousands of replacements needed each year for the teaching, preaching, and pastoral activities of the clergy throughout the world are to be assured. Not all the clergy need to be great philosophers. Consequently, the textbook was designed primarily to provide the irreducible minimum demanded of everybody. Had a genius been given the task of writing such a manual, he might have escaped the pedestrian matter-of-factness of content and style that distinguished it. Hickey was not such a genius.

But our professor was more ambitious. And gradually he carried us, or most of us, to higher peaks. Bit by bit, starting where I did in the middle, I began to piece together the jigsaw of facts, theories, and opinions which form the body of knowledge elaborated by the great Middle Ages schoolmen, following Aristotle and Plato. I learned first of all to define words and analyze the elements of each definition. Then I got a picture of what life means as contrasted with nonlife, what the soul as contrasted on the one hand with the body, and on the other with forms of spiritual life not naturally correlated to a body, what the immortal human soul as contrasted with the mortal souls of animals and plants. A thousand subsidiary problems and concepts unfolded themselves by inference or necessary relationship while the meaning of these first concepts was revealing itself. Finity, infinity, materiality, spirituality, activity, passivity, matter, form. They began as vague, meaningless words, unlovely in the misfocus of the soupy fog out of which they loomed. But the breath of the spirit dissolved a little more each day the haze of ignorance, giving form and beauty and precision and attractiveness. Gradually our unconventional professor stirred in us the enthusiasm of the search, made us feel the existence of problems and the need for answers. One of his most successful experiments, daring in the environment in which it was made, was to introduce us almost at the outset of our questings to Bertrand Russell's *Introduction to Philosophy*.

Russell was already well launched on his spectacular

and unconventional career both in and without the realm of philosophy. Most of his fame and notoriety rested on activities ill suited to the edification of budding monklets, but in this semipopular little volume he had succeeded better than most in putting into language that made sense to the high school level of intellectual development what it's all about. What becomes of the table when you cover it with a tablecloth? What color is red in total darkness? How sweet does the rose smell when nobody's smelling it? What must you stand on to find out where you're standing? Frivolous, flippant questions when asked by Bernard Shaw. But down-to-earth fundamentalism when one is on the treadmill of a subjectivism that rejects even the testimony of one's senses.

Relatively unorthodox as was this particular professor in his efforts to stimulate our curiosity and make us understand that philosophy wasn't just an intellectual exercise, he was an orthodox exponent of the scholastic system in his definition and presentation of the meaning and scope of the subject. The scholastics have always extolled human reason, but only the human reason that is properly trained and that recognizes religion as a guiding principle of the whole educational process. They safeguard the genuine validity of human knowledge, the unshakable metaphysical principles of sufficient reason, causality, and finality, and the mind's ability to attain certain and unchangeable truth. They consequently reject the skepticism of Descartes who believed each man must start anew and alone to find the truth, as also his dualism between thought and matter which became in Kant the divorce between reality as revealed by faith and reality as revealed through the senses.

For us such an attitude was even less thinkable than

the possibility of getting two different answers to an equation through solving it by two distinct methods. We knew the answer came out wrong simply because a mistake had been made in the calculation, and so we crossed it out and tried again. If we thought of the philosopher as a specialist, we thought of him as that paradoxical impossible person, a specialist in everything. It outraged us that anyone could set up seriously as a philosopher on the basis of a schism between facts and values, between the realm of science and the realm of art and religion, between the secular and the spiritual. We did not think it possible that anything better than acute intellectual indigestion could result from the type of curriculum given in many modern universities which seemed to think of themselves as elaborate cafeterias offering the student indiscriminate choice of innumerable intellectual tidbits. Such an approach destroyed the organic unity of truth, failing to recognize that the parts have value by virtue of their place within the whole, and that God is the ultimate and controlling reality through which all else derives being and through which consequently human knowledge derives significance.

Philosophy affected each of us differently. Two of our class of ten never made the least sense of it. One of these had an I.Q. well below average. His inability to master abstract thinking came as no surprise. But another who had made a reasonably good showing in the humanities of our high school course was almost equally at sea. And a third who might reasonably have been expected to be one of the class leaders never even established contact. He was one of two students in our class who had had an interval of a couple of years between secondary schooling and entering the novitiate. Late vocations we called them. Both of them had fought—on opposite sides—in the civil war Lloyd George had machinated as his parting gesture after the United States had forced him withdraw his Black and Tans. That civil war had divided Ireland deeply, hurting us most by incubating all the meannesses and spites that had been cold-stored during the glorious preceding moment of bare hands defying the world's greatest empire in its hour of supreme strength. Partisan politics were absolutely barred in the monastery and in any case were relatively remote because of our isolation. But the immediate experience of these men, both of whom had held rank and responsibility in the contending armies out of all proportion to their youth, created tensions that made more noticeable the ability of the one and the incapacity of the other to make an impression on and receive an impression from philosophy. It was ironic that the more intelligent, practical, well balanced of the two in dealing with the normal affairs of life was the one Saint Thomas stymied. My political sympathies were not with him. The broad division in Ireland in the civil war had been between the upper and lower middle classes, the two dominant and in fact almost only classes in the country. My family belonged to the former and had suffered accordingly in the part of the country longest under the military control of the other. But my feelings were not so bitter as to influence my decision when he appealed to me to coach him for the examinations that would decide his future. He was not my fellow novice, having started a year earlier. But he had failed his first philosophy. And a second failure would mean the end of his ambition to become a priest.

I didn't welcome the request. I had already more than enough on my hands. I was giving several hours weekly to another of my backward classmates and in addition was teaching English to the first of my Flemish pupils. Besides, I was beginning to get the savor of knowledge. There was so little time, so much to learn. Saint Thomas hadn't yet made a great impression. It took a little longer before I began to appreciate the profundity enshrined in his deceptively innocent objections to his own theses or to realize the tensile strength of the slender threads of argument from which he suspended his deductions. But I already knew I must for my own satisfaction read all those ponderous volumes in which he had collected the sum of his wisdom. And I had found in the library a beautiful Latin volume of Aristotle with copious and illuminating commentary by a medieval scholar whose name I have long forgotten. Mercier and Chesterton and Belloc and Maritain had become more than names. I read slowly, for I had discovered that for me the best way to understand and retain was to summarize in writing the argument as I went along. There were other branches of knowledge, too, that I had decided could not be neglected. I was becoming aware of the relationship of philosophy and the natural sciences. Man was not pure intellect and he lived in a world that was not spirit. Both scholasticism and the many other systems of thought about which we had to know something in order to demonstrate their error or inadequacy continually made assumptions or deductions about matter and its nature. As an adjunct to our major course in philosophy we did a summary survey of physics, physiology, and astronomy. But I was not content with that. I wanted to learn all I could about the mysteries of the universe and the forces of nature. I was conscious of the constant flux of knowledge in regard to such subjects as heat, light, sound, electricity, of the need for information on the latest discoveries and developments. It was a perennial, though only partially if at all justified, criticism of the scholastics that they paid little attention to the changing theories of the physicists when they discussed the relationship of the material and the spiritual. I was conscious of the charge and anxious to avoid the possibility it might ever be leveled at me. When I look back today to what the scientists of twenty years ago regarded as definitive in their field and see the complete disruption of their first principles atomic fission has caused, I wonder if it wasn't largely wasted time to humor them by dignifying with so much attention their gropings.

All these interests, fitted into a week scheduled to allow for almost no free time, kept me operating at high pressure. Nevertheless, I couldn't refuse the request of a confrère, little as I liked it. I thought at first I might take him at the same time as another classmate I had already begun to help. But it didn't work. I soon found out it was wasted time to try to make either understand what it was all about. They didn't have the intellectual equipment to appreciate abstract discussion, and the most that could be hoped was to get the essentials into simple formulas to be learned by rote as answers to questions likely to be asked in examinations. The first thing was to boil down each tract and thesis to its barest elements, then by dint of endless repetition hammer each item into those two heads, taken one at a time. It was no use trying to keep the two in step. Nor could they be left to learn anything by themselves. For the one, the written page dissolved into crotchets and quavers and he floated off into the dream world of music where lay his genius. For the other, footnotes and abstruse objections became more important than the heavy type. He would confound his confusion by trying to absorb everything before he knew anything. To keep him on my tracks was a perpetual struggle. He would importune me to help him with side issues. I couldn't deny his argument that some questions would hinge on them, but I also knew my simplification would scrape him through if he would only be content to concentrate on it. I finally compromised by undertaking to return to the fine print when he had mastered the bold. A day which, of course, never came.

But I got them through. It was a close shave. So close in fact with one that the examining board couldn't make up its mind. I don't know what transpired at the examination, a terrifying experience even for those who knew their subject well. Each presented himself in turn before a board consisting of professors and of superiors of all the houses of the Province. The proceedings were entirely in Latin. That evening our professor called me to his room and asked me for my conscientious opinion as to whether this student really knew the rudiments of the course. He was under the terrific emotional strain of knowing that failure was final, and his answers had been so confused that they could not decide whether to blame nervous tension or ignorance. The other examiners apparently left it to our professor to make the decision as the one familiar with his year-round performance. He was an honorable man who knew he was impatient of stupidity. He feared his own bias and wanted to be just. But for me the question was a dreadful one to answer. We all had had dinned into us ad nauseam the priority of the common good over all personal or particular claims. Could I justify casting a vote for one whose philosophical inadequacy I knew only too well? But my humanity—as I see it in retrospect, my common sense—prevailed. Yes, I said, I believed he had the bare rudiments.

My answer trapped me. I had promised myself tutoring was for this one examination, that I could then go back to my intellectual den. But I no longer dared. I had assumed responsibility in my conscience for this student by vouching for him. I had to see him through. And I couldn't help him without also helping the other. So the next year and the next and the one after that, and until they were both finally ordained priests, I continued to spoon-feed them. One practical benefit. I succeeded after much negotiation, for it was a dangerous departure from tradition to permit a student such a novelty, in getting permission to borrow a typewriter a couple of times a week to transcribe for them the summarized notes of the various courses; and I taught myself to type.

But in the final analysis I didn't regret it. There is nothing so mysterious as Providence. All my efforts to prepare myself for the activities of a missionary priest were to be wasted as far as the object I intended was concerned. Only the by-products proved significant, and important among them was the contribution I made to the journey of these two, at least one of whom—humanly speaking—could hardly otherwise have reached the goal. For twenty years I have neither seen him nor corresponded with him. Yet all that time he has been preaching the good tidings of salvation, in four different languages (for though no philosopher, he was a gifted linguist), doing more than a man's share each day to bridge the gulf between heaven and earth and to make amends for the pettiness and villainy of our generation by offering God the mystical sacrifice of his Son in the Mass. My part I do not regret.

And I still found time to continue my personal task of building on the basis of scholasticism an intellectual foundation for my faith that would be as complete as the emotional foundation it was the object of the noviceship to create. It was the fashion of self-styled intellectuals then, even more than now, to deride the idea of a person adopting an intellectual position and then purporting to examine that position to prove its correctness. The only logic they could see was the skepticism of Descartes who wanted every man to start anew and alone to find the truth, abandoning not only hope but knowledge as he entered the ink-black cavern of inquiry. The scholastics argued differently when they contended that the best light by which to guide the intellect along its road to natural truth is the light of faith. But they were conscious of the difficulty of distinguishing between faith and prejudice at each step of the journey, no less than of the danger that half knowledge all too easily joined with pride to challenge truth as revealed by faith.

Our superiors and spiritual mentors were particularly alive to this second threat. For many of them philosophy was an all but superfluous imposition, to be accepted because the Holy See in its wisdom so directed, but to be played down as far as consonant with carrying out the letter of the law. They didn't encourage too much prying into the depths. Above all, they insisted that the desirable approach was to regard the study as a preparation to meet objectors and doubters in later life rather than as a vital and personal examination of one's own attitudes to life and religion. For this, the emotional development was all they seemed to think necessary, reflecting once again that mixture of Italian emotionalism, French Jansenism, Counter-Reformation (as opposed to Catholic Reform) last-standism, and Irish protective defensism which constituted the distinctive characteristic of our ruling class.

Even to show too much interest in the critical problems of the relationship of philosophy and theology, not to be happy to accept the traditional dictum that the former was the latter's handmaid and leave it at that, was to render oneself suspect. One classmate worked himself into a state over the proofs of the existence of God. He read everything he could lay his hands on, and insisted on discussing his doubts with whoever would listen. I don't think it occurred to any of us, certainly not to me at the time, though today I'm pretty sure such was the case, that he was sincerely unable to satisfy himself as to the validity of the traditional proofs and was trying to struggle back to certitude. All we knew was that no normal person would get so excited about a purely formal chore. We wrote him off in our own minds as a little queer, and I think few were surprised when we learned he had left. I knew better than to behave like that in public, and when I suddenly crashed into intellectual doubt on my own account, I kept it to myself while I laboriously worked out my own solution.

But that was later. In the first stages of exploration everything for me fell easily and naturally into its proper place. I had no great difficulty in deducing from an analysis of man and the world the existence of the corporeal, material nonthinking element and the spiritual, thinking element, of the body and the soul, in recognizing the soul as free from such characteristics of the body as extension, corruptibility, and necessary death, yet subject to such evident limitations that it could not be seriously thought of as its own cause or an end in itself.

It was scarcely more difficult to accept the inevitability of the existence of God. None of the six or seven—the scholastics themselves never agreed on the exact number—

traditional scholastic proofs, when expressed in the crude logic of a syllogism, carried at first overwhelming assent. The syllogism is a magnificient device for channeling the cogitative processes, but it asks too much of a single mechanism and strait-jackets unreasonably the straining after truth of the human mind to insist, as many of the scholastics would, that if it can't be demonstrated syllogistically it can't be so. Indeed, as far as syllogisms went, I always thought the most convincing was Saint Anselm's argument, rejected by the main stream of scholastic thought. God is by definition a being greater than whom cannot be imagined. But if God did not exist, then a greater being could be imagined, namely one who added existence to all God's other attributes. Therefore.

But the other arguments also took on substance and gradual conviction when one allowed one's mind to dwell long enough on the deep significance of each word and realize the implications of every claim and of every apparent escape from the inevitable conclusion. Little as we knew then or know now of the essence of matter, there is no evading its self-insufficiency. It cannot but have a cause outside itself. Whether the universe began as an immeasurably diffused gaseous substance, its particles so widely dispersed in the near-infinite expansion of space as to exert no appreciable push or pull on each other, as we then suspected, or whether it began with the entirety of matter concentrated into a single speck more tightly packed than a cluster of angels on a pinpoint, from the explosion of which we are now hurtling outward with ever increasing acceleration to the annihilation of the speed of light, as many scientists of the atomic age prefer to imagine, it began. And it didn't begin itself. I could and can never see any *but* or *if* or *maybe* about that. I have only a mixture of pity and contempt for the skeptic who won't look long enough at this uncomplicated fact to see its inevitability. He is not being unreasonable, only unreasoning. Movement, change, development, evolution, make sense only in relation to a first mover depending for no attribute or power or energy on any outside source, endowed with life, with intelligence, with limitless power, with all the perfections and none of the imperfections of what we see and hear and feel and know. Creation needs only to be defined to be self-evident, and creation demands a Creator.

There were as many aspects to this argument as to a finely cut diamond, new light flashing from each brilliant facet, and all the beams illuminating the same road. There was need for a sufficient cause for the effects we observe each day. There was need for a prime mover for the movements of which we form a part. There was need for a beginning of the series of movements which would inevitably have long ago ended if they had never begun or if they had begun an infinitely long time ago. There was need for an infinite to justify the finite, of an all-powerful to make sense of existing limited power. There was need for an adequate object for the audacious yearning of the human soul, never fully satisfied with any created object, ever searching for something more worthy of its love and affection, ever seeking to sate its own desires with Saint Augustine, yet ever confessing with him at the end of its breathless whirl of experiences that it can find no rest that is not in Thee. In his day-to-day routine of microscopic investigation of the details of reasoning the tired-eyed philosopher is a world apart from the wild-eyed poet, but the two meet and join their voices in harmonic unison in the ultimate reaches of metaphysics where truth, beauty, and goodness, symbolic trinity of absolutes, join to form the cause, justification, and end of us and our questings.

That was the positive part of philosophy's contribution to theology, the establishment of first foundations. The rest of the proof of the truth of our faith was primarily historical, that Christ existed, that his claims to be God had been substantiated by actions impossible except to God, that he established a church to which he gave the right and duty to teach his truth for all time, that the church he established was the Catholic Church. But in all of this long chain of reasoning philosophy was constantly needed to clarify and justify, to define (for example) what is a miracle and show the possibility and reasonableness of miracles, to define what is a mystery and show the reasonableness of mysteries, to show that none of the mysteries proposed by the Catholic Church for our belief is contrary to truth or right reason.

One of the many things that constantly impressed me about scholasticism at its best was its unconcern at the claims of exponents of related sciences to have made discoveries that destroyed its foundations or that proved the falsity of the religion it gloried in buttressing. At our particular moment the fashion was evolution, and its exponents were shouting themselves hoarse about what they had established and what they had disestablished. The reaction was always the same. Maybe there is some truth in this. Maybe the scientific part is entirely true. It is not inconceivable that all forms of vegetable and animal life evolved from one simple cell by gradual evolution or by natural selection and survival of the fittest, or even that each species came from one before by jumps without intermediate forms. It is not inconceivable that man evolved from the ape. We are open to persuasion, but not by theories or assertions or inconclusive remains. Where are the facts? Show us the evidence. And if your theory is true, so what? Even if you prove that man descended from an ape, you must still recognize the difference between the two. Somewhere along the line came rationality, came the soul as we define it. Your theory not only does not exclude God but adds to the wonder of his ways.

Sometimes I used to think, as I suppose many another has thought along the way, that at times the unconcern was overdone, that it would be better to accept once for all what the natural scientists seemed to have established definitely, rather than drag always behind like a dead weight on scientific progress. Yet when I reflected, I could not but recognize that such was inevitably the function of the philosopher. And the subsequent story of evolution has more than confirmed the wisdom of waiting. As I write, Mortimer Adler is proclaiming in Chicago that Darwinism is as dead as Darwin. He has discovered what we took to be self-evident, that only man makes artistically, that only man machinofactures, that only man communicates ideas, that only human society is constitutional and political. His language is more vivid but his conclusion is the same as ours when he proclaims that men and apes are as far apart as a square and a triangle, that there can be no intermediates, no three-and-a-half-sided figure.

Wisdom the Catholic Church proclaims to be the first of the seven gifts of the Holy Spirit, and a thing that struck me more and more forcibly as I studied the teaching of the Church was her own uncanny wisdom, her amazing ability to distinguish between the essential content of her teaching, which she defended with uncompromising determination, and the accidentals which she utilized or discarded or left to the free play of discussion as circumstances dictated. The outsider is usually conscious of the insistence on dogma, but much more evident to the insider is the deference to individual opinion. Thus, the Church insists that man has free will, that he himself makes the decisions that decide his eternal destiny. But her philosophers and theologians fight among themselves and work out their own explanations as to how free will operates, skirting according to their disposition the Scyllian rocks of predeterminationism by affirming that God moves the will to act freely in the fullness of his prescience, or tacking in the Charybdian shallows of denial of the principle of causality by holding that the will determines itself in the act of choice.

The Church's attitude to miracles reflects a like reasonableness. To one who accepts the principle that God created the universe and set it to work out according to a predetermined pattern its daily development through the centuries and eons of time, nothing is more reasonable than the notion of a miracle. A miracle means an exception to this natural law. In the government of human affairs we admire the ruler not only for giving his people intelligent and wise laws but also for administering these laws wisely and intelligently. History and language have reserved a special category for the laws of the Medes and Persians, not because they were particularly unjust or particularly vicious, but simply because they were inflexible. They admitted no exception of equity or mercy. Roman Law and English Law, on the contrary, developed into great and lasting systems because their administrators learned to temper the literalness of the text to suit the countless variety of circumstances of time and incident. It would be strange if the omnipotent and omniscient Creator and first source of all law was so subject to the laws he had made that he could make no exception to them.

The point is one of many on which people have very strong views on one side or the other without ever having bothered to think why they have them. Many grow up taking miracles as normal. Many others grow up taking them as nonsense. Once you define the terms, you can see almost without further examination that they are neither normal nor nonsensical. They are the height of common sense but highly exceptional. Each one requires proof as to the fact of its occurrence, which is the point where we move again from the realm of philosophy into that of history and evidence. In practice the only way to be sure that a miracle occurred is to have the testimony of the Church that it did. The legal processes of scrutiny to which the Church subjects each claim to a miraculous occurrence are quite enough to satisfy any reasonable person that the verdict is accurate. For the Catholic there is still stronger motive for acceptance of that verdict. Since he believes that God gave the Church the duty of teaching all men, he believes that the Church's teaching carries the guarantee of truth.

Various teachings of the Catholic religion involved exceptions to the physical laws of nature, that is to say, involved miracles. As philosophers we had to examine these teachings, not as to their dogmatic or historical content, but solely as to their reasonableness. We were not asking if they were dogmas of faith or if there was in fact evidence as to their happening or having happened. We were concerned merely to see if they involved repugnance to right reason. That is the extent of the philosopher's right in regard to what theology claims to present as revealed truth, to judge if it is unreasonable. If it is, then he can reject it because truth is one and indivisible. If a thing is repugnant in the natural order, it cannot be other than repugnant also in the supernatural. Such has always been the Catholic Church's defense of the rights of reason, even when Luther stormed against Aristotle as the unholy rampart of the Papists. So, when the Evangelist said that Jesus stood in their midst, the doors being closed, he raised a problem as to the compenetrability of matter. Could two physical bodies occupy the same space at the same time without one or both losing their identity? It looks at first glance like a job for the physicist, but when you appeal to the physicist he can give very little help. He will perhaps agree to distinguish between the substance of a thing and the accidents, between what makes it what it is and what presents itself to the senses as taste, color, shape, weight, extension. But today less than ever, when his theories equate mass and energy, is he prepared to say which if any of the accidents is inseparable from the substance. True, the imagination cannot visualize one body as interpenetrating another, since the imagination feeds only on sense perceptions. Yet even the imagination today is not so stunned, thanks to the theories lately elaborated by the physicists to explain the facts of the atomic age. No longer do we think of physical bodies as continuous and impenetrable. Rather we have learned to visualize them as constituted of protons, neutrons, and a dozen other infinitesimal elements held in ever-changing association by electrical and magnetic forces while spaced relatively further apart than the planets in the solar system or the stars in the heavens. Though it be no more than a metaphor, it may help to light the infinity of possibilities available to the One who controls nature's laws and can as easily make an exception as the rule.

Failing more help from the physicist, the philosopher must develop his own theories of substance and accident, theories that will stand up to what is known from faith no less than to what is known from reason and experience. Particularly has he to take account of the profoundest of all faith's mysteries, the real presence of Jesus Christ under the species of bread and wine in the sacrament of the Eucharist. The scholastics didn't try to avoid such issues or brush off inquiry with a dogmatic affirmation. They never forgot that Saint Thomas started to discuss God's existence with a sheaf of arguments calculated to deny or question it. They tried to go as far as reason would carry, but with enough humble realism to recognize that reason could go so far. That limit on reason, human reason that is, didn't upset them unduly either. They saw it as an easy deduction from the primary notions of the infinite and the finite. By definition what is finite has limits. That there should be limits to what man can understand is no more extraordinary than that there should be limits to what he can lift. No more does such recognition invalidate his reasoning within its limits than it negates his strength within its limits. And within those limits philosophy could make some definite clarifications about the meaning of the Real Presence, showing (for example) that while the change of one substance into another without a corresponding change of the accidents or appearances through which corporal substances are normally revealed to us, while contrary to all human experience, is not demonstrably outside the realm of possibility.

Suffering was another mystery we batted about with

the facile insouciance of inexperienced youth. Yet wiser men than us had written the commentaries, and enough clung of the principles to justify their formulators when the bitter day of knowledge put them to the test. That God could have created a world in which suffering played no part was undeniable. That those who might inhabit it would be so essentially different from those who do as to make every being's innate instinct to self-preservation reject the transformation involved in belonging to such a world was scarcely less evident. Suffering in the physical order is animal's and man's first weapon, the cry of the infant for food, the mother hen's call of threatened chicks to her sheltering wing. In the intellectual order, it is the bond of friendship, the temperer of the fine spirit, the restorer of the pride-strayed mind. And to all of this we had still to add the testimony of revelation's supreme mystery of suffering to redeem the fallen and atone for sin. The abuse does not take away the use, even though by reason of the finity of the animal or human individuals, suffering in extreme cases went unbearably beyond the limits of usefulness. That God by a miraculous intervention could prevent such abuse of suffering could not be denied. That any, least of all those who scoff at the notion of miracle, has a right to demand such intervention or to usurp God's right to decide how out of evil ever to bring forth good is an impertinence recognizable in its formulation.

It was a grand life. There was a constant sense of satisfaction, of each day producing something important and each morrow crowding on to unfold its more significant secret. It was that most satisfying of human experiences, fulfillment tinged with expectancy. Every hour had its occupation, work or prayer or anticipation. We trampled underfoot the crisp, crackling leaves of the copper beeches as they stripped for action at the onslaught of the winter winds. We saw the crocuses peep through melting snow in early spring. We took time out from our work on bright May afternoons to sit on the daisy-studded grass of a hill-side and enjoy the sights and sounds of nature's slow awakening: droplets on the whitethorn glistening in the sun, cooing pigeons hidden in the soft, young leaves of the trees, excited rooks following hard on the heels of the plowman turning over the dark, peaty furrows. We watched the giant dragonflies reflect the fragrant light where they hovered over the lazy mid-summer meadows. In the shade of the peaceful oaks atop the eskers we hoped for a breeze to cut the oppressive heat of dog days on which by custom we revised the examination texts outdoors instead of attending afternoon classes. A whole year whirled by at a timelessly proper rate that was shorter than an hour yet longer than a lifetime. Second-year philosophers started theology. We first-year philosophers moved into the second year. A new group arrived from the novitiate to open for the first time the brown-backed unlovely tomes.

I think mostly everybody one time or another experiences intellectual doubt. I know I did, and the experience was extremely disconcerting. Everything up to then had fitted beautifully. What I learned from reason not only made sense with but gave more sense to what I had known from faith. Then suddenly the crisis. It was in my second year of philosophy. We had a new professor, young, serious, devout, very unimaginative. He didn't think I was as interested as I ought to be in my classwork. Perhaps the fault lay in the dry bones of the treatise on logic with which the year opened, but I found equally little to inspire or even hold attention in the long commentaries he read mournfully from authors as heavy as himself. In any case, he selected me to prepare a thesis to be defended, according to custom, before the entire community. And the subject he selected was the existence of the nonego.

It sounded to me not only absolutely uninteresting but positively futile. We had already read the first chapters of the treatise on ontology of our textbook, which dealt very summarily with the problem, and it had seemed scarcely worth dignifying with the name. But of course I had no choice. I went back and read it all over again. Then I had a look at Reinstadler and Mercier and a few other textbooks that were lying around. One reference led to another and in a week I had accumulated a sizable bibliography. And gradually one conclusion formed and clarified itself in my mind. There didn't seem to be any proof that realities outside and other than the thinking mind existed. Like Descartes I had sealed myself in a vacuum. Only it wasn't the same vacuum. I didn't have even Descartes for company. I was alone.

I wasn't excited as yet. I didn't really believe I was in a trap. I knew it looked like a trap, but of course that was absurd. The thing to do was to keep my head, walk casually up to the man in charge of the maze, and ask to be directed to the nearest exit. That's what I did. I took my review of the situation to the professor, analyzed for him the various syllogisms by which the various authors sought to present their conclusions, and showed the unacceptable assumption each argument seemed to me to contain.

"That's perfectly true," he commented. "You can't really prove it."

I was flabbergasted. "But . . . ," I stammered.

He smiled his dry smile, indicating with a gesture this was an unimportant detail. "Now we just have to go ahead and prove it."

I had no doubt as to his meaning. The whole thing was for him a pure formality, a piece of play-acting. But I couldn't see it that way. It didn't yet seem to me to be particularly important—that was to come a little later—but my stomach revolted at the idea of being a party to a sham, a negation of the intellectual process we were pretending to follow and defend. But again I had no choice. I went back to my authors and set out to string together the required number of words in the proper form, to assemble all the conflicting opinions and pulverize to my own satisfaction, or at least to that of the orthodox, both them and their authors. I dreaded in anticipation the entire performance for which I was preparing, the reading of my thesis in the presence of the priests of the community as well as of the students, and its defense against whatever objections anyone might wish to make. I couldn't get enthused because I knew the answer I had was *not* the answer. It was at least a consolation when I discovered that none of the other parties to the performance was making any effort to take it seriously. The students designated to prepare criticisms didn't bother going deep enough to find that there were any. They assembled four or five stock objections, which a kind friend passed me in advance so that I'd be prepared for them. In due course we assembled, and in due form I read my composition in Latin, starting with the state of the question, explaining what the problem was, what different philosophers had thought about it, what was the true teaching which I proposed to defend.

Then came the syllogisms in which had to be expressed

the essence of the defense. I had frequently observed that the more uncertain an author was about a particular attitude, the more alternative syllogisms he presented to bolster his viewpoint. That's how I felt and that's what I did, gliding lightly over the light patches in the explanatory development that followed each. Then came the pages devoted to demonstrating the falsity of the assertions, assumptions, and deductions of Kant, Descartes, Hume, Berkeley, Russell, Santayana, and as many others as dared depart from the true and alone admissible teaching that real substances really exist outside and independent of the thinking mind. And so the end of my text. A student stood up and presented his objection. I had the answer by rote and reeled it off. He expressed his satisfaction and another took his place to be disposed of in like fashion. Then came the third. He was a confrère I never liked. It was one of those natural antipathies which constitute a main trial of religious life. I'm not sure that it even was mutual, though I suspect it was. If it was, he certainly worked at least as hard as I did to keep it in place; and indeed if my memory doesn't play me false, it was he who had passed me surreptitiously the list of objections. At this moment, in any case, he didn't let me down. Although the objection he now presented was precisely the one I knew was to come, I realized with a sinking heart as he proceeded that I didn't have the slightest notion how to deal with it. My mind had gone blank. Feverishly I struggled for time, resuming slowly what he said as though I were anxious to get his point exactly before disposing of it. Then I had a brain wave. After all it was only a game, so I'd better play it. "It seems to me," I said gravely, "that this particular point has already been dealt with." I flipped back the pages of my thesis and reread two long paragraphs from the middle. "Doesn't that answer your objection?" He knew as well as I did that it had no bearing. "Thank you," he answered. "That seems to solve it." Nobody else had even been following.

So ended the public disputation. But my personal problems were far from solved. I had been so busy reading, annotating, and writing during the previous weeks that I had put to the back of my mind the implications of my conclusion that it was not possible to prove the existence of the nonego. Now it was time to see where I really stood. Even such fundamental truths as the existence of God, which had previously seemed securely anchored in their place, were again floating in uncertainty if the outside world itself didn't really exist as it seemed to. The arguments from causality, from order, from succession of events, and the rest started out from the assumption of a world and a universe as really existing in the way they seemed to common sense to exist. I was frightened, but there was nobody to whom I felt I could talk. I have already mentioned the environmental atmosphere of condemnation of any suggestion of ideas or attitudes other than the normal. If we had thought my friend a bit queer because he was unduly interested in the existence of God, what would be thought of me if anyone knew I doubted the existence of men?

The person to whom I could have properly turned and to whom I did attempt to turn in the first instance, my philosophy professor, had refused to take me seriously, which in all the circumstances was perhaps just as well. It was up to me. I went back over the whole subject as tranquilly as I could. I thought for long hours and I prayed for long hours. It was then I first found the works of a writer whom I slowly but surely began to appreciate and who ultimately rose in my opinion to a very high level. I cannot understand why he is not better known in the history of philosophy.

Jaime Luciano Balmes was born at Vich in Catalonia in 1810 and died only thirty-eight years later. It was a short life, but genius and wisdom are measured neither by mathematical symbols nor by mechanical divisions of time. Balmes was a man of many parts, priest, politician, patriot, thinker. In philosophy he was an eclectic scholastic, seeking to integrate the positive contributions of Leibnitz, Descartes, and Reid into the system of Saint Thomas. I think his *Criterio* helped more than anything else to place solid ground again under my feet. His method, rather than syllogistic, was discursive and explanatory. The most abstract and abstruse ideas were developed in simple language that stripped off each ambiguity and irrelevancy until the kernel of the problem lay under the microscope of the intellect. Even Kant's profound mystifications, on which he commented at great length, began to be intelligible if not intelligent. But his supreme achievement, as far as my concern went, was his analysis of the Berkelian theory that the entire corporeal universe, including our own body, is a dream. He didn't say it couldn't be a dream, philosophically speaking. But he took up the two suppositions, that the world is a dream and that it is what common sense tells us it is, and paralleled the inferences and implications of each. Then he took up in turn the notions of doubt, possibility, probability, and certitude, the kinds of certitude that apply to different orders, the mathematical, the metaphysical, the physical, the moral.

He didn't have to draw conclusions. By that time I was beginning to see the way out of the maze. The fundamental error was in trying to prove what is immediately and directly obvious once the terms are explained. While it is true that ordinary knowledge consists for the most part of mere opinions or beliefs based on more or less adequate foundations, it implies a hard core of certain knowledge. This category includes the data acquired through the senses, for example, that bodies possess length, breadth, and height. It includes such self-evident axioms as that the whole is greater than the part, or that whatever happens must have a cause or reason for happening. And finally it includes certain consequences which can be deduced immediately from these axioms, for example, the fact of freedom of the will. These and similar certainties belong to the common sense of mankind, deriving from the natural and primitive judgment of the human reason. The only men who do not possess a natural certainty about such truths are those whose ability to reason has been damaged by a faulty education or some intellectual vice.

Having thus erected myself a scaffolding, I was in a position to rebuild the edifice of philosophy that had come toppling about my ears. I was prepared to recognize there were truths in philosophy as in all the sciences so immediate they neither needed nor were capable of proof. In philosophy they include the so-called principles of identity and contradiction, that what is, is; that what is not, is not; that a thing cannot be and not be in the same way at a given time. They also include the existence of the thinking mind and of the object of thought, the ability of the mind to think and reach conclusions, the accuracy of such conclusions in certain circumstances. These are first principles, which we must assume and which we can rightly assume in discussion. If I deny them, you can feel sorry for me, but you cannot unconvince me. If like Descartes I question all facts and all principles, I must logically stop right there. Descartes wasn't logical because he didn't stop right there. When he resurveyed the position, he declared there was one fact too obvious to be questioned, the existence of the thinking mind: and from that single principle he went on to prove the existence of substances outside of and other than the thinking mind. But there again he wasn't logical. As I had realized, and as Berkeley properly pointed out, if the subject doesn't know real external substances but only his ideas of them, he has no right to conclude that outer things apart from his ideas of them really exist. To give them an external rank is a complete gratuity, prompted only by the inadequacies of language. The Cartesian compromise is alike unreasonable and useless. It is unreasonable because the existence of the nonego is just as obvious as that of the ego and far more obvious than the adequacy of the thinking mind to think properly. It is useless because as a starting point it leads nowhere. The choice is accordingly between universal skepticism and a system which recognizes that first principles require no proof. Now nobody can really be a universal skeptic, though many pretend to be. As Santayana said, it is an exercise, not a life. Indeed, doubt only has meaning as a secondary attitude which presupposes prior certitudes. It is both theoretically absurd and practically impossible for the universal skeptic to doubt that he is doubting, thereby immediately ceasing to be a universal skeptic.

One could go on talking forever about and around this subject, as Coffey does in the two heaviest tomes produced since the Middle Ages when they did it to keep fit, and as every philosopher and sophist for the past two centuries has done. But there in a kernel is the process by which I argued myself out of my vicious circle, and I was and am so happy to be out of it that I have no wish to start all over again. There was so much more worth-while activity, so many things to be learned, that it was grand not to be transformed into a cracked phonograph disc condemned to spin in the eternal discord of a single groove. What I pursued most fervently was information calculated to revise the predigested views of life, people, and things I had absorbed as a by-product of having grown up within or at least on the fringe of the Anglo-Saxon sphere of cultural influence. As Mr. Dooley had discovered before I did, it's a pretty gruesome business this knowing things the way they ain't. And that happens every child. Even if it is his rare fortune to be instructed by saints and sages, every fact imparted to his mind implies a judgment of values that cannot but be slanted. And what child is in fact so fortunate? First books of history are ever a potpourri of sanguinary episodes and shady deals presented and interpreted to show the statesmanship, valor, and integrity of certain individuals, classes, and nations, as highlighted by the absence of these qualities in other individuals, classes, and nations, usually those the former did down. The child imbibes feelings of antagonism toward religions, national groups, and races with which he never came in contact. He picks up qualitative opinions about machines, manufactures, foods, drinks, standards of living, things to do and not to do, which are justifiable on no possible objective standard.

The Anglo-Saxon culture, British variation, for example, left us knowing that the important things in life were the things Britain had done successfully, the conquest of inferior nations (proved inferior by the fact of conquest) by means that were always proper (proved proper by the fact of their success). It taught us that the important virtues were those that insured material success, that the fact that the British had a higher standard of living than any other people showed how much more virtuous they were. It taught us that Italians, Spaniards, French, and in general all Catholic peoples were poor and backward and ignorant partly because Providence had denied them the natural resources to do any better and partly because as Catholics they were so interested in the life to come that they didn't want to do any better. It taught us that the Americans were uncultured and uncouth, that even if they had built themselves skyscrapers it was all show and unsubstantial, that their automobiles and machines were a lot of junk that fell apart when you shook them. British goods were best and that was a law of nature. Even the Germans, who were nearly the same thing as Britons, if it hadn't been that talking a different language made them foreigners, recognized that by trying to make their things the same way as the British. But they made the mistake of putting substitutes instead of the real materials, so naturally their goods couldn't be expected to last so long. It taught us to admire the great heroes who had contributed to world progress by their piracies on the Spanish Main and their opening up of China to the opium trade.

Naturally we as Irish children hadn't taken all of this without a grain of salt. We didn't absorb it as unquestioningly, say, as did our English contemporaries. We had first of all the advantage of knowing something of two languages, and few things are more conducive to balancing an outlook. We also had the advantage of having our own version of our history as well as the English version. Incidentally I have long thought that the possession by the Irish of both versions of Anglo-Irish relations while the English have only their own has been a major if not decisive factor in enabling the Irish to continue their resistance century after century against hopeless odds. And when the official version told us that Ireland had no industries because it lacked the natural resources and the will to work, we knew the actual reason it lacked them was that they had been wiped out by *force majeure* in the first half-century of the Industrial Revolution because they competed too fiercely with those of politically and militarily dominant England. We knew that Irishmen were poor, not because they didn't work, but because military and political control had deliberately been used to create a social and economic system in which they had to work two to three times as hard as their neighbors to win the same monetary results. What we knew wasn't much but it showed the cloth wasn't all of one piece. It made us ready to question everything and to make ourselves the answers that suited us because we were in no position to establish the facts. If imperialism had retarded our development as a nation when it pretended and perhaps even believed it was promoting it, shouldn't we assume the same to be true of its dealings with uncivilized peoples? Which may have been the case, but certainly not in the way we interpreted it.

All of this slowly developed line of thought had at least made me realize there were answers to many important questions other than those I already had. And in addition, there were new questions constantly seeking answers, some stimulated by my reading of philosophy, others just arising naturally out of the strains and stresses of growing up. A book of Balmes, discovered in preparing my thesis on the existence of the nonego, was just what I needed to give me some orientation on the modern world, where it is going, and in particular where it has come from. It was a hundred years out of date, which also should make it appeal to Mortimer Adler who has since done people the kindness of distinguishing between out of date and out of focus. This book, which I still keep recommending to those who are interested and those who are not, is called *European Civilization* and subtitled *Catholicism and Protestantism compared.* I don't think it would appeal particularly to those who believe that everything that has happened in history has happened immediately for the better, in the wildly sentimental sense in which evolutionists so believe. But it did appeal to me. It gave a picture of the different aims which men and movements envisage and of the means they will use to realize those aims. It distinguished between the ends which different leaders consciously sought in the clash of personalities and ideas that characterized the splitting up of European thought and culture in the sixteenth and seventeenth centuries, and the results that necessarily flowed from the philosophical and theological doctrines they championed and propagated. It marshaled the advantages and disadvantages both from the point of view of man's happiness and well-being in this life and from that of the primary object of his sojourn on earth, the salvation of his soul, of the systems which give primacy to material comfort and the development of the practical arts and sciences, and of those that place the spirit first and reverence knowledge for its own sake.

Of the hundreds of books I read in those years, I believe the one that made the deepest impression was the autobiography of Johannes Jörgensen. He was a poet as well as a thinker, a man who saw beauty in the clouds, in the air, in the fields, in books, in houses, and above all in the brown dust thick on the roads of Tuscany, roads I have not yet seen but which I have walked and smelled and loved with him, who saw the image and likeness of God in all those things God had created in his own image and likeness. With Jörgensen I lived the joys and fears and childhood disappointments of his Lutheran home in Denmark, the searchings and doubtings and abandonment of faith of his university days, the long, lonely, insistent, intense search through many years and many lands, through many philosophers and many claimant faiths, to the rest and peace and contentment and certainty he found at Assisi in the shadow and the spirit of a saint who rejoiced in the blossoming flowers and the dumb beasts of the fields and the brown dust on the roads because they praised God with their entire being and consumed themselves utterly according to the laws of their respective natures to his glory.

I found Jörgensen just at the right moment and he was a valuable counterweight to philosophy. The philosophers or at least the scholastics proclaimed emphatically that man was not intellect alone, that there existed in him an essential dualism, of body and spirit, of matter and form, of intellect and will. Even Aristotle had isolated and identified all that was positive in the first of the three laws on which Marx set up his system of dialectical materialism: the law of unity of opposites. I had been made conscious of the omnipresence of balancing forces in nature, of the perpetual dying which maintains life, of the sloughing-off and rejection of self in metabolism, the reaction to the challenge of environment, the secretion of the antitoxin in the presence of the toxin, the uneasy equilibrium of the sympathetic and parasympathetic nervous systems. But I was conscious of them in an abstract, detached way. They had been sterilized and anesthetized by the probing intellect. Jörgensen saw the same things but with the poet's eyes. They were still the same, but vastly different; instead of mass, energy; instead of persons, people; instead of sensation, suffering, joy, love. New overtones, shades, nuances. Suddenly I was aware that it was not enough to know in order to understand, that in dealing with people, the rules by which to judge their conduct remained important but not more important than knowing how to apply them. I saw a new and vastly more attractive way out of the mental isolation of which I was already conscious but which I had been attacking from a sense of duty. It still remained a duty but now a delightful one because people had become interesting, a worthy object not only of study but of love. In terms of Adlerian psychology, of which I had just become aware at this same time through Rudolph Allers' *The Psychology of Character*, it was necessary to direct my will toward others as well as toward myself.

Allers' book was a lucky find. It took me a long time to summon up courage to ask permission to read it. Not that I was ever refused permission for any book for which I asked. But there were certain well-beaten tracks outside which it was not wise to stray too far or too often. The worst thing could happen to one was to get the reputation of being a lover of novelties, and of all novelties the most dangerous was psychoanalysis. We were simple folk and our mission was to simple folk. Our Congregation had been founded to tend to the spiritual needs of the goatherds of the Abruzzi, and the nearer we kept to that tradition, the less likely we were to harm ourselves or anybody else. Nevertheless I decided I wanted to read *The Psychology of Character*, and I haven't regretted the decision.

Allers was quite an extraordinary man. He was at that time reader in psychiatry at the University of Vienna. A student of Alfred Adler, he had decided quite properly that Adler's system of individual-psychology, with slight modifications, fitted into and complemented the teaching of the scholastics regarding the soul and mental states. Perhaps the greatest criticism that can be leveled against Allers is that he plays down excessively the importance of the sex instinct in human behavior. Historically, this is understandable as a proper but excessive reaction against Freudianism. And as far as my acceptance of his views was concerned, it was perhaps an advantage. It was a confirmation of the extremely narrow attitudes on this subject traditional in Ireland and traditional also in the Congregation. As such, it conditioned me to accept more readily what Allers had to say about many other subjects on which I had a relatively open mind.

It is not easy to decide which of these was most important, but I think I should give first place to his emphasis on the normality of the normal. Freud was again probably partly responsible. He had built his system by assuming that the healthy human mind behaved according to the same rules as the sick, that pathological states merely revealed openly the motives for conduct which the rest of humans successfully hid by doing violence to their nature. Allers on the contrary showed that the traditional scholastic notion of man as essentially and naturally good but prone to follow against his own better instincts the temptations of his lower nature made scientific sense and provided a more reasonable interpretation of such empirical evidence as modern psychology had been able to assemble. This was a valuable corrective to the more negative aspects of asceticism, exalting as it did, in the spirit of Saint Thomas for whom all that exists is good, the positive element in living, giving meaning to every act, and justifying the natural pleasure of having done well. While developing the sense of personal value, Allers also brought out that the complete realization of himself by the individual is possible only by an equal development of the will to community, love of his neighbor and every kind of love, thus giving a new clarity to the divine commandment to love one's neighbor as oneself.

On a more specific level, I also learned from Allers a lesson that I have daily found valuable, that the main problem most people have is discouragement, and consequently the main help one can give others is to encourage them. To encourage, one must want to sympathize and understand. In other words, one's feelings toward others are more important than one's action. For this he set up a simple test. Can you accept a favor with as much pleasure as you do one? It took me years to pass that test, but I never stopped trying.

CHAPTER 6

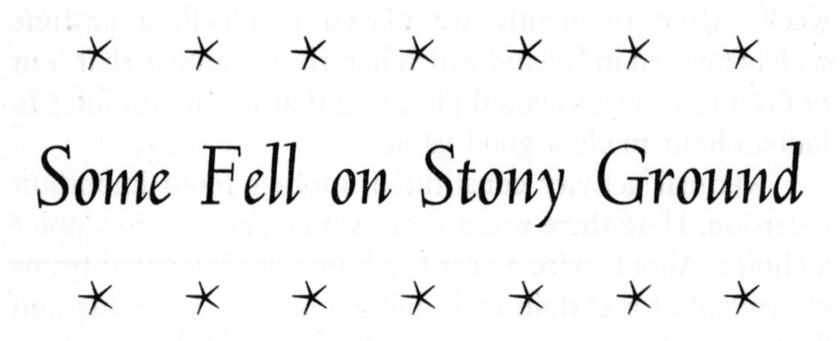

Some Fell on Stony Ground

Few interruptions counterweighted the routine of study and prayer. The rules forbade games, a prohibition rigidly enforced for those of chance and amusement, and even for such semi-intellectual activities as checkers and chess. The sole exception was in favor of a few outdoor games, tolerated rather than approved as physical exercise. There had been a group of Australian students at the house of studies until a few years before my arrival. Irish members had established the Congregation in Australia, and while that province was in the formative stage, aspirants came to Ireland after their noviceship. They had brought their national game, cricket, and the equipment together with a few boomerangs survived their going. But cricket, though we occasionally played it, laying a crease of coconut matting, ceased to flourish with the departure of the last Australians. Irish nationalism of that period frowned on foreign games, and as far as cricket is concerned, that attitude retains my sympathy. Instead we played football a couple of times a week. More frequently we played handball, a pastime widely favored in Ireland which had the advantage that four or even two persons could play, and that twenty minutes to half-an-hour made a good game.

Manual activity constituted another more important diversion. Here there was a wider variety, and up to a point a choice. About twice a year the Superior designated teams of students for certain continuing activities, sweeping and dusting of classrooms, care of garden paths, of the cemetery, of different flower and rock gardens. Over and above one's assigned duty, one might help others or undertake a special activity.

Of the recognized special activities, the one I preferred was planting trees. Our grounds were laid out between and around two low sandhills known as eskers. These eskers, believed to have been formed by the receding glaciers at the end of the Ice Period, stretch right across Ireland from near Dublin to Galway. It is theorized that a pause in the temperature rise which drove back the glaciers caused the southernmost fringe of the ice to stand on this line for a period of centuries. Rivers of melting ice flowing southward across the glaciers deposited mounds of sand and small stones where they cascaded down from the ice on the land below. Our eskers rose twenty-five to thirty feet above the level of the flat surrounding countryside, were about two hundred and fifty yards long from north to south and thirty to forty wide, and lay about a hundred yards apart and parallel to each other. They differed little from their neighbors in the chain except that they were tree-clad. This was an important difference. Only a couple of inches of soil covered the surface, and little moisture was retained in the porous sand underneath. The average esker had accordingly merely the thinnest surface of low-quality grass which parched out and bleached whenever the sun shone on two consecutive days.

Tree-planting required special techniques in such soil. Not only did the ground contain practically no nourishment, but it provided little hold for the roots. A top-heavy tree in an exposed situation would be whipped out of the ground by the first storm. When the monks settled here some fifty years earlier, they began the uneven fight, and by ingenuity and perseverance had established a firm cover of oak, ash, and beech. Most of the trees were thin and scraggy, but they survived. And the beeches in sheltered spots near the foot of the inner sides of the eskers were noble specimens. Nothing I have seen in nature remains so vivid in my mind as the soft, fresh green of the beeches for the first four or five days after the buds burst in spring and spread their beauty to praise the Lord. There was an ecstasy about those April days when the bright sunlight broke the rain pearls on the tender leaves into gleaming diamonds and the birds interrupted their nest-building to sing joyous love songs that made life's galloping chariot pause in a timeless anticipation of the rapture of eternity. And again the copper beaches were beautiful in the fall when, languid from the excess of lazy sunlight, we saw them across the football field through a perfumed haze heavy with apples and honey.

No wonder I loved the trees. But I loved them too because to me they spoke of permanency and also spoke of unselfish activity. The man who planted a flower or a crop planted that himself might reap. To plant a tree was to work that those who came after might enjoy. Or so at least I then saw it. For the young think of fifteen or twenty years as more than a lifetime. And as I planted my trees, I dedicated each sapling to the future when I should not be there to see, and to the successive generations of students who should pray and study and lift up their souls under the shade. In the sandy soil there was plenty of spontaneous germination. One had but to search and scrape a little among the weeds and undergrowth to find seedlings suitable for transplanting. But they had to be moved early because they did not survive long the drought and lack of food.

Success was best insured by filling to within half a foot of the surface with heavy peaty soil carted from the adjoining fields a hole a couple of feet in diameter and a couple of feet deep. Here the selected sapling was planted below the level of the hillside, receiving some shelter from the winds and more than its share of the moisture. As it grew, it sent out long roots in the sand to spread and form a mat with those of adjoining trees so that the whole hillside became bound together with roots underground. Additional shelter was provided at exposed points by windbreaks of laurel and variegated holly and hazels, all the tough bushes that knew how to survive in poor soil, drawing their nourishment in large measure from the air and the sunlight. Suiting the remedy to each developing situation, we lopped off dangerous branches, cut down trees that showed signs of trunk rot, replaced those torn up by the roots in storms, and gradually extended our plantings outward from already wooded areas to those not yet covered. For fifteen hundred years monks had been taming nature and learning by experimentation to make things grow where they had not grown. It was one of the important civilizing by-products of their mode of living, and it made us feel good to continue in that secular tradition, showing to the people who lived in the shadow of the monastery that it was possible to get more beauty and well-being into their surroundings than they had previously known.

There was a relationship between the fundamental, almost primitive, way we approached the problems of planting trees and our entire life. We took a pride in working from scratch and making something from nothing. We were radical in many respects, emphasizing the ability of the individual to make his own way with a minimum of reliance on others, while in another sense we were as highly organized as a beehive or an anthill. And it may also have been deep down a gesture of rejection of modern mechanized society which esteems each member for a narrow specialty. Whatever the reason, we took delight in achieving results with the simplest tools and materials, with no outlay of money or dependence on others for labor or technical direction. What I am trying to say is that the conditioning we were receiving included a more or less conscious protest against the complication of the modern world from which we had withdrawn and an eagerness to prove by example that the simple life which we thought of as having been led not only by monks but by everybody in an earlier and, in our minds, a holier age could still be led by those willing to make the effort. It wasn't altogether logical, this attitude. If we had read aright the history of Christian monasticism, we should have realized that the monks living in primitive societies then and now were and are the pioneers of the development from the simple to the more advanced in material as well as in intellectual progress, that they were and are the ones driving men to that greater domination of nature which the tractor represents no less than the hoe.

I had graduated to tree-planting from rock-gardening, which had been my first assignment. All over the grounds in most unexpected and sometimes most unsuitable places flower gardens had been laid down, usually in combination with some emblem or element of religious significance. All down one side of one of the eskers were laid out the fourteen stations of the cross, each built into a niche in the hillside. It was a well-planned and well-executed project, for which I understand some Australian students had been mainly responsible. Between and around the stations were flower beds and flowering shrubs. Another major area of decoration was the cemetery, the emphasis on the light and pleasant and peaceful reflecting the attitude to death. My particular area of operations was a life-size Calvary group, Christ on the cross looking down on his Mother and Saint John, which constituted the centerpiece of a formal rock garden. It was set deep in a hollow at the southern end of the esker immediately adjoining the classrooms. The hollow, I presume, had been excavated to supply sand when the buildings were going up. Trees and bushes all around the semicircle combined with the buildings to exclude almost completely the direct sunlight, so that when I came on the scene, weeds and slugs were well ahead in the battle between man and nature.

I threw myself with enthusiasm into the struggle to redress the balance, starting off by reading everything on which I could lay my hands on the subject of rock gardens. Most of my reading had a sobering effect. The best authorities at my disposal agreed that in addition to rocks and well-drained sandy soil, of which I had an abundance, sunlight was essential to success. The landscapers among them, in addition, deprecated the suburban middle-class technique of placing equal-sized rocks equidistant throughout the area, urging a treatment with bold extensions of outcrop or simulated outcrop broken irregularly by islets of suitable flowers and ferns. I couldn't do much about the sunlight but at least I thought I could give rein to my artistry, and accordingly proceeded to pull the whole thing down. Nobody tried to stop me, but before I had got much further than transplanting into temporary beds all the various plants and ferns I discovered under the weeds, in the process disposing of myriad slugs, the time came for a reallocation of activities. Somebody else took charge of the Calvary, restoring it in due course to its previous middle-class respectability, while I, left without fixed assignment, proceeded to amuse myself with planting trees.

Up to this time I had been working mainly on my own, but I shortly embarked on an undertaking which, if nothing else, taught me a great deal about a subject in which we should have had and didn't have much instruction. And I naturally learned the hard way. For the first time I had to lead a group activity. Not only had I no knowledge of how to do it but not even the slightest suspicion of my unpreparedness. It started very simply. A retaining wall on the lower side of the path leading along a slope of the esker to the stations of the cross was being pushed out by the roots of trees growing higher up on the other side of the path. The priest responsible for seeing that buildings and grounds were kept in repair was one day bemoaning the undesirable development.

"You know what you can do," I said. "Instead of trying to build up that wall which will be pushed out again in a few years by the tree roots and the rain seepage, why not take enough filling out of the hill to make a sloping bank between the two paths, then cover over that bank with a rock garden?"

I was full of enthusiasm. Here at last I could do something that would be remembered as a major contribution to the beautification of our home. The bank would have a sheltered southwestern aspect, catching the sun for the greater part of the day but protected from the bitter north and northeast winds. The fill needed for the bank would leave a hole in the esker on the upper side of the upper path about thirty-five feet across, fifteen feet deep from front to back, and fifteen or eighteen feet high at the back. A short time previously I had seen and admired the beautiful shelters built by Ranji Sinji, the famous Indian cricketer, on his estate not many miles away. They were intended to be mainly decorative but also to shelter his salmon-fishing guests from the showers without which no West of Ireland day is complete. Using only the materials at hand on the estate, rough-hewn logs for framework and rustic seats, lighter branches for lattice walls and rushes to thatch the roof, he had achieved the flavor of his own exotic India. I had been fascinated. What most tickled me was the fact that only labor and unworked materials had gone into securing the sophisticated effect, confirmation of my wishful thinking that modern technocracy was superfluous. My idea was that in the same way, using only timbers available in our own woods, we could build a rustic summerhouse where the priests at recreation might sit to drink their after-dinner coffee.

My plan approved, I assembled six or eight volunteers

to speed the work. It looked easy. The main job, it seemed, was to move one hundred and fifty to two hundred cubic yards of sand and gravel an average distance of ten or twelve yards. We started enthusiastically with picks, spades, and shovels. I outlined the general idea and for several days we worked the two half-hours of recreation during which manual labor was permitted and put in a couple of extra hours on Thursday, our free day. We tore out a couple of small trees and did other preparatory clearing. Then gradually, for reasons that were very simple but which I didn't understand clearly until much later, the cordiality began to sour. The fundamental reason was that I was treating my volunteer helpers like a gang of slaves. I was making a lot of assumptions that one can't make in dealing with people. I had a very definite idea of what I wanted to do, but instead of trying to get my idea across to the others by explaining in detail what I had in mind and stirring them with my own enthusiasm, I assumed they would accept my division of function, leave the thinking to me and to them the execution. I was guilty of the very type of conduct which we, in our sociological discussions, regarded a basic fault of modern mass production: that the workers have ceased to have any intelligent or even emotional part in what they do, being reduced to repetition of uninteresting and psychologically unsatisfying operations.

My companions' more than normal spiritual development undoubtedly helped them for a time to put up with my unnecessary peremptoriness. They had likewise a great deal of self-control and would have regarded it an unforgivable fault to criticize me directly for what I was doing. I think that was one of the great defects of our whole setup, that in our determination never to be unkind, we could be cruelly unkind. For all our spirituality, each was entrenched like a little god in his own mind. There was no technique for reaching in there short of cutting into it with a knife. It was as though a criminal code had no sanction but capital punishment. Some of them may have whispered among themselves. Some may even have given me veiled hints of how they were thinking. If they did, it made no impression. The wine of authority had gone to my head. I ordered them around like menials, moved them hither and thither like puppets. And one by one they reacted the only way they knew. They dropped off. Some invented excuses, others just didn't come. Soon only two or three were left. One mild, self-effacing person didn't seem to mind taking orders, perhaps didn't realize he was being pushed around. Another probably welcomed the humiliations to which I thoughtlessly subjected him as an opportunity to progress in self-effacement and spirituality. Neither of these was up to much as a worker. Either could put in a half-hour with a shovel without making any observable impression on a cubic yard of gravel. There was one other, a powerful lanky youth, who stayed with me because he admired my determination and single-mindedness of purpose enough to tolerate my dictatorialness. He tried more than once to make me understand what was wrong with my methods, but I was so deeply entrenched in my self-righteousness that each time I brushed him off. Understanding was not to come so easily. Afterward I realized how deeply he grieved each time I made a fool of myself.

While my help was dissolving away, I suffered another serious setback. I had thought up a wonderful scheme to mechanize the operation by means of an aerial cable to carry the fill from source to destination. The theory of the project was excellent. Two carrier cables running from a tree above to a tree below, the two separated by the width of the tree trunks, would each support a detachable scoop of a size to carry about a hundred pounds of gravel, each scoop attached to one end of a lighter cable running through a pulley affixed to the trunk of the upper tree. When one scoop was loaded, its own weight would cause it to run down the cable on which it hung and simultaneously pull the empty scoop up the other cable to be refilled. From various dumps and workshops I assembled the materials. But MacEoin's Folly wasted many precious hours. The trees gave so much that the cables sagged under the weight of the scoops. If the cable was tightened enough to take up the sag, it invariably snapped under the load. Even I was forced to acknowledge failure of Operation Perpetual Motion and return to the tedious but trusty wheelbarrow.

Then the same thoughtless ruthlessness I had visited on my helpers was visited on me. One day I arrived on the scene to find a couple of workmen had been brought in to finish the job. The superior responsible hadn't even bothered to break the news to me in advance or to make any effort to let me down easy. It never even occurred to me that he should have, for the subjects were much more conscious of the need for blind obedience than were the superiors of the wisdom of intelligent command. Nevertheless, the mortification and loss of face were bitter. In a few days the workmen built a containing wall and ran up a summerhouse much more practical than my conception because usable in all weathers, but an architectural monstrosity utterly out of harmony with the landscape. Hugging my unpalatable lesson to my bosom, I went back to planting trees, dreaming the while about the virtue and learning that fifty years thence would shelter under their spreading branches.

There I was joined by a companion who no longer entertained such dreams. From the age of thirteen we had been classmates, keen rivals in examinations and at sports, but always pals. For him I had decided, early in my noviceship and in the first days of his, that the spirit of the law authorized me to dispense with the letter so that he could let off steam to me in those moments of dizzy bewilderment and I could assure him it was easy once you persuaded yourself it was easy. Now he was again bewildered. Even I, who refused to see anything but what I wanted to see, was worried. His brother had just left. One day he was in his place in the oratory, the dining room, the class. He had been sitting at the table during recreation stitching together the pages of a textbook, plastering glue from a dirty iron double-pot over the stiff cardboards that tomorrow he would enclose in brown imitation leather. And tomorrow he wasn't there. That was all we knew. That was all we ever knew. But I had been able to think back and make deductions. He had been a novice a year before us, which meant his final six weeks overlapped our first six. Then he had been more than a model of observance. His fervor had been frightening. He went about each duty as though life itself depended on the exact performance of every detail. Never was a fold of his habit even a fraction of an inch out of place. The long rosary beads always hung in perfect match from his cincture, and he fondled one between his fingers as he went with downcast eyes along the corridor on his way to and from the oratory or walked measuredly in the garden, wrapped in thought and oblivious even of the rich-hued flowers lining the paths and the chattering of the birds as they picked at overripe pears in the fruit-laden trees. At mealtimes, he was of all the most austere, and his penances were the severest and most literally carried out. In the morning he did his utmost to hide the tell-tale limp that revealed the wearing of a sharp-pointed cilicium on the upper part of his leg. If one passed his door just before lights out at night, one could hear the rhythmic plash of the discipline as he scourged himself.

In the house of studies he threw himself into philosophy with the same abandon. His previous academic record was above average, but he had always been overshadowed by his more brilliant brothers. As a young boy he had lost much school time because of his health, and he had always had to struggle to make up. Now he fought hard to reach the very top. The same machine-like drill that had characterized his straining after piety in the novitiate was transferred to his study. Not a minute was wasted. At the end of recreation he was nearest the door so he could rush straight to his room. Even the short visit to the oratory we paid before starting study was cut to a minimum. On a free day he never left his desk beyond what was absolutely necessary. The devotions imposed by custom over and above the stated obligations of the rule were trimmed closer month by month. Always reserved and withdrawn into himself, he now grew noticeably more morose. We knew he was working up to a crisis, but the inviolable taboos forbade any mention of it either to one another or to him. He had to fight his battle alone though in full view, and we knew he had lost only through the vacant chair in the classroom and the removal of his name from the notice board in the hall.

Now it was the turn of his brother, my friend. The details of the process were different but the direction was obviously the same. When he had first joined me in the novitiate, we had still been able to talk about his problems. But no longer were we able to exchange ideas with the old freedom. Certain things one did not discuss. Even after he had made his decision and was just waiting for the completion of the negotiations which freed him from his vows and permitted him to return to the world with a clean record, he respected my sensibilities and never breathed a single hint of his intentions. In fact we talked little. Often we would work for an entire period without exchanging a word. Or if we happened to be together at recreation, we would walk in our file for as much as a quarter of an hour without speaking. But the silence was neither embarrassing nor tedious. He relaxed through the mere fact of not being obliged to make a pretense and keep up appearances. And I was happy just to know that he had a respite from the unending strain of wrestling with his conscience.

No decision could create such tensions as the decision to leave the Congregation. I presume that all religious orders and congregations have similar attitudes and similar defenses in order to maintain the continuity of their existence, and discourage persons from joining who might seek only the benefits of a period of membership. But I suspect that few place so great emphasis on this point as did the Congregation to which I belonged. A historical reason explained the origin of such an attitude. In its first years its existence was threatened several times by secession encouraged by internal factions led by men whose ideas of the objectives on which to concentrate the work of the members differed from those of the founder and who were supported by powerful political cliques in the Kingdom of Naples, at that time at loggerheads with the neighboring

Papal States. An upshot of these clashes was an emphasis on unquestioning obedience to every command of a superior. Another was the emphasis on the importance of perseverance to death. To highlight this concept, to the three usual vows of religious life, poverty, chastity, and obedience, were added a vow and oath of perseverance to death. It was not easy to define the precise additional binding force of this vow and oath of perseverance. The difference between the vow and oath was clear enough, the vow being a solemn promise to God and the oath a solemn promise, which God was called upon to witness, to the Congregation. But the vows of poverty, chastity, and obedience were themselves for life, and anybody who would not shrink from violating them was unlikely to be deterred by the further grave obligation of the vow and oath of perseverance. And these last, like the others, were always subject to dispensation under the circumstances defined by the rule and by Canon Law.

The practical effect, and this no doubt was what motivated the decision in the early days of the Congregation to introduce them, was to emphasize the importance of perseverance and to render more heinous in the eyes of those who remained the crime of any who fell by the way. The same historical motives impelled the founder, one of the Church's most distinguished theological and doctrinal writers, to recur to the subject of perseverance in his exhortations to his companions and in booklets he wrote to encourage them to greater fervor in the spiritual life. Any who loses his vocation through his own fault, he once wrote, is in grave danger of losing his soul, because when he realizes what a serious and irrevocable error he has committed, he is likely to fall into despair and give up the battle to lead a good life and remain in the state of grace. This tenable proposition had in course of time been shortened by superiors in their conferences to novices and students, with more zeal that exactitude, to the simpler but much more alarming statement that anyone who lost his vocation was damned. In the light of Catholic theology, with its emphasis on God's readiness to pardon the most hardened sinner right up to the moment of death, such a proposition is not worth the breath with which it is formulated. Yet the official voice of superiors, spiritual directors of the students, and retreat masters continued to defénd it, making certain concessions and circumlocutory explanations when it came to a discussion of the subject in theology class, but withdrawing them again when returning to exhortations during spiritual exercises.

I remember there was quite an upset about this teaching at one point while I was a student. The Pope or one of the Roman Congregations had put out an instruction concerning candidates to the priesthood which stressed that vocation to the priesthood in the final analysis is the call by the bishop to ordination. Perhaps the actual instruction had been issued earlier, but if so, it came up at that time in the form of some reminder or in some important article in a religious publication. In any case, it cut right across the official attitude within the Congregation as to what had been the founder's teaching on vocations. One could not challenge directly what Rome had said, but immediately an effort was made to distinguish between the vocation to the priesthood and the vocation to the religious life, a distinction which at that time seemed to me very plausible but not nearly so plausible a little later. And in any case, the discussion was soon conveniently forgotten and we were back to the old simple if alarming statement that anyone who lost his vocation was damned. We were never allowed to forget it for long. We could be reasonably sure to have a conference on the subject the Sunday morning after a student disappeared. There would be no reference to the one who had departed, but the connection called for no special exercise of intelligence.

The cumulative effect was profound. Even if my reason, basing itself on general theological principles and the reservations made by theologians when they wrote on or around the subject, told me no such proposition could be defended as true or certain, or even more probable, the repeated impact caused the will to acquiesce in accepting it as the only safe and commendable opinion, making it impossible to weigh rationally the motives and circumstances which might impel an individual or group to decide to leave. There was for example the case of the Paulist Fathers, established with the blessing of Rome by a group of priests who had left the American Province of our Congregation because of differences with the Father General and his advisers over what the seceders considered an unreasonable refusal to adjust the original objects and practices of the Congregation to meet the requirements of Catholic life in America. Not only had they the blessing of Rome, but the record of their apostolic work indicated the blessing of God. Yet we were not convinced. We simply refused to look at facts that would not fit our theories.

Against that background, there was nothing I could do for my friend except hope and pray that his difficulties would solve themselves. I could give him no positive help, neither express or even allow myself to feel any solidarity with him in a struggle which *ex hypothesi* was his own fault and had no right to exist. And when he did leave, silently, I could but redouble my prayers in thanksgiving for the Providence which had dealt with me so much more kindly, and try to turn my grieving thoughts away from the wicked world that had swallowed him up.

The wicked world was a cliché belonging constantly in the conferences on perseverance. One of the strangest elements in our myth was this wicked world which one day we would be called on to do our part to convert. Afterward, when experience had clarified for me some of its actual characteristics, I thought bitterly that one of the reasons missionaries fail to influence more profoundly its earnest yearning after the good and after the forbidden is a misfocused concentration by many of them on windmills of their imagining.

Often as the picture was word-painted for us by successive spiritual lecturers, its lines remained as blurred as the canvas of a subjectivist painter: crowded with capricious slices of a carnival abandon of luxurious living, indolent ease, the self-indulgent epicureanism of decadent Rome and a mad rush to the pleasures of the gin and sin palaces of gaslit side streets of glamorized cities where jazz-mad millions thought of God but to blaspheme him.

I was destined later to learn the facts. I was to share the desperate struggle to make enough money to survive which dominated the lives of all who in the Depression years grew to manhood and womanhood in far from glamorous cities. I was to see the crowds of able-bodied unemployed hurry from signing the register in the euphemistically described Labor Exchanges in order to be in time for the last weekday Mass in the nearest church. I was to learn the enthusiasms and the sacrifices of the social workers who shared their poverty for the love of God with starving families in bare, bug-infested rooms. I was to see in perspective the innocent and hard-won distraction from daily dullness of a party, a hop, a movie, or a bottle of stout. Why anyone should want to misrepresent those normally edifying and often heroic lives, adding to the mental torture of any who for whatever reason was questioning the propriety of his continuing as a member of our brotherhood and warping into impotent aloofness the attitudes of the rest of us at a moment when—more than any other—solidarity was an obligation, remains to me a mystery.

CHAPTER 7

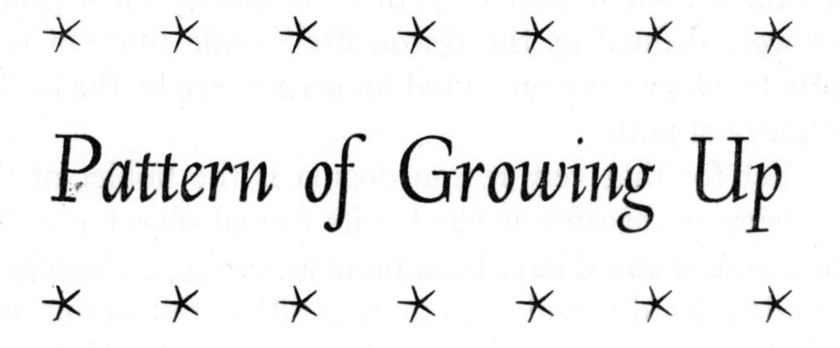

Pattern of Growing Up

Dogma was dull. For two years we had scaled the heights and plumbed the depths of knowledge in the company of the world's greatest thinkers, no rein to the flight of the intellect save those itself established. A heady experience, from which we emerged with a full measure of confidence in our own ability to perform the proper function of philosophy: to judge of all things. And after that to find oneself back within the narrow guide rails of a glorified catechism was more than something of a come-down. Boring, too. Not that the subject was empty of all interest. As of philosophy, the scholastics made of dogmatic theology a science in the exact sense, an organized body of knowledge concerning a given subject set out in an ordered way, starting from a set of first principles and by logical induction developing from them their proper conclusions. Knowledge always attracts the mind. And order pleases it. What distinguishes formally the two sciences, while making dogmatic theology the less absorbing of the two for the reason or at least for the intellectual, was that philosophy's first principles were defined by the reason itself while those of dogmatic theology were presented for acceptance by the higher authority of faith.

Yet for that very reason dogma is the nobler of the two sciences, because it has for its formal object revealed truth. And it could have been more absorbing if the official attitude toward it had been more positive. But in our own special way our approach to every subject and activity was pragmatic. We saw no purpose in dogma other than the fulfillment of the requirements of Canon Law. Our founder, Saint Alphonsus, for all that he was one of the greatest theologians of all time, one of that handful of learned men on whom the Church had conferred the title of Doctor, had established his Congregation to preach to goatherds. The subtleties of predestination or the relationship of the divine and human natures in Christ would help little to that task. And so we, heavy with the weight of tradition, continued to think. Besides, the day seemed past when people could get worked up about the nature of grace or the existence of purgatory. Not that people had stopped denying the truth of Catholic or even of Christian dogmas. On the contrary, non-Catholic Christian leaders could publicly deny belief in eternal punishment or original sin or the divinity of Christ. What had happened was that intelligent argument about these things had practically ceased. The lines had been drawn. One either accepted the Catholic teaching or one didn't. And as far as our anticipated field of operations was concerned, it was simply accepted. The Irish people, to whose spiritual needs we were preparing ourselves to minister, had no dogmatic problems. By and large, they were happy to believe what the Catholic Church proposed for their belief.

Nevertheless there was a textbook to absorb and lectures to attend and propositions to formulate and objections to answer. And it had to be done seriously and conscientiously because our life was posited on seriousness and conscientiousness. Nor was it all without relief of appeal. Even the stern-faced Fathers at Basel and Constance and Trent, fulminating against heretics and anathematizing backsliders, at times relaxed their features to become distinguishable as human beings using human means for divine ends. Even with them a sluggish liver was a mighty deterrent to clear thinking. And a split-instant politician's sense of timing was as useful in squeezing through a definition as it is in transforming a great white hope into a presidential candidate at a Democratic Convention. And out of all of this came a clear-cut picture of what constitutes the teaching church. I do not now mean an appreciation of the relationship of private judgment and of authority which anyone must establish who wishes to accept intellectually a revealed religion. The function of private judgment in determining that God exists, that he gave a revelation in and through Jesus Christ, that Christ founded a church and bequeathed to it a teaching office, belongs partly in philosophy and partly in history. Once these points are accepted, one must hope to advance further not by reasoning but by learning. The inquiring function becomes limited to analysis of what is taught and by whom. This is the core and distinguishing feature of the Catholic system, the notion of a continuing and continuously teaching church, a moral body instituted by Christ, holding and teaching infallibly the truth from that moment to this, now emphasizing one aspect, now another, gradually bringing into fuller definition what earlier was held implicitly, yet never changing or adding to the deposit of faith. And that teaching takes place in many complementary ways, by the formal definitions of General Councils and of Popes, by the less formal decisions of Roman Congregations (the government departments of the Church), by the agreement of theological experts, by the fact of active belief by the body of the faithful.

The impressions I retain of this as of all the subjects I was taught are necessarily conditioned not only by the way they were presented but by the people who presented them. So much depends on the professor. And we had them of all sorts. I already mentioned the philosophy professor whose delight it was to share the experience of intellectual discovery. Then there was the professor of sacred scripture who, assuming that everybody started with his own quite substantial grounding in the subject, devoted his time and ours to review at lightning speed the latest commentaries on obscure points on which he frequently had reached no opinion and which we still more frequently did not even understand. And the canonist who loved to talk himself out of difficulties but never to solve them. Normally, however, the professors thought of themselves mainly as taskmasters, their function performed when they had split the textbook for the term into as many sections as there were classes and satisfied themselves that we had memorized each day's allotted section.

That put a premium on memory, and gradually I came to realize it was essential to the continuance of all my extracurricular activities to put my memory in order. Slipshod or imperfect answering was tolerated from those known to be devoting all their time to the subject, but it was a clear understanding that outside studies might be undertaken only without sacrifice of the official ones. Already in philosophy I had discovered I could best remember by abstracting the outline of a proposition or presentation and writing down this abstract, a practice I followed systematically even when reading books. But I felt the need for a perfected technique that would trim ever more finely the minutes necessary to be able to present myself in each class with the day's lesson at my fingertips. One day by pure chance I got the outline of an idea. A professor, who as a student had studied in the national seminary at Maynooth under a professor of international reputation as a theologian and canonist, mentioned in conversation that he understood this man used a system of memory pegs. He had only the vaguest notion of the system but from what he told me I developed my own method. Its essence consists in taking a series of objects, each known intimately and containing a large number of clearly defined characteristics. The objects must be envisaged as existing in a definite order. The subject to be learned is divided by chapters or sections to correspond to all or any appropriate number of the pegs, and then each element of each section is attached to one of the characteristics of that peg by means of some superficial association. The more fantastic or absurd the association, the more easily it sticks. For my pegs I selected the living members of my family, who including my parents were ten. Since each had an indefinite number of distinctive characteristics, once these were fixed and placed in an arbitrary order, the whole machine was ready to turn over. It worked like magic, enabling me to reduce to twelve minutes the time of preparation of a lesson to which the average student devoted two hours. Nevertheless, I don't recommend it. I believe the excessive concentration it involved was a major element in a nervous upset I subsequently suffered. I then abandoned its regular use, though even today I occasionally call on it to enable me to record almost verbatim a discussion or interview at which it is inconvenient to take notes. Curiously enough, the theologian from whom I derived it in the very indirect way I have just described ruined his health to a much more serious degree through his excessive application. Many years later I came to know him well when he was living in semiretirement and we both contributed to a religious weekly publication. More than once, with the presses waiting, I batted out the material to fill the space allotted to him when he couldn't concentrate to write his column.

Some spiritual writer has observed that members of a religious order are like people in a boat headed for the land of perfection, so that even the lolling passengers are carried forward together with the sweating oarsmen. A pretty figure that can easily be misinterpreted and also easily overturned by conflicting metaphors drawn from equally serious sources. But within its limited justifiable meaning it has validity. The pooling of spiritual assets was graphically illustrated for me by the events just described. Round about the same time there occurred a very different event which had also its mystic meaning. We celebrated the silver jubilee of membership in the Congregation of one of the priests.

Father John was unique. For more than five years we lived under the same roof, ate in the same refectory, prayed in the same oratory and church, walked in the same garden, tended seedling oaks side by side on the sandy eskers. I consequently know him as intimately as it is possible to know somebody with whom one has never conversed. For in all that time, I didn't exchange half a dozen sentences with him. That wasn't peculiar. Since he wasn't a professor, the only time we students might talk to him was on the rare feast days when we had common recreation. And for reasons I could only surmise he always avoided students on such occasions. But that was the least of his peculiarities. The first to come to my knowledge was that he smoked. I never did see him smoke. Even he, who at times did and got away with incredible things, didn't dare interpret liberally the extraordinary permission that enabled him to smoke a pipe in his room. The reason for this exception was the state of his nerves. It was bad, as was evident to anybody. Father John was a shy, timid, fragile creature. I suspect it was shyness kept him away from students on days of common recreation. He was also scrupulous. It was piteous to serve his Mass and see him work himself into a tenseness of stammering indecision in his concern to avoid a mistake in the words of consecration. And his life, perhaps in consequence, was hopelessly ineffectual. Apart from preaching occasionally in a high-pitched voice, and three or four times a year initiating with a ten-minute paper the weekly thirty-minute discussion of an ascetic or dogmatic subject, his only regular external activity was to say Mass each day. He neither heard confessions in the public church nor left the monastery like the others to give missions and retreats, nor had he done so for years. Shy friendliness shone in his every action, his salute as he passed in the garden, his hours spent in coaxing timid chaffinches to fly down and pick pieces of cheese out of his hand, his gentleness in handling even an injured branch of a shrub or in making a windbreak to shelter some delicate plant. He spent endless hours in the garden, engaged in such trivial activities or just wandering about by himself doing nothing at all.

Nobody seemed to interfere with him, not even the superiors who nevertheless could not entirely hide their concern with his prodigal waste of time and refusal to stay within the narrow lines of conduct the rule prescribed. Not that there was anything positively outrageous, but rather an inability to think details important. One day he would be in his place for morning meditation and the next wouldn't show up; one day at spiritual conference and another not. He might stay in his room during the time of common recreation and, just as the bell rang instructing everyone to retire to his room for the following prescribed activity, emerge and make his way to the garden, a hesitant smile on his face as he sidled past the others (who were headed for the door) that seemed to say, "I know this makes no sense to you, and neither does it to me."

Our tradition was opposed to making allowances for such human idiosyncrasies. We interpreted in the narrowest sense the notion of invincible ignorance. Once it was brought to a person's notice that a thing was right or wrong, to be done or to be avoided, the question was answered, according to our interpretations of moral theology. We might make theoretical concessions to the complexity of psychological processes, yet found it hard to draw any practical conclusions therefrom in favor of one whose scales for measurement of duty happened to differ slightly from the normal. We skated over Saint Paul's lament that the evil he willed not, that he did, to concentrate on his ruling that the spirits of the prophets are subject to the prophets.

Yet we students, though it ran counter to the intellectual conclusions from the theoretical principles we accepted unquestionably, still knew that a career such as this could not be summed up in a balance so neat. Though the reason continued to proclaim that good was entire and ceased to be good with any lapse from entirety, the heart with Pascal still had reasons the reason knew not of. No doubt the superiors had come to the same conclusion, since on such they seemed to base the acceptance in practice of a stalemate. At the same time, they remained uneasy about the effect on the community and particularly on us youngsters of too ready a tolerance of such deviationism. And it was precisely when the twenty-fifth anniversary of his profession as a member of the Congregation approached that the situation threatened to get out of hand. This silver jubilee was a big day in each member's life. Not, of course, like the fiftieth anniversary which the jubilarian celebrated with extra-special solemnity in each house of the province, but important enough to merit a free day in the community to which he belonged and tributes from his confrères at dinner.

No sooner was the day for the celebration fixed than the students began to get to work. There was no conspiracy and certainly no intention of turning the occasion into a homage to the recipient's nonconformism. It was something much more simple and spontaneous, a feeling that for the first and probably the last time in an unknown life there was a chance to bring to the center of the stage for a brief spotlight bow one consigned by destiny to perpetual obscurity and gloom. But the superiors were alarmed. It was typical of the system that nothing was discussed in express terms in relationship of cause and effect. But those who were planning the decoration of the refectory with plants, streamers, and flags, those who were organizing poetic tributes in the entire range of languages at our disposal, and those programming a sensational concert for that night were quickly brought down to earth by a clarification of the relative unimportance of the celebration and the direct relationship between its importance and the splendor of the pageant. Yet, even if he didn't know the reason for the abbreviated expression of solidarity, he didn't fail to recognize the sincerity of the tribute. I think the only time I saw behind the quizzical defensive smile to an inkling of the emotions it hid was in his apologetic high-pitched reply to our demonstration at dinner. We had caught him off guard.

The transfer from philosophy to theology marks in the life of the student for the priesthood the ending of the remote preparations and the start of the proximate. This change is emphasized by the ceremonies that normally occur about that same time, the conferring of the tonsure and minor orders. Once these ceremonies had considerable practical importance. The shaving of the head by the bishop marked off in an unmistakable public way the candidate. He could no longer hide in the crowd but had to conduct himself wherever he went in the manner demanded by his state. The minor orders qualified and authorized him to perform certain minor functions about the altar and the church, as assistant to the priest. Today the ceremonies are symbolic rather than practical. The clerical student is already identified by his dress even before the crown of his head is shaven. Most of the functions formerly reserved to those in minor orders are now exercised by the laity, while others, formally conferred, may not be exercised by the recipient without a further express authorization of the bishop which in practice is no longer given.

Yet even for us these rites served a practical purpose. They were a milestone on the way, a reminder to renewed effort to prepare. Elements that had formerly seemed unimportant or so far away as safely postponable assumed significance and urgency. For me one such element was constituted by preaching.

The art of public speaking was at a low ebb in Ireland. The very existence of such an art was questioned. In the national seminary of Maynooth, from which come the great bulk of the diocesan clergy of the country, the point had been reached where a student who exhibited oratorical gifts in the elocution class was laughed at and ridiculed by his companions. The results were evident in practically every parish church. At that very moment dramatist Paul Vincent Carroll was delineating them in *Shadow and Substance*, a play which was to offend so many the cap fitted when it was presented a few years later in the Abbey Theatre. His suave, cultured, worldly-wise Canon, able to manipulate and modulate language to his purposes, the product of an old European university, was giving way to a boorish, half-baked curate, with more facts than knowledge, more self-satisfaction than self-assurance, more words than ability to express them. When he stood in the pulpit, he stammered self-consciously. Often the words were gems of wisdom but so delivered that they failed to reach the last row even in an edifice seating only a few hundred people.

With us, things had not quite come to this pass. We had a reputation as preachers, blood-and-thunder or hell-fire preachers to be sure, but nevertheless preachers. We took our weekly public practice periods seriously, and nobody laughed at a student who spent half-an-hour before breakfast bellowing out his vowels in an empty classroom.

But even with us the whole business was haphazard. Nobody taught elocution as a subject, nor did there seem to be a realization of the need to teach it. It was accepted that everyone should work out a technique for himself, and let the devil take the hindmost.

I've never read or heard a discussion of the origin of this attitude in a country once famous for orators and still addicted to words, but I have a theory. By the early part of the present century, the efforts to impose the English language, first given legal sanction by Poynings Law in 1494 and continued uninterruptedly from that date with all the material and moral force at the disposal of the invaders, had borne substantial fruit. English had become the vernacular of most of the country. But acceptance had never been wholehearted. Irishmen tried, usually with only a modicum of success, to express the nuances and subtleties and modes of thought of their old tongue in the new one. And when the national revival made itself felt in the first ten years of this century, it included a conscious effort not only to restore the Irish language but to accentuate the difference between English as spoken in Ireland and the King's English. Misguided enthusiasts saw no incongruity in throwing out the baby with the bath water. The result was the production, principally from the otherwise magnificent high schools of the Irish Christian Brothers, of a generation (destined to become the *bourgeoisie* and public officials of the Free State to be inaugurated in 1922) which rejected as un-Irish everything that happened to be held in esteem by the English. I remember as a boy of not more than ten or eleven being so impressed with a doggerel poem printed in a boy's magazine—comparable to the Donald Duck and the Superman and the Lone Ranger types of the present younger generation—published by the Christian Brothers, that I learned it by heart. The poem was called *Reading for the Bar*; its theme, the deriding of the graces and amenities of cultured living, and in particular of the efforts of students who misguidedly believed their prospects in life would be improved if they learned to pronounce English according to the norms of good taste then still recognized by the leaders of the legal profession in Ireland. That campaign was so successful that today it is quite impossible to correlate accent and social standing in Ireland, whereas in England accent remains an automatic guide to the class to which the speaker belongs.

I began to be conscious of the existence of this whole curious state of affairs as a result of a bitter experience the first time my turn came to preach. That was early in my first year of philosophy. On Sunday evenings the entire community, students and priests, assembled in the common room to hear and criticize. Several students performed at each session, so that the turn of each came once in two or three months. The new arrivals skipped the first turn but the next time they were supposed to be ready for their début. I was so satisfied with my imagined preparedness that I looked forward eagerly to the impression I was going to make. In fact, I was rather disappointed that we were not permitted to compose for ourselves the brief sermons we were to deliver. The text had to be an extract from some approved book of sermons. I picked what I considered a forceful exhortation with well-rounded sonorous cadences and in due course found myself looking into the sea of curious but not unfriendly eyes of my audience. They were not impressed, nor was there in truth any reason they should have been. The first critics contented themselves with ambiguous generalities about first performances that would with practice and experience blossom into oratory. Then came one priest who spoke his mind unmincingly. He criticized the selection of the piece for delivery, the interpretation or lack thereof, and finally and most galling the lack of a voice with which to propel the words. Unless I did something drastic about it, I wouldn't be able to fill the smallest church in the country. What hurt me most about it was that the critic himself was no great shakes as a preacher. He had a beautiful singing voice, which we generally regarded —and I think with reason—superior to that of John McCormack. But he guarded it so carefully that when he preached he never imposed the slightest strain on his vocal chords. However, the truth was the same wherever it came from. The more I studied the performance in retrospect, the more I was forced to recognize the justice of the criticism leveled at me.

It took time to decide how to overcome this obstacle. That I should and could overcome it never was in doubt in my mind, but the method was mainly one of trial and error. As usual, I fell back on the library for inspiration, and there I found a number of books on voice production and public speaking. Their counsels were often unclear, sometimes contradictory. But they agreed on the primacy of practice and provided me with a series of exercises to develop breathing and clear enunciation.

Effort gradually began to have its reward. I never reached the top ranks of preachers, for some with little or no apparent effort or application were able to turn in quite notable performances. But within a couple of years I at least reached the point where those of the priests who were known themselves as preachers of note commented on my efforts in terms that showed they recognized something worthy of constructive criticism and capable of improvement. And that was sweet after such ignoble beginnings.

As I went along, I came to see the problem as one not merely of technique but also of outlook. To carry conviction, one had to know how to appear convinced oneself. The answer was the drama. Previous generations of students had performed different Shakespearian plays during the Christmas vacation, but all they had left behind them was a quantity of mainly home-made stage props. Why not revive the tradition, I asked myself; and having asked, proceeded to action. But my previous experience as an organizer had not been entirely fruitless. I set my sights on one of the more senior students. I knew he was a tremendous admirer of Shakespeare. I did not know but was to discover that he was also a magnificent actor. He took some persuading, for he had far more idea than I had of what we were undertaking. But when he did agree, he really got things moving. There was the question of permissions. Because it was a revival of something that already had a long tradition, the only obstacle placed was that important parts should go only to students whose studies were not going to suffer. We had fixed on *Macbeth*. It had few feminine parts, and those such as could be interpreted fairly accurately by men. Then began the selection of actors, the allocation of parts, the hatching of many elaborate projects, most of them to prove quite unfeasible, for staging and production. I had chosen my director well, however, and he kept a firm grip on enthusiasms. In recognition of my important contribution to initiating the project, he allocated to me a fairly substantial part in the first distribution of the roles, that of Banquo. I thought I was doing fine in the rehearsals, but then I began to notice that I was being singled out for a lot of individual coaching. I was learning to take a hint, so that it wasn't a complete surprise when the director, who was himself playing the lead as Lady Macbeth and making a fine job of it, broke to me very delicately the suggestion that it would be better if I concentrated on stage-lighting supplemented by a walk-on part as a page boy. That was a part that suited me down to the ground, and I was highly commended by those in a position to judge for the air of childish terror I carried with me on stage to assure my Lord Macbeth that they were ten thousand soldiers and not geese that were bearing down purposefully on us from Dunsinane.

We bought nothing but the canvas for a curtain, a substantial quantity of a neutral color cloth for scenery, and a still bigger quantity of brightly colored satins for costumes. The rest was our own work, the shields, swords, and spears, the paraphernalia for the witches' cauldron, the lamp reflectors cut from old tin cans. The framework for the stage already existed and rollers for the curtain on which a student with more application than art reproduced the arms of the Congregation to the admiration and edification of all.

It was a terrific night. More terrific than the performance itself was the victory party that followed. With night prayers at the end of the evening recreation came the Great Silence, as solemn, immutable, and inevitable as night itself. But after the more than two-hour performance, when the audience filed away to prayer, silence, and bed, the players remained to divest themselves of grease and disguise, and to relax and celebrate the job well done with a good supper and a bottle of wine. The situation was so unusual and the spirits so high as a result of the success of our enterprise that the customary barriers of reserve and formality fell down so far as to reveal a friendliness and fellowship and goodness that normally remained hidden behind the mask of common life. Sitting around a log fire, we relived every moment and every excitement of the rehearsals and the performance. Most of all we laughed about a near-last-moment development that for a time threatened to undo all our plans, the discovery that there existed a ruling made many years earlier by a General Chapter or a Superior General in Rome that no member of the Congregation might appear in any theatrical performance, even—as in our case—before an audience composed exclusively of his brethren, except wearing his habit. We had heard of Hamlet in modern dress. But Macbeth in religious habits! However, one of the professors had come to our rescue with the solution that had been proposed and accepted when he was a student. They had got a number of old habits brought back by returning missionaries from the Philippine Islands, white in color and made of the lightest cotton cloth as demanded by that climate. Having cut off the sleeves and shortened the skirts to knee length, they used them as the foundation on which to build the costume of each. And so did we, obeying the letter of the law though I know not whether also the spirit.

A couple of glasses of wine all round added mightily to the jollification. Somebody had the idea that each in turn should do an act, the implementation of which worthy proposal brought forth a series of talents the official performance had scarce hinted at. The highlight came with a parody by the three witches, still attired mainly in their tattered robes, of the interpretation the leading players had given of their roles.

The following year we did *Julius Caesar.* I was beginning to understand a little of the secret of acting, for I was given a not unimportant secondary role and subsequently had the word brought deviously back to me that some who had no reason to be prejudiced in my favor had been impressed. It was then, as it has always continued to be, my belief, at first quasi-instinctively and gradually more consciously held, that there is nothing you can't do if you want to badly enough and consequently try hard enough. Jörgensen had said in the very first pages of his autobiography that every man gets what he really wants. Like many another generalization, it has to be mixed with brains, but at least as a formula for action if not for living, it isn't a bad one. The important thing is to realize that each of the arts has to be learned before it can be practiced. Otherwise one continues to make oneself look ridiculous all through life by appropriating to oneself qualities one doesn't possess.

These activities assume in retrospect a pattern not in any way visible while they were taking place. It is the pattern of growing up, of being affected by one's intellectual and cultural environment in a way that forms strong habits of thought and attitude that in turn impel one to react on the environment and shape it further in the directions in which one has oneself been oriented. And the intellectual influences were still hard at work. During the third and fourth years, in addition to the dogmatic theology already mentioned, the principal subject was Sacred Scripture. This I found vastly more attractive than dogma, partly at least because of the unbounded enthusiasm of the professor whose own intellectual curiosity carried him endlessly and disorderly over the range of specializations required to find the meanings of a series of books written thousands of years ago in at least three different languages and by people with diverse social, cultural, and intellectual criteria. Greek, which we had studied for four of the five years of our high school course, became again important. And Hebrew, now studied for the first time, revealed to us ways of thought and expression never hinted at by any of the main languages of western Europe, though strangely enough exhibiting several curious similarities of construction with our native tongue.

Of the many impressions developed in the Scripture classes, I think the most profound was the emphasis brought to bear on an aspect of the teaching Church which few even among Catholics appreciate, its reluctance to say the last word on any question, whether linguistic, historical, philosophical, or theological, while at the same time guarding fiercely its right to the last word if the question is one within its competence.

Earlier, when studying the natural sciences, we had experienced a very different approach to the development and propagation of knowledge. The elder Huxley, author of our physiology textbook, had no trouble at all in developing an elaborate theory, propping it up with a scaffolding of semi-controlled experiments, and transforming it in a few pages into an article of scientific faith. Sir James Jeans, in astronomy, performed similar sleights of mind. They left me with many big question marks about the literal or traditional interpretation of the origin of the world and of the species; and when we went to work on Genesis in our Scripture course, I was frankly disappointed at first at the apparently negative approach of the Scripture experts, the people who as lifelong students, professors, and writers were entitled to express an opinion, and those who as members of the appropriate papal commission could formulate binding decisions. These latter had lots of opportunity to lay down the law if they felt so inclined. The masses as such, whether Catholic or Protestant or Jewish or pagan, have never been particularly interested in freedom for others. Once they agree on some viewpoint, for whatever reason, they want to hear no more nonsense about it. And even if they are not agreed, they prefer the lazy way of having some higher tribunal, some Huxley or Jeans or papal commission, do their thinking for them, tell them such is so and such isn't.

Such tendencies get little comfort from the papal commission which constitutes the court of appeal on questions of scriptural interpretation. "Not proven" is the judgment that closes nearly every investigation. It is irritating because it challenges the ability of the individual to assemble and compare the facts about any particular problem, reminding him constantly of the limitations of his knowledge and the vastness of his ignorance. Yet one grew by degrees to see it was more positive than negative, designed less to humble today's investigator than protect tomorrow's searcher. Even the famous and famously misreported Galileo trial exemplifies perfectly this attitude. Galileo wasn't rapped on the knuckles for proclaiming as true something everybody later agreed was true, but for teaching as certain something he couldn't certainly prove.

Likewise, when we wanted to show whether the seven days of creation had twenty-four hours or twenty-four eons each, whether the species had been created separately with their specific characteristics or had evolved endlessly from lower to higher, whether all animals had really trooped two by two into the Ark, whether the Flood covered the whole land surface of the earth. No matter who claimed that the facts now available gave a definitive answer in this sense or in that, the decision remained still the same: "not proven." Almost never "not true" but only "not proven." It was a new and, once appreciated, pleasant concept of the Catholic Church as guardian of the rights of the intellect to continue endlessly to seek truth in defiance of barriers erected by self-appointed fallible censors, a practical reaffirmation that original sin, if it had clouded, had not vitiated the human reason.

Of all my professors, none has left so lasting an impression as one rather uncouth old man with whom I don't remember ever having had five minutes of private conversation. *Mac Con na Mara* was the way he wanted his name and not in the meaningless anglicization McNamara. For the name says, in the Irish language he taught and reverenced, Son of the Sea Hound. To the Irish the hound has always meant nobility. Hero of the greatest of their great folk tales, a hero with the unusual distinction of having been given by the anonymous historians the victory that eluded him on the battlefield, is Cuchulainn, the Hound of Ulster. Oisin, old and blind, rejoicing in memories of the great days of the Fianna, recalls that Fionn dearly loved his hounds, Bran and beautiful Sceolang, courageous and of good achievement. And later, when the youth flocked into the medieval schools in chase of knowledge, they were still hounds, yapping Irish hounds with sharp-filed teeth of grammar. Such was he in his mind, this Son of the Sea Hound, even if specks of brown snuff smeared the front of his old habit as he shuffled sloppily along like one suffering from the dropsy, which he did. We used to laugh about that. It seems impossible to kill the association between dropsy and good living, and one thing of which nobody could accuse him was good living. Instead, he died well. And that was what more than anything impressed me. He wasn't remarkable for any particular attribute, except perhaps that he was never idle. But he was devoted beyond belief. When I try to put my finger on the qualities in him which impressed me, I find it hard to be more precise. He was not a bigot. His conviction that what he did was the right thing to do carried no overtone of stricture on others who might think otherwise. He was free from guile. He was humble.

I was not even conscious of these qualities while he lived. It was in his death he became to me a symbol. There was nothing notable about his death. He was an old man, looking older and more feeble than his age because of his dropsy. One day he didn't leave his room. Then came visits from the doctor. We knew he was seriously ill when at the end of our night devotions the superior asked our prayers for a happy death or a speedy recovery. One evening shortly afterward our study was interrupted by the ringing of the bell. Seldom was the measured rhythm of the day so disturbed. It was a summons to one of the Church's most impressive rites, the administering of the Sacrament of Extreme Unction, the symbolic cleansing and polishing of the weapons through which man expressed himself, the five senses of sight, speech, hearing, taste, and touch, for the use or abuse of which he would soon account.

Yet even this act was not final. We knew the rite, designed primarily to prepare for death, often served psychologically as well as spiritually to encourage recovery. But a couple of days later the great bell again clanged out unseasonably. Again we assembled silently and rapidly, yet not so quickly that the start of the prayers for the dying could be delayed for everyone to be present. As we filed in to fill the bare cell, the overflow kneeling along the corridor outside, the candles by the bed were already casting their flickering light on the bloodless face, immobile so that one wondered if the spirit still clung within, and we could hear the words of the liturgy, consoling for one who is ready, terrifying for one who is not, the words no longer of admonition, or of entreaty, but of command:

"Go forth, Christian soul, from this world, in the name of God the Father almighty who created thee, in the name of Jesus Christ Son of the living God who redeemed thee, in the name of the Holy Spirit who sanctified thee, in the name of the glorious and blessed Virgin Mary Mother of God, in the name of Saint Joseph her illustrious spouse, in the name of the angels and archangels, in the name of the thrones and dominations, in the name of the principalities and powers, in the name of the cherubim and seraphim, in the name of the patriarchs and prophets, in the name of the holy apostles and evangelists, in the name of the holy martyrs and confessors, in the name of the holy monks and hermits, in the name of the holy virgins and all the holy men and women of God . . ."

The only sound was the sonorous voice of the reader giving out the deep music of the Latin prayer, the only movement that of his hand as he turned the pages. But all eyes strained to read the signs in the motionless face on the pillow, all minds concentrated to add their quota of urgency and spiritual value to the call for the soul struggling silently in the agony of dying.

"May the shining choir of angels hasten to meet thee, the court of the apostles come forward to plead for thee, the triumphant army of white-robed martyrs receive thee. . . .

Mild and favorable may the face of Jesus Christ appear to thee, and may he count thee for all time among them that swear fealty to him. Mayest thou remain a stranger to the tremblings of darkness, the hissing of flames, the agony of hell. May ill-favored Satan keep from thee, he and his satellites. Let him tremble at thy coming escorted by angels, and be driven into the dismal netherworld of everlasting night. . . . Let the just be glad and rejoice before God. Hell's legions slink away to hide in their confusion, and let not Satan's cohorts dare impede thy journey. . . . Mayest thou see thy Redeemer face to face, be for all time in his presence and gaze in beatific vision on divine truth fully manifest . . ."

The voice rose and fell. There was a pause for silent prayer. One of the older priests, a contemporary of the dying man, rubbed an eye repeatedly, trying to give the impression he had got a speck in it. Another contemporary, selected to pronounce for a last time the form of the Sacrament of Penance, blew his nose loudly several times in a big colored cotton handkerchief, part of the stock in trade of snuff-users, before he came forward to hold an indulgenced crucifix to the slightly parted lips. Each strained forward, mentally rather than physically, to catch some flicker of recognition by the corpselike central figure of the solemnity of the rite, some external expression of acceptance, of willingness to accede to the urging of his brethren to welcome, not shrink from, Brother Death. One couldn't really say whether the movement one seemed to see was on the ashen face or in one's own imagination. But it didn't seem to matter much. In a sweep of intuition one expanded upward, higher and yet higher, a Jacob's telescoping ladder of lifetime devotion, of conviction, of acceptance, of daily contribution of simple ordinary acts. No doubt remained. As one heard the low-spoken familiar words of absolution, "I absolve thee from thy sins in the name of the Father and of the Son and of the Holy Ghost," one knew that here was one soul that had successfully bridged the gulf from time to eternity.

Somebody rose and blew out the candles whose smoke had been adding to the closeness of the crowded room. The doctor came forward from the corner where he had knelt unseen. Lifting the powerless hand, he felt the pulse. Accustomed as he was to death in many forms, he was visibly moved by this scene, seemingly sharing the universal if unexpressed reaction that now it didn't really matter whether the heart had already stopped or would flutter on a few more minutes. Yet he had still his professional duty to do, and automatically he did it. His brows puckered slightly and his sensitive fingers moved almost imperceptibly over the veins. Then he nodded slightly to himself. The guttering candle of life still flickered.

We went each about his business solemnly, I at least carrying with me a new understanding of the fitness and properness of death in the economy of life. Not that I had ever an exaggerated consciousness or horror of death. Children who grow up in the country, if their elders don't create abnormal reactions by trying to shield them (and elders themselves living according to the traditional norms don't make that mistake), recognize death as properly a fact of life as sunshine and spring and the mating of the birds and the birth pangs of a heifer whose calf has grown misplaced in her womb. In the economy of nature death already revealed God's intelligence. Now, as I knelt in the darkened chapel, watching the glow before the altar of the symbolic light that proclaimed the real presence behind the tabernacle veils of God miraculously hidden under a humble disguise, I marveled at the revelation of death as a discloser in the economy of grace of God's love. Such meditation filled the hours while I waited for the bell to summon us once more to lend the sympathy and mental outpouring of brotherly adhesion in the final struggle. But he didn't struggle. When the bell rang it was to announce that the wick had simply fallen sideways in the emptied candlestick.

Death is compelling, even on the purely material level on which it imposes an immediate obligation to dispose of what undertakers so properly call the remains. Yet that same compulsion which prevents the living from lingering over the moment of death no matter how final they may think it, reduces the impact of death by spreading it, by forming a bridge back to everyday life. Psychologically, the spiritual rites perform a similar function. The majesty of the prayers for the dying had seemed to sever with finality the bonds between us and him with their recurrent, insistent "Go forth, Christian soul, go forth, go forth . . ." Yet we were soon to be reminded that membership in the mystical body of Christ and brotherhood in the Congregation perdured. We were reminded by the offering of the Mass for the Dead with its solemn chants which blended mystery and confiding fear and hesitant assurance, the body of the dead brother lying before the altar in plain coffin flanked with candles. As his brothers we set out in the silent, surpliced procession that wound along the walks past the eskers to the trim cemetery, where the choir sang out the poignant words of the burial service, words designed to pierce the curtain now hiding but not separating us from him. "O death, where is thy victory?" Often had that line recurred in the recitation of the Divine Office. Now the question was meaningful. The victory was not to death but over death. Which the Rule recognized appropriately by decreeing two free days for the community whenever a member died. We celebrated them reservedly but joyously.

CHAPTER 8

By the Western Sea

Only by a stretch of imagination or of language can one describe as mountains the range of hills known as the Twelve Pins that run parallel with the shore of northwest Galway, for few of the bare, pointed peaks rise to a height of more than twenty-five hundred feet above sea level. The strip of marshy land dividing them from the Atlantic is seldom more than a couple of miles wide. If you leave the winding road that leads from Galway town to Clifden just after you have passed the elaborate castle on the salmon stream at Ballinahinch restored by Indian cricketer Prince Ranji Sinji, and take an unmetaled trail on the left, you will a few miles and much dust later find yourself in the seaside village of Roundstone.

It is best you should walk those miles, for so you will have absorbed by your arrival an accurate impression of this barren, inhospitable land. You will have been able to study the water-sogged bogs and see the tedious processes of cutting, spreading, turning, footing, clamping, and ricking that turn the muddy peat into the briquettes of friable turf which is the fuel of Ireland. You will have got a picture of the heartbreaking labor involved in creating little quiltlike patches of vegetation among the outcropping rocks wherever the land rises a few feet higher than the water table, the innumerable loads of kelp harvested on the rocks at low tide and carried by patient barefooted men and women to provide a little plant sustenance and lower the acid sourness of the peat so that a handful of oats or rye and potatoes may be coaxed into germination and nursed to a slender harvest, the countless mounds of stones upturned by the spades of the diggers and piled high by the petticoated children on the bigger rocks. You will unquestionably have left the dusty road for a few minutes to climb on a rock or hillock and looking westward recall the vision of Finn after he had eaten the salmon of Knowledge . . . "Finn, what do you see?" . . . And he said that he saw May Day and swallows skimming and haze on the lake and the rushes talking, heather and black peat, and the sea asleep . . . And you will also undoubtedly have been enveloped in the soft, warm, clinging mist that drifts landward with the turning tide to merge land and sea and sky in a friendly mystery that seems a miracle when the sun again emerges to shatter its dancing beams on the raindrops clinging to the big, bold, flaming-red flowers of fuscia hedges.

But do not make the mistake of assuming in the people along the way a harshness or inhospitality like that of the terrain. This is not really their land or their way, and nobody knows that as they do. The children, it is true, carrying their tattered books from school, will sidle shyly past a stranger, their eyes studiously concentrated on the ground as

Indian-file they pick their barefoot way, to break into a nervous giggle when they think they are out of earshot. But their elders will express their old-world courtesy, paying you the compliment of addressing you in what they assume to be your language, the language of the stranger, spoken in a vowelful, melodious brogue and translating literally the phrase of greeting which reflects two basic elements of their habitual preoccupations, the weather and the supernatural: "Fine day, thank God" or "Soft day, thank God," as the circumstances dictate. Their lives are spent wrestling on sea and land with the weather, but 'tis still something for which to thank God however it comes, never bad or rough or intolerable but at worst soft. They know the wisdom that they must live with it, and better as a friend.

But if the man is working, whether loading the sods of turf into the panniers astraddle the patient donkey's back or with a crescent sickle affectionately garnering the golden stalks of corn into a sheaf, then don't forget it rests with you to prosper his task with a "God bless the work," which will be returned in a grateful "And you, too" to ease your road.

More fortunate you if you can phrase the blessing in their tongue, soft as the mist, colorful as the fuscia. It will serve not only as introduction but establish forthwith a bond of friendship and quick communication of deep long-brooded thoughts, so that before you gaze on the decaying trawler hull which constitutes the last surviving indication of the original purpose of Roundstone harbor, now serving solely as inspiration for artists in search of atmosphere, you will have sat before more than one fire blazing on the open hearth of an earthen-floored kitchen and drunk the strong peat-flavored steaming mugs of tea or even a fiery dram never blessed or watered by the Department of Excise.

That is the country, those the people. There each month of August we shook off the cobwebs of learning and, shaking them off, learned still more. Miraculously, the sun always shone on the day of our departure. This was a very necessary intervention of Providence, for we journeyed the forty-five-odd miles from our monastery to the seashore on an open truck which belonged to the community. Five or six students had gone ahead the previous day in the same truck with camp beds, tents, folding tables and benches, and other supplies, which left thirty or more in the main contingent. My first and second vacations we still had an early one-ton Ford truck with small tires and no springs to mention. How we all got aboard and kept aboard is now an unsoundable mystery. But we made it and we enjoyed every minute of it.

The road was metaled from the time we reached the little medieval town of Athenry, dreaming in the shadow of its ruined walls, until we turned left on the last lap beyond Ballinahinch bridge. The surface of the metaled road was passable, so that on the occasional straight stretches we'd open up to a good twenty miles an hour. But it would have been sheer lunacy to do other than crawl round the sharp bends that were never far apart. Any one of them might hide a tiny donkey holding steady to the crest of the narrow road, his red-petticoated driver sleeping soundly in the high-wheeled cart or sitting stolidly in the center of the sideless vehicle with back to the animal and eyes fixed sightlessly on the road behind.

Usually some business to be done in Galway city allowed us to stretch our legs and walk to the famous bridge near the university to watch the salmon lie flank to flank from edge to edge of the river just below the weir. Between one thing and another, the journey took a good half-day. But we didn't mind. We had finished another year, struggled limply through the examinations in the dog days of July, returned the textbooks to the library. It was vacation, and we hadn't yet been able to forget what vacation has always meant to schoolboys. Passing through the towns and villages we behaved with the decorum demanded by our clerical dress, but in the open country we gave rein to our high spirits and shortened the road with stirring renderings of "The Stein Song," "The Queen of Connemara," and "Marching through Georgia," which last—I hasten to add—was included for its technical attributes without thought to or even knowledge of its political implications.

The month was to be spent in a fairly spacious one-family house standing on its own grounds just north of the village of Roundstone. A big entrance hall made an excellent recreation room. Behind was the dining room, facing the kitchen, and still further back another room which served us as oratory. There was one upper floor with four or five rooms which we packed with camp cots, as many as each would hold. The rest of us overflowed at night into a big tent pitched among the elder bushes outside. The house stood empty the rest of the year, except when its owners managed to let it another month to some other religious community, for no private family would think it a vacation to furnish and make livable so elaborate a summer home in a place so remote. We were young and unaccustomed to refinements. The canvas cots were no more unyielding than the straw pailasses on which we slept at home. It was no hardship not to have running water, since even in the monastery we didn't have it in our rooms. As for the rest, the folding tables and backless forms and other items of furniture and equipment, army surplus from the first World War, differed little from the strictly utilitarian furnishings of the monastery. And in any case, we spent most of our days out of doors. Perhaps the worst thing was the primitive sanitation. The mountain torrent that cascaded behind the house after heavy rains dried up in a couple of days when fed only by the soft mists. Here for the first time in my life I saw and experienced a mosquito.

Vacation called for a new and not easy adjustment of one's ways of thinking and acting. Its purpose was relaxation and the restoration of the physical energies needed to carry out our duties. It would be wrong not to relax, not to put out of one's head as fully as possible all thought of studies past and future, not to eat heartily and sleep soundly. Yet we had to keep clearly in mind that such concessions to the frailty of the flesh had to be made with as little sacrifice as possible of the spirit of mortification, without forming attachments for comforts, without growing lazy and soft. One could never let go, had to stay constantly on the alert.

Yet it wasn't quite as difficult as it might sound. In this, as in everything, there was a well-defined tradition which established down almost to the last detail what one should and shouldn't do. The day started as usual with a half-hour's meditation in common, followed by reception of the Blessed Eucharist and attendance at Mass. That marked the end of silence and also of prayers in common (other than a brief Examination of Conscience before midday dinner) until evening meditation held immediately before supper and reduced from its ordinary half-hour to fifteen minutes. Night prayers followed after-supper recreation as usual; but then, instead of the Great Silence of the monastery, we became bound by a less strict silence which tolerated a little sniggering if somebody's camp cot collapsed under him when he got into bed, or even a syllable of ironic advice if a mosquito hunt developed during the hours of sleep. Apart from the common exercises, the only obligatory ones were a half-hour's spiritual reading, the recital of the rosary, and a ten-minute daily visit to the Blessed Sacrament.

Our regular bathing place was about a mile away, a long, narrow inlet with rocks rising on both sides and a sandy bottom. It was a perfect swimming and diving pool, the low cliffs permitting divers of varying skill or daring to choose whatever height they preferred. And we also put up a diving board. Nobody else ever came to bathe there, though we had no legal rights. But there were miles and miles of shore, long stretches of sand separated by reefs and low cliffs, enough and to spare for the few people holidaying in the neighborhood. Our privacy was interrupted only by a couple of fishermen who tied up their home-made primitive rowboats in this natural harbor. Once a day they went out, taking short, gawky jabs at the water with their straight, narrow-bladed oars, to lift the lobster pots and transfer the catch to the trap submerged in our inlet, from which a dealer picked them up once a week and shipped them off to delight the gourmets of Paris and London.

This cove was our center of operations. We might go there any time from breakfast to supper, except that we had to be home for midday dinner and the common recreation that followed. And there most of us spent the entire day, starting out immediately after the postbreakfast chores had been done (for between us we cleaned, made beds, cooked, and did all the rest of the maintenance work) and again immediately after midday recreation to spend several hours morning and afternoon in the water or lying on the cliffs, reading, talking, or just resting. As was perhaps inevitable, some of the intenseness of our normal life carried over into our vacationing.

Roundstone had none of the organized pastimes that the up-to-date seaside resort offers to the typical holidayer, and even if it had, we should not have participated in any of them. Nevertheless, as can be seen, we were never at a loss for a way to keep ourselves occupied. Saint Alphonsus Liguori, founder of our Congregation, had made a vow never to waste a moment of time, and our monastic life was inspired by that attitude which carried over into our vacation. Even when it rained, as it did to a greater or lesser extent nearly every day, a fine, warm, friendly rain that drifted like foam in from the sea and that seemed in some obscure way linked to the changes of the tides, we still went about our activities indoors and out. Few could shake off entirely the sense of urgency, the desire to be able to record in definite form a concrete benefit to show that time hadn't been wasted. For some, this urge was satisfied by reading a certain number of books. The area within bounds included not only the cove but a nearby beach about a mile and a half long with a series of low sandhills on the land side. The readers would usually retire to the sandhills after a quick dip. Others concentrated on diving or learning the crawl or physical jerks. Long-distance swimmers were cramped by the rule that forbade swimming beyond one's depth except inside the cove, but one enthusiast thought of a way to test his endurance and persuaded me to join him in a swim parallel with the shore of the beach, keeping close enough to the edge to be equivalently within the terms of the regulation. Even on the hottest day of summer the water at fifty-four degrees north latitude whether off the coast of Ireland or off that of Alaska, has a bitter sting. Five minutes is enough to spend in it unless one has the protection of a substantial layer of blubber, which I didn't. But I stuck with him for more than a mile, by which time my limbs were numb. When I made shore I couldn't stand on my feet, and my companion was in little better shape. However, we supported ourselves staggering along the deserted beach till we got back to our clothes, dressed, and made our way home, I at least seriously chastened.

One important product of vacation was the establishment of more informal relationships between ourselves. This was true of our mass relationships which inevitably took on a lighter tone in the rough-and-tumble camp life. It also was true of individual relationships which the rule of the Congregation, strongly fortified by convention and practice, tended to maintain throughout the rest of the year on a near-absolute impersonal level. In its insistence on being all things to all men, there was no room for David's friendship for Jonathan, nor even the special affection Christ had shown the Beloved Disciple. During vacation that rule remained unchanged, but the interpretation was a little less rigorous. Any two students might wander off by themselves along the beach or find a secluded sandhill to sit, read, chat, and soak in the sun.

They might even get permission to go off bounds to explore the coast or the mountains, so long as the same two did not make a practice of being together. In those circumstances one naturally gravitated to the company one found more congenial. As one sat on the rocks with a companion, watching the breakers beat out their restless hearts on the impassive rocks, eating biscuits and honey, and forgetting past and future in a breath-taking present of sea and air and sun, one discovered or developed common dreams and interests, one learned to pour hesitantly and tentatively into a friendly ear some of the deep, half-formed thoughts that spring from every young man's fancy, and to experience the wonderment of pleasure that comes from a sharing of the perplexities and soul-searchings of others.

We shared a sense of corporate solidarity as members of the Congregation, and we had the additional outlet of the intimate but impersonal relationship with spiritual adviser and confessor. Yet for me, as I think for most, that left a chasm. There was a realm of aloneness which we were encouraged and which we tried to fill by treating with God and the Blessed Mother and the saints as our personal friends. Students of mystical literature, familiar with the lives and thoughts of the great mystics, know that they in many cases were successful in precisely this endeavor. Yet the spiritual writers of the Catholic Church are the first to admit that the mystic state is an exceptional one vouchsafed to few. The rest of us can no more do without natural friendship than without food or sleep. I know that for myself few hours stand out in those years as bringing more satisfaction and contentment, more of mental awakening and self-revelation, than those spent with one or other of half a dozen confrères, sometimes talking, often merely listening to the lazy roll of the restless Atlantic.

Vacation time had yet a further dimension. It brought with it a partial relaxation of the rule that forbade us to speak to outsiders. As an aid to our study of Irish, we were authorized to converse in that language with anyone who spoke it. The storekeepers in the village of Roundstone itself did not fall into this class. About a century earlier it had been a center of one of the sorriest and most despicable of the many sorry and despicable efforts made by the English to uproot the religious and cultural roots of the nation they had enslaved but never conquered. Seizing on a significant detail of this project, the Irish gave it a name which damned it from the start. Souperism looked mighty benevolent in the cruel famine years of the middle of the nineteenth century. Any starving peasant might fill his hungry belly in Roundstone or any one of a hundred other centers in famine areas. It didn't cost a penny. All he had to do before grabbing his mug of hot soup was to bow his head and join in a form of prayer of a religion to which he didn't belong. So the soup went cold in the kitchens and was poured down the drains, while the poor people continued to die by the roadside, their mouths green with the grass and weeds from which they had vainly tried to suck a little nourishment. A century later there remained as monuments to the soupers only a great resentment among the descendants of the survivors and little English-speaking villages like Roundstone, out of which they had operated.

The people in the tiny cottages on the hills and in sheltered spots along the shore mostly understood English, but in their daily lives used the old tongue. Most of them were fishermen as well as farmers. Using small home-made rowboats, they set their lobster pots under the cliffs and caught fish that constituted a substantial part of their diet. At low tide in the late summer and fall they dragged seaweed up the rocks to cure above the high-water mark and be carried later on their backs or on those of sturdy little donkeys for spreading on patches of land reclaimed by laboriously picking out the smaller stones and piling them on the big ones until each tiny field was dotted with cairns to the indomitable spirit of their owners. Economically, they were practically self-sufficient on a subsistence level. Tobacco, tea, and a little flour were the principal items requiring cash. Even clothing was provided by wool from their own sheep spun by the women and woven by the men.

None of the circumstances existed which normally encourage the creation or maintenance of high cultural levels, none of the accumulation of capital or commercial activities necessary for the development of architecture, sculpture, painting, or the dramatic arts, not even the knowledge of reading and writing and the leisure which constitute the prerequisites for literature as known in Western civilization for thousands of years. Yet they were cultured people, the ultimate repositories by a quirk of history of a tradition that stretched back in time to the dawn of history and east in space across Europe and Asia to the Indian subcontinent, and that reached its culmination in Ireland's Golden Age twelve hundred years ago. One reason it had managed to survive at all was that even in the period of its flowering it had leaned but slightly on material supports. Unlike the civilizations of Greece and Rome which had grown up in wealthy industrial centers, that of Ireland had always been rural, depending on the modest material support provided by a prosperous agricultural economy. Even while it was expanding spiritually eastward to give birth to English literature and stimulate the first stirrings of the vernacular French in the eighth and ninth centuries, it was already being undermined at home by the successive inroads of the Danes, the Anglo-Normans, and the English, each in turn obeying the historic urge of the strong to go west. Year after year and century after century the invaders drove the Irish toward the sea beyond which they could not go. All they could carry with them was their learning and that only in the frail receptacles of their memories. But to this they clung with all the pathetic determination with which the dispossessed cling to canceled title deeds of former splendor, for it was indeed the only remaining title deed to their inheritance, the proof that to them rightfully belonged not only the material wealth of Ireland but the even more valued spiritual descent from kings and princes, from saints and scholars.

So long as any vestiges of their social structure survived, they nurtured a high level of formal education in spite of poverty. In the eighteenth century an itinerant laborer could still draft a letter in Greek, Latin, English, and Irish for the wealthy planter for whom he worked, when neither the planter himself nor any of his family knew how to write a line in any language. But the nineteenth, with its artificially created great famine, completed the erosion of that society, so that nothing survived beyond an oral tradition in Irish actively shared to a remarkable extent by all survivors of the old order living their secluded lives along the western seaboard, and guarded and handed on from father to son by professional storytellers in each community. Their homes were the social centers, taking the place of the movie houses and variety theaters and poolrooms of more sophisticated societies. In the long winter nights around the blazing turf fires, they wove their spell about ever-appreciative audiences. The crouching barefoot children stilled their skittish giggling in the far shadows as they heard the heroic tales of Finn and the Fianna. The weather-beaten men stopped sucking on clay pipes as the narrator's magic conjured up in the bluish flames on the hearth the beauty of Helen of Troy, and the laughter died in their strong eyes when they listened to the prophecies of Columcille with their promise that the wrong of centuries would one day be undone.

These storytellers we sought out. Sitting at their feet on low three-legged stools in the dim-lighted smoky kitchen-living rooms of their homes, we listened entranced, often groping for the meaning of the archaic language they poured forth as evidence of their professional status, as they repeated one tale after another, some in heroic meters that had long since ceased to be composed, some in a prose almost as fixed as the verse through the conventions that guided their art. They were poles apart, this crystallized folk culture and the book learning of the schools on which our highly specialized education was based. Yet many of us found inspiration in it, in its formalism, its idealism, perhaps even in its remoteness from reality. To some extent we were taken aback, as one always is who finds beautiful paintings in tarnished frames. For there were many things about this petrified culture that produced disillusionment or even disgust. Not only the extreme poverty, in some cases accompanied by dirt and the acceptance of actual conditions of life as unchangeable frequently found in those who live on the subsistence level, but often an obvious inability on the part of the storyteller to appreciate the essential of his art. We debated freely those firsthand experiences in our going to the people, comparing our personal impressions with those of modern Irish playwrights, poets, and writers, like Synge, Pearse, Douglas Hyde, and Lady Gregory, who had extracted from the same sources the material of their inspiration. Not a few remained unimpressed. Others, including myself, came away with not only a sense of nostalgia but a mystic enthusiasm for the civilization which even in its ruins made people live with noble dreams, able to lift themselves above the miseries of their condition. If such the ruins, we told ourselves, the building must have been stupendous. So it was we went back with renewed zeal to our monastery at the quick end of our vacation to dig deeper in the library and learn more about the noonday of that learning, of the sixth century when the Irish schools were the most famous in Europe so that scholars flocked thither in boatloads from the Continent, following the old trade routes from the Loire to Cork or sailing up the Irish Sea to the monastic university of Bangor, so that it became a commonplace of European biography to say that such a one, forsaking his own country, sojourned in Ireland for the love of God and of learning, all of whom (as Bede the Englishman testifies) the Irish willingly received and saw to it to supply them with food day by day without cost and books for their studies and teaching free of charge.

Not everything we learned was edifying within the limits of our strict orthodoxy. There was the story from the *Book of Lismore* of the nun who loved a clerk and when her time was come sent him away so that he might escape the curse that would be pronounced when she could no longer hide the scandal. So she was cursed, and she died in childbed and was buried in unblessed ground in the middle of the Bog of Leighlin. But her lover could not long stay away. Coming again to seek her, he discovered that she had died, and he built a hut of wattles by her grave, where he prayed day and night for her soul. More than a year went by, and one day Saint Fursa came to visit Saint Molaisse who had pronounced the curse. And as the two holy men sat talking, gazing the while across the bleak expanse of bog, Fursa of a sudden interrupted their pious discourse to ask who was the great saint buried yonder. Saint indeed, growled Molaisse in indignant surprise at his friend's lack of spiritual sensitivity, no saint but an idol, a devil of a nun. But still a saint, persisted Fursa, for I see a service of angels between heaven and her grave. So the body of the vindicated nun was transferred to consecrated ground, and the clerk—his vigil done—followed Fursa who in due course made of him too a saint.

More impressed were we by what these early Irish monks had done to help incorporate into the Christian heritage of West Europe the unbaptized natural splendor of the spirit that was Troy and Athens and Rome. The problem is one that Christian thinkers from the earliest ages had felt the urge to solve. Having foresworn sensual delights, they needed the more such sensuous delights as could cohabit with their austerity. Saint Jerome had seen the dilemma. He fulminated against the pagan poets, yet admitted his inability to write a paragraph without an allusion to them. Saint Augustine, trained as a teacher of rhetoric and convinced that his subject was the basis of all sound education, proposed—though not without misgivings—the compromise on which subsequent practice was based. As the spoils of the Egyptians were to the Israelites, so by right the Christians might bespeak to themselves the grace of style of the pagans. The Irish monks took him at his word. As Colombanus and his disciples spread over the west and center of Europe, the more than one hundred monasteries they founded became the strongholds of classical learning of the early Middle Ages, giving eternal fame to such names as Luxeuil, Bobbio, Saint Gall, Saint Bertin, Jumièges, Saint Riquier, and Remiremont. They had a feeling for classical literature. Sensitively yet fearlessly they handled the spoils of the pagans. Colombanus, for all his personal austerity, was a lover of Ovid. Beguiling his old age with experiments in Greek meters, he left us verses that are mosaics of the old mythology.

So we adorned our ivory towers, picking eclectically from so many disparate sources, yet ever striving to synthesize the odds and ends of information into one organic corpus of learning. That we were creating for ourselves mental worlds with almost no relation to the life of the twentieth century didn't upset us at all. We were already convinced of the superiority of the self-sufficient, simple life on the material level over the complexities of modern industrial living, and on the intellectual it was still easier to be persuaded that our own times represented nothing better than a threadbare debasement of a long-gone Golden Age.

CHAPTER 9

A Dream That Was Dreamed

Some memories of those years remain sharp in one plane and vague in another, open-lens close-ups on ultra-rapid film with one narrow band in focus and all in front and behind blurred. I recall a day I sat at my desk a long, long time doing something young men have been doing a long, long time. I was trying to compose a poem. The theme is blurred, though I believe it had to do with the second most popular of subjects of poetic effusion, the wonder of the reawakening earth, the extravagant beauty of new buds, the swallow returning thousands of miles to create from mud a miniature masterpiece of architecture on the next rafter to that on which last year he first looked wide-eyed and hungry at the world.

The room itself is sharp. Once a year rooms were re-shuffled. Some fared well in the reallocation, some badly. But all were uprooted, a reminder that nobody had a right to anything. It served, too, as a spring cleaning. Surplus books went back to the library, and to the common stock socks or a shirt or a towel lost in a corner. It was understood each would leave his room in the state he hoped to find the new one. Presumably my predecessor didn't hope for much. It was a dark room looking northeast into a little quadrangle, without too much ventilation. One day I opened the window shutters to find to my horror that behind were clustering thousands of hibernating flies. How they got there I can't imagine, but I know one of the most disgusting things I've ever done was to sweep them down and dispose of them, some dead, others crawling wearily as in the last stages of loathsome disease, others again with energy to buzz around my head and try to land on me or whatever object came in the way of their seemingly sightless flight. Not even to scrape masses of bluebottle maggots out of the wool and flesh on a sheep's flanks is so nauseating, since they at least are fully alive.

Much Jeyes Fluid and much soap and water finally made it habitable, but it was never other than dark and unhomely. And there I sat on the day I mention, which must have been a free day to justify an occupation so frivolous. No inspiration came, and I wanted to forget the whole affair, for nothing is more thankless than trying to write poetry without inspiration. Yet something held me, a great weight bearing down on my body as well as on my mind, pressing heavy, insistent. It was always dark in that room into which the sun never penetrated, and I was too stifled to be clearly conscious that it was growing darker and that reaction was to external physical conditions. No sound came from nature or from man, but within my brain a mighty orchestra built up inexorably to a deafening crescendo. Then, just as the shriek of brasses and the clash of drums became unbearable, I was conscious of a deliverance. At first I didn't hear the soft raindrops but only savored the fragrance of fine, dry dust touched by a sudden shower. Then the rain rushed, faster, heavier, more insistent, eager to lose itself in the ardent embrace of the welcoming earth.

I did always love the rain. I became conscious of it only one typical, gray, misty day I met in the garden a visitor, a tall, lean priest who had spent twenty or more years in Rome. He strode along vigorously, his shoulders back, his face lifted to get the full benefit of the light rain. All those years he had gone without it. Unlike the tropical torrents, falling from great heights to strike the ground in huge, hurtling drops; unlike the snow-flecked, stinging rain of New York driven by icy winds through the marrow of one's bones, the clinging mist of the west of Ireland is companion and friend. The drops on the blades of short green grass or the petals of the primrose might be tears, but always smiling ones soon to sparkle as they dried in the never-faraway sun. This mist enveloped our life, a spectrum scattering ever so slightly the colors of all objects captured whether by the body's or the mind's eye to give them a rainbow quality of ethereal beauty, a suggestion of even fuller content than what we grasped. It embraced the quick years each punctuated by changing seasons, liturgical fasts and feasts, examinations, vacations, football games, and strenuous hikes through the loose stone-walled sheep fields and the rock-strewn, scrubby hillocks of fox-hunting East Galway, five days of silent recollection each Holy Week and again after summer vacation, the yearly departure in July of the final class and the arrival in September of a new one full of the ingenuous enthusiasm and dedication the novitiate engendered.

Studies, spiritual conferences, and devotional exercises combined to keep in the forefront of our thoughts the fact that all was a preparation for the goal of priesthood, a fact highlighted each year by the ordinations in late September. These ceremonies took place a few weeks after the arrival of the first-year student from the novitiate. I then saw them almost as an outsider, impressed primarily by the magnificent liturgical spectacle, the pomp, the loving attention to detail. Each year I shared more importantly in preparing and celebrating the rite whose principals were the senior students with whom I lived as a brother. As my turn neared, the impact deepened, became more personal. Finally, it was the turn of the class immediately preceding ours. They were the chosen ones.

For ten days, while we kept our normal routine of study and class and recreation, we saw them pass with downcast eyes in silent meditation, preparing themselves to be sealed with the indelible mark that consecrated forever the priests of the Lord and conferred on them the mysterious power to renew the self-immolation of Christ on the cross as a worthy sacrifice of praise and atonement to God each time they should speak the words of Consecration in the Mass, and the only less awesome power of binding and loosing the sins of their fellow sinners. We held our breath through the eternity-long moment of silence that followed the command of the bishop to all present in church to reveal what any might know making a candidate ineligible or unworthy to receive the Sacrament of Orders. We chanted the responses, carried the candles and incense and ritual books, attended the bishop and held up the flowing purple train as he moved from the altar to his throne in the sanctuary and from his throne back to the altar in ritual procession, girded each neophyte in white alb and cincture, and added at the appropriate moment in each ceremonial the other vestments, the maniple, the stole, the dalmatic of the subdeacon, the tunic of the deacon, and finally, at the third, crowning ceremony (after the prone prostration, the anointing with sweet oils, the invocation of the Holy Spirit, the imposition of hands and the delivery of the sacred vessels), the chasuble of the priest. We knelt to receive the blessing of the newly ordained. We served his Mass, bowing in wonderment that today one who was yesterday but as ourselves could by a few whispered words over a particle of bread perform the miracle of transubstantiation, only to remind ourselves that tomorrow, within all too few days for all the things that were still to be done, we should be as they had become. For we were now the *ordinandi*, those to be ordained.

The year already begun would make demands more exacting than any that preceded. To the usual quota of theoretical studies would be joined a stiff schedule of drilling in the ceremonial the priest must know to the final detail to celebrate Mass and administer the Sacraments, the ceremonies not only of Low Mass but of different Solemn Masses, the liturgical chant; endless repetition to insure that under no matter what circumstances or stress there would be no slip-up in performing the Church's rites.

The studies I found more interesting than any since we left philosophy behind. A large part of the priest's working life is spent in hearing confessions, deciding according to the evidence the penitent presents whether or not the conditions are present that entitle and oblige him to speak the words of pardon. Each confession he hears he acts as a judge, and in order to judge in the first place whether a law of God or of the Church has been violated and second whether the penitent possesses the proper dispositions to receive absolution, that is to say, is truly sorry for his sins and has a firm purpose of amendment, he must be an expert in the applicable law. Moral theology is the science that equips him for this task.

As my experience in dogmatic theology and Scripture studies had led me to anticipate, I again found here that within Catholic orthodoxy there is a solid core of definitely accepted principles, surrounded by a wide area of conflicting opinion in which different schools of theology interpret and apply, more or less strictly according to the traditions of each, the principles on which all agree. Typical of the area of disagreement is the approach of confessors to absolving a penitent who continues after confession to fall into the same sin. All accept the principle that for absolution to have effect the penitent must have true sorrow for having sinned, and that true sorrow includes a firm determination not to sin again. But how can the priest know if the penitent is truly sorry? Through what he can learn by examining him, plus the presumptions of law which moral theology, a most elaborately developed system of criminal law and one which leans strongly in favor of the accused, provides. The penitent's profession of sorrow normally creates a presumption that he is truly sorry and consequently determined not to offend again. Only if, on his own admission, habitually and without making a serious effort not to fall he relapses into the same sin is this presumption voided. So far all theologians agree. They agree further that in those circumstances, the penitent is obliged to give some special evidence in order to rebut the contrary presumption which has now arisen that proper dispositions are lacking.

But they most emphatically do not agree as to what constitutes the special evidence sufficient to rebut the presumption.

Our Congregation took an extremely rigid stand on this matter, claiming to base that stand on the teaching of Saint Alphonsus, its founder, both as enshrined in his writings and as handed down by tradition within the Congregation from one generation to another. They held, for example, that in many cases absolution should be postponed for a substantial time so that the penitent could show by actual performance that his promise was serious. It fell to me to prepare and defend in public before the priests of the community a thesis on the point. This was a far more serious undertaking than defending a thesis in philosophy or dogmatic theology. Few of the priests continued to follow those theoretical subjects actively, while all of them had to brush up their moral theology regularly because they had need to apply it all the time.

As was expected of me, I prepared and defended without mishap the thesis in conformity with the viewpoint regarded as traditional and official in the Congregation, but my research and reflection on the subject left me much less certain in my own mind about my conclusions than could be suspected from my manner of presenting them. The position of Saint Alphonsus, recorded in his *Moral Theology*, demands only that there be some indication of purpose of amendment more than that required of one who is not what is technically called a *recidivus*, a relapser. What is something more than a normal protestation? The Jesuits, who—as is widely known to sinners anxious to recover the state of grace with a minimum of effort—represent the mildest, the most human, or the laxest (the choice of adjective depending on one's viewpoint) school of theology, insist that Saint Alphonsus means precisely what he says, that if a mere protestation suffices for an ordinary penitent, then for a *recidivus* a repeated protestation, or a protestation expressed with evident fervor or determination, since it represents something additional, is adequate; and that, accordingly, the confessor—who has a grave obligation to absolve the penitent confessing with proper dispositions—has no right whatever to defer absolution. Our official interpretation placed Saint Alphonsus with the strictest schools of theology, whereas his polemical writings had been directed against the contemporary rigorists who, under the influence of French Jansenism, had all but ousted their opponents from popularity. And there was the curious additional testimony of Saint Alphonsus himself that he had never in his long pastoral experience sent away a penitent unabsolved, which would indeed be extraordinary if his theory was as we claimed.

That leaves standing one further very strong argument, the tradition of the Congregation that claimed to go back to the close companions of the Saint, an argument additionally weighty because of the persistence, not to say obstinacy, of traditions within the Congregation. Yet one's view of the extent to which his companions formed their attitude on his must be tempered by the admitted fact that they expelled him at one point from the Congregation, and though they subsequently readmitted him he spent his final years not as a member but as the bishop of a diocese.

For every one of us the study of moral theology was a serious matter, and we knew it. It was now no mere question of working for a pass mark or to make a good grade, not even of feeling that we had to do the best we could because that was our duty as religious. This was going to mean more to us than anatomy to a surgeon or his cultures to a chemist. Our success or failure as ministers of the Gospel would inevitably vary according to the extent to which we succeeded in equipping ourselves professionally as moral theologians. We consequently worked under tension. And there was a further element of strain. We had always assumed, from the moment of deciding to bind ourselves for life by the vows of membership in the Congregation, that in due course we should undertake the additional obligations of the priesthood. Nevertheless, as the day approached, it brought a clearer realization of the seriousness and irrevocability of the responsibility. And years of continuous application had left us with slight reserves of physical strength. This strain now revealed itself in the development or accentuation of nervous idiosyncrasies, loss of weight, more or less neurotic ailments, insomnia, moroseness, scruples.

And there was always more to do than time to do it. My two fellow students I was helping with their studies continued to make heavy claims on me. My mind never had a moment to relax. When at ten-thirty the moment came to turn it off and abandon myself for seven short hours to sleep, it would refuse to coast to rest. No weariness is like that weariness that rejects its remedy, no discomfort like the lonely, dark discomfort of tossing on one's hard paillasse. There was absolutely nothing one could do. It was forbidden to switch on the light after hours, or to leave one's room. These hours were for sleep and nothing else. But sometimes it would pass enduring, and then softly, to avoid disturbing sleepers in adjoining rooms, I would tiptoe to the window and look out across the square to the sleeping trees on the eskers and let something of the peace of the pale moonlight seep through my burning eyeballs into my burning mind. And then perhaps sleep would follow, a coma of exhausted unconsciousness from which in a few hours the big bell would summon to another day of feverish insistent activity. That many of my companions were feeling a like strain I have no doubt, but just how deeply it affected each or in what ways I cannot say. Each had to plow his own furrow and hide his secret thoughts behind the same mask of the common life. There was one who made many efforts to communicate to me something of what he was experiencing but he never found words to convey to me more than the knowledge that he wanted to talk of intimate problems which the unwritten law told us one discussed only with one's spiritual director; and I, bound by that convention, never encouraged him. Yet I don't think that he or any of us was seriously worried about or even seriously thinking about the correctness of the decision made in the far past to become priests. To bring that into question even in our minds we should have considered a kind of treason. We had all long since accepted the postulate that the very fact that Providence had made us members of the Congregation automatically signified that we had received the vocation as a consequence to persevere to death and therefore indirectly to become priests. The worries and questionings were—at least consciously—about minor things, one's worthiness, one's motives, one's assiduity in learning all the things to be learned.

That year we had a new superior. It made no important difference in a routine fixed in such deep grooves by the detailed prescriptions of the rule that the Superior's function was largely mechanical. There were, however, small changes of emphasis. The previous Superior was an outdoor man, tall, slight, athletic. He loved to lead us on long walks across country at breakneck speed, laughing loudly at the discomfiture of those who couldn't keep up with him. He was shy, awkward, and unemotional. The monthly private talk which the rule prescribed he reduced to the merest formality. In a couple of hours on the monthly day, the first Friday, of silent recollection, he got through all forty of us, asking each if he felt well, ate well, slept well, had any problems, and directing those he thought needed extra food to take an egg beaten up in boiling milk in mid-morning and a cup of tea with bread and butter after the afternoon class. His successor differed from him in being a glib and voluble talker, and also in having been brought up himself under the semimilitary discipline of a father who was a member of the Royal Irish Constabulary. Like an amateur detective, he would pop up at the most unexpected moments, and one could sense his chagrin at finding on such occasions that nothing reprehensible had been going on. He had an equally irritating habit of trying to pry into everyone's mind, using a rather crude third-degree method of cross-examination. The monthly private talks expanded from a couple of minutes to a half-hour, an hour, or more. I never was quite sure what he was looking for. Apparently at one time the superiors had claimed the right to interrogate the students at the monthly conferences, not only about their actions, but also about their beliefs and attitudes. But the new Code of Canon Law promulgated in 1918 and Instructions subsequently issued had made it clear that the conscience of each was his own domain, subject only to whatever guidance he chose to seek from a freely selected confessor and spiritual director. Only if the student of his own initiative chose to reveal his problems and worries could the superior concern himself with them. With the previous superior I had done just that, perhaps precisely because he hadn't welcomed it. In any case, going to his room at special times apart from the routine monthly talk, I had discussed with him in minute detail all my doubts and concerns about the religious life, none of them of any consequence, and obtained his assurance that my attitudes and interpretations were orthodox. I had no wish to go over that ground again, and besides I felt no slightest temptation to unburden myself to this new superior, not feeling any of that sense of mental attunement which at best any given individual can have with few others. I believe he would have welcomed the invitation, but he knew his Canon Law too well to insist.

So our monthly talks, though he managed to spin them out to fifteen or twenty minutes or more, never did develop anything of consequence, neither about myself nor about anyone else. Much of the time went in talking about others. He would ask all kinds of questions about various students, how they studied, what they did with their time, what their views were about this subject or that. What he hoped to discover or establish beyond what he could find out by his own observation I could only suspect. But it never concerned me particularly. It was only once a month, and all perfectly pleasant and friendly. I went through the prescribed formalities.

As a reminder that the vow of poverty meant that one owned nothing as one's personal property, permission had to be renewed each month to use whatever items were necessary in the ordinary course of business, needles and thread to sew one's buttons, pencils and ink, and so forth. This was also a convenient time to get permissions for other things, shoelaces or tooth paste, or a letter one wished to write. Another monthly formality was to receive authorization for the customary private acts of mortification, the same rule existing as in the novitiate that no acts of corporal penance might be undertaken on one's own responsibility. Having cleared up these matters, the interview was over as far as I was concerned. Others, as I learned much later, did not get off so easily. The previous superior had left reports about different things concerning them that had come to his knowledge, and the new one reopened cases long closed and cross-examined them unmercifully about things they had all but forgotten. Presumably my records provided no material of this kind, for I never had any such experience. As far as I was concerned, these monthly talks were always perfectly friendly if lacking in any sense of cordiality.

And so this last preordination year slipped by, each month disappearing more rapidly than the previous one. I remember I used to go during the half-hour intermission after the afternoon class to a quiet part of the garden with a companion who was a leading exponent of Plain Chant. With infinite patience he repeated the parts sung by the celebrant in the common liturgical offices. It needed all his patience. I could talk learnedly with him about major thirds and minor sevenths but I never got closer than a rough approximation to the prescribed chants in their simplest forms. The more elaborate ones we didn't even attempt.

That was but one of the hundred final details that were gradually settled. Early in the summer the bishop of the diocese confirmed he would be available at the normal time in the fourth week of September. The number of guests each might invite was agreed. This depended on the total number to be ordained that year, the reception rooms for the breakfast that followed the ceremony accommodating not more than about fifty people, even in two relays. We passed the word to our families and left it to them to work out for themselves who to offend by omitting. Since in my case the seven or eight invitations did not even permit the presence of all my brothers and sisters as well as my parents, the problem could be resolved without discriminating between outsiders. Wording of the customary commemorative cards was decided and designs selected from printers' samples.

With a deep gasp of relief each of us welcomed the day early in August when we set out for what would be our last month by the seaside. The examinations were over. Everything had been done. We could put it all out of our minds and build up some strength for the final couple of weeks after we got back when there would be a hectic last-time repetition and polishing-up of the ceremonies, as well as ten days of complete seclusion and silence to give us a chance to complete the spiritual preparations and present ourselves to the bishop for ordination with proper dispositions. The month passed quickly. We swam in the sea, climbed the mountains, wandered by the cliffs, crossed over to a wind-swept island off the coast in search of folk tales.

By September 1, a day or two before the five-day retreat that marked the beginning of the new study year, we were back at the monastery, on the top of our form, fit, rested, full of energy. We were anxious to squeeze the last ounce of pleasure and relaxation out of the vacation, to maintain the spirit of it right up to the start of the retreat. Once we had rearranged our rooms and stored the equipment brought back from Roundstone, we were free to do whatever we might like. And consequently, on the morning of September 2, some twelve of us obtained permission to go swimming and boating on the lake.

CHAPTER 10

Secret Decision

The lake was on property belonging to the monastery but outside the enclosure. Up to a couple of years before it had been nothing more than a stagnant bog-hole, a small water-logged depression such as one finds everywhere in the peat swamps. Then one of the priests got the idea he could make something of it. Gathering a squad of students to help him, he started a program of draining and dredging, building up the edges with weeds and dirt dragged from the center, making a couple of causeways and landing stages by driving piles and surfacing with gravel drawn from an adjoining sandhill, cleaning out channels to encourage a flow of water through the lake, and finally getting a small rowboat which we launched with much ceremony to proclaim the fact the mud pond had become a stretch of navigable water. It never did amount to much as a bathing place. There was only a slight flow of water, scarcely enough to keep it fresh. Its color was the dark brown of the bog, and if one dived too deep, one came up covered from head to foot in the muddy peat that formed its unstable floor. But there was nothing to compare with it in the neighborhood. It seemed a thing of beauty on this September day. The alder trees that had been planted on its marshy banks had already grown enough to cut off the bleak expanse of bog. The giant dragonflies were streaks of orange and silver and blue-green on the surface of the water. The sun shone warm out of a clear sky, the air was rich with odors of fresh hay and honey and the fullness of harvest.

The morning passed pleasantly. We swam, took turns at rowing the little boat, sat in the sun, discussed the progress that had been made on marsh-draining and beautifying projects while we had been away, and exchanged views on future action. Somewhere about mid-morning a late arrival from the monastery brought word that Father Provincial had arrived. The news caused some slight murmurs of surprise. We had not heard that he was expected. But the interest quickly subsided. There was no likelihood his visit would affect us in any way. Our routine looked after itself, and the comings and goings of the Father Provincial were almost always related to the affairs of the mission priests.

A little later another student arrived, with word that the Father Provincial wanted to see me. Even this summons didn't perturb me. He had been superior of the high school when I first went there at the age of thirteen. A stern-faced, unbending man, he had not been particularly liked by most of the boys, but I had always got on well with him and he had subsequently shown a continuing interest in my progress.

One thing in particular I had admired about him, especially after he had ceased to be superior of the high school and I could appreciate by contrast the value of his method. He trusted us. We had quite an unusual method of maintaining discipline in that school. The superior each year appointed a senior boy as captain. He was assisted by aides called guardian angels, each of whom had five or six boys under his direct supervision. The guardian angel showed the new boys in his charge the ropes and instructed them in the rules. But both his powers and those of the captain were strictly limited. Beyond a verbal reprimand they could only direct the culprit to report to the Father Superior a breach of the rule. He then had twenty-four hours in which to do so. I still recall the icy horror that seized on me the first time my guardian angel issued the dread order. I had been fighting with a classmate. And without warning he came on the scene. For several hours I felt as one sentenced to death. I couldn't do it, I kept telling myself, I wouldn't do it. I knew perfectly well that my guardian angel would not report the incident to the superior, though he was entitled to do so, and my human instincts urged me to forget all about it. But I couldn't do that either. It was a matter of honor. And so I wavered back and forth undecided, cursing my class fellow, my guardian angel, my fate, everything and everybody but myself for getting me into this mess. But in the end conscience triumphed. I did my duty. On my knees in the superior's room I accused myself of my breach of rule. There followed a lecture, the first of many, and the imposition of a punishment. Corporal punishment had no place in the system. Instead, the superior directed the student to take his tea without milk or without sugar at the next meal, or to eat his bread without butter. For more serious offenses, the meal might be limited to dry bread and black unsweetened tea. The carrying-out of the punishment was likewise an obligation of honor. By and large, the system worked excellently, simply because the superior trusted us and consequently brought out our best instincts. When he was replaced by a man who had a poorer idea of the honor of boys and accordingly lost no opportunity to spy on us, it quickly turned into a battle of wits in which we became extremely adept at not being caught.

I had always retained my affection and respect for this man who was now Father Provincial, and accordingly I set off in high spirits the moment I learned he wanted to see me. But this time there was no smile of welcome as I kissed his hand. With scarce a word of introduction he performed his duty, which was to tell me it had been decided I was not to be ordained. For a long time I sat in dumbfounded silence. Through my mind was running a confusion of unconnected thoughts. The words couldn't mean what I had understood by them. Why should they want to postpone my ordination? How could I break the news to my family? What reasons could I give them? How could I face my companions? What would they think?

I wanted to shout out that there had been a huge mistake, that they were all wrong, that I wouldn't take it. But there had been years of rigorous drill, of meditation on the principle that the will of the superiors was the will of God, that their decisions had to be accepted without question whether pleasant or bitter. This was the moment of testing and I must be equal to it. I did not cry out. I did not break down and weep. To what extent this absence of external reaction reflected a true interior acceptance, to what extent merely a cloaking over and hiding from authority as a result of years of conditioning of feelings that did exist but were instinctively known to be unacceptable, who can say? What is the difference between the soldier who admits and the one who denies fear in battle, if both behave alike?

Father Provincial did not try to precipitate reaction or comment. He let me wait all the time I wanted. He let me pray silently for guidance. Finally I knew what to say: that the disappointment was grievous, but that I did not question the decision. I would of course accept whatever further probation period might be thought necessary.

Father Provincial now looked really pained. Apparently he had not explained himself as clearly as he had thought. He had not been talking about a postponement but about an irrevocable decision. He was sorry, but it was better I should understand clearly, and once for all. I should never be a priest.

We sat silent another long time. This was really back to the wall. How could I accept it without a struggle? And yet what could I do? Now it had become all-important to know why. True that was a question one never asked. One accepted. But this time I had to know. How could I fight it if I didn't know?

This man had been my friend. In all the years I had known him, I had met him in many roles and with many duties to perform. Yet never till this moment had I doubted of his friendship. Now I saw for the first time a chasm between us. Whatever he may have been thinking in his own mind, or whatever his part in or personal attitude toward the decision he was conveying to me, I realized intuitively I could hope for no help from him. Yet I was going to try. I plucked up courage to ask whether he would not tell me the reasons. He was obviously prepared for that question. Without hesitation he replied that Canon Law provided that the superiors of a candidate for ordination might decide not to recommend him without stating any reasons, and that the decision in my case had been made under the provisions of this canon.

That kind of sharpened my wits. I had of course been conscious of the existence of provisions of Canon Law governing the relationship of superiors of religious orders with their subjects, and had studied the more important of them. But such things had had a merely theoretical interest. It was something new to have a superior quote me a provision of Canon Law. It meant I'd better watch my step. He was proclaiming a new relationship between me and him, a relationship not now of friendship but of legal rights.

Cautiously I asked the next question. What then did the superiors propose? The answer to this one also came smoothly and precisely. Only one course lay open in the circumstances, he said. That was to ask a dispensation from my vows and leave the Congregation. He was authorized to assure me the dispensation would be granted immediately. The only delay would be the days it would take my letter to get to Rome by air mail and Father General's authorization to come from there.

Stunned no less by the awfulness of the suggestion than by the cold matter-of-factness with which the solution to my problem was presented, I asked for time to think. Father Provincial didn't seem in the least pleased. The matter was closed, he insisted, and there was nothing to think about. But he had infected me with his own approach of cautious unfriendliness. Reluctantly he agreed to give me time to make up my mind.

Only one thought remained in my mind. Though in less than fifteen minutes the bell would ring for dinner, I must immediately talk with my spiritual director. Fortunately he hadn't left his room. I can still remember his shocked amazement, and I can also still remember the definiteness and spontaneity of his reaction. Already I felt better. I was no longer alone. I must by no means ask for a dispensation, he told me. This was a mistake that could and would be cleared up. We would work out a plan of campaign, writing to the Father General and getting all the priests who knew me to write also.

How I got through that dinner I can't imagine. It was the last day of vacation and that evening we were to start our five-day retreat. Accordingly, we were dispensed from the usual reading and silence. What I wouldn't have given to avoid that ordeal of conversation! They were all in the same high spirits in which I had been two hours earlier. I tried to smile, to be gay, to wonder what was the object of Father Provincial's visit, to hide my feelings and my confusion, and the shame I felt at the thing I knew that all soon must know.

Each following day the same horror. Outwardly all went on as usual. Behind the scenes, feverish activity. My family had to be told the ordination was not coming off. There was no more I could usefully tell them, a vague, uncommunicative letter that left them up in the air, even as I was myself. Those whose support might carry weight, professors and former professors, my Master of Novices, my former superior, had to be approached directly or by letter. In almost every case, the first reaction was the same, the conditioned reaction of people who like myself had been taught to take for granted the correctness of the decisions of those in authority. Surely I must know or at least suspect what lay behind. But the sincerity of my bewilderment must have been convincing, for most of them promised to make representations to the Father Provincial or Father General, and several went to work with enthusiasm. Only one or two refused to be convinced. The superiors must have had good reason for their decision, they insisted. There was no point trying to buck them.

My most terrible interview was with my Novice Master. He was a man of fierce loyalties, and loyal to the Congregation before all else. In response to my letter he secured permission to visit the house of studies. But he didn't come to defend me. He opened the interview with an upbraiding such as never before or since have I received. I had been, must have been, unfaithful to all he had taught me, all I had undertaken of my own free will. Then step by step he took me through each day and year since I had left the novitiate, questioned and cross-questioned me on my thoughts and my actions, my relations with my superiors and my companions, my studies, my prayers, my attitudes, my convictions. Not once did he betray any sentiment of friendship or approval. But when he finished, he, too, was convinced. He, too, urged me to fight and not to stop fighting until I had exhausted every resource.

One thing gradually clarified by these discussions was the anomalousness of my legal position. Canon Law clearly gave the superiors the right to decide as they had. But it equally clearly did not authorize them to exclude me from the Congregation. And the rule made no provision for the situation. It took for granted that the course of studies would be followed by ordination.

My spiritual director, after discussion with several canonists, summed up for me. "You cannot be expelled," he said. "And you are not bound to ask a dispensation from your vows. At the same time, in view of the extraordinary circumstances that have developed, circumstances unanticipated when you took your vows, you certainly could ask for a dispensation with a good conscience."

That threw back on myself, unused to making decisions, the supreme decision. Fresh from my interview with my Novice Master, I knew what I would do. I would fight on until I had exhausted every resource.

But my resources were meager, and among the most meager my physical strength. The month by the seaside had built me up a bit. I had even put on a couple of pounds and was sleeping well. Now all that changed quickly. Day and night I could find no moment's mental quiet. The solid earth of my world had suddenly parted, leaving me on one side of a chasm and those who were yesterday my friends and brothers on the other. Who were my friends, who my enemies? There was no way to know. Even when it gradually became public property—as it had to—that I was not to be ordained with my classmates, I could still breathe no word of what was going on behind the scenes to any fellow student. We had to live together as though nothing had happened, filling the long hours of common recreation with empty words. My immediate superior washed his hands completely, professed absolute ignorance. I quickly realized that from that direction I could expect neither help nor sympathy.

From the semidarkness of the organ loft I watched, a dryness in my mouth and in my heart, as the ordination ceremonies were enacted day by day, raising my comrades to the dignity of the subdiaconate, the diaconate, and finally the priesthood. They were kind to me, those companions of my studies. When I knelt to receive their first blessing, I could feel they placed their hands with special tenderness on my head, and I knew that—though they could only surmise what was happening, did not even know if my absence from their ranks was my decision or that of another—they were praying I should one day share the joy that then was theirs.

There was a further year of studies for the newly ordained priests before they would leave the house of studies. And so classes began again. The Superior gave me to understand that as far as he was concerned he didn't see any point in my returning to class, but he didn't insist when I told him I'd prefer to continue as usual until there was an answer from the Father General to the letter I had sent him, a letter I knew had been reinforced by others. So everything went along externally unchanged for a few weeks. Then one morning I got up, after a night that like the night before and the night before that had been one of fitful sleep, with an excruciating pain in my left side and shoulder. I dragged myself to the oratory for morning meditation and from there to the church for the Mass that followed, every slightest movement a torture. As the day advanced, the pain grew worse. I could not lift my left hand above my waist; and to climb the stairs to my room, bent almost double, resting on each step, was a refinement of agony that even now repeats itself when I dwell on it. Finally I had to go to the Superior. He took it casually, suggesting it was a product of my imagination, as it may well have been. I accordingly had no choice but to force myself as best I could to carry out my normal duties, dragging myself to church and classroom and dining room, limping along with a companion behind the others at recreation. After a couple of days, however, the Superior relented and sent me to the adjoining town to the doctor. I didn't think much of him or his knowledge. A few years earlier he had examined a finger broken at football and prescribed for it rubbing with olive oil, which of course did nothing to prevent ossification of the cartilages and permanent loss of the joint. This time, nevertheless, he did help me, strapping the entire side so that when I breathed I filled only the right lung, and thereby making life once more tolerable.

A couple of days later the Superior came to me with a completely different attitude. He had become worried, he said, about my illness and had decided to send me to the Provincial house in Limerick where I could be examined by a specialist. At the time I didn't realize it, but he was unloading a problem and simultaneously putting pressure on me to abandon the unequal fight. My student life was over. From here out I was on my own.

CHAPTER 11

Last Stand

A very small circle, it was still full circle. In Limerick, eleven years earlier, I had for the first time seen a Redemptorist on the day in September, 1922, I started high school. In those eleven years the city had changed, prospering as it hadn't in centuries. Modern stores now stood where then were skeletons of buildings burned by the Black and Tans in their terror campaign during the just-ended Anglo-Irish war or destroyed in the still-raging civil war Lloyd George had engineered as a parting legacy. Replaced, too, were potholed, dirt-littered roadways by tree-shaded concrete streets. Trade had flourished with the construction nearby on the Shannon by German engineers of a hydroelectric station to feed a national grid, a project British coal interests had delayed thirty years. And people, their imaginations stimulated by all this newness, had begun to talk of the further business the projected Shannon airport, European transatlantic air terminal, would throw their way.

Limerick had changed. But the monastery had no more changed since I first saw it than had the battlemented castle built to guard the ford by the signer of Magna Charta, or the block of weather-beaten granite that commemorated the Broken Treaty on its pedestal across the rapids from the castle. It was the same stern, cut-stone building squeezed between the big revival-Gothic squat-towered church and the newer, brighter high school. The same gloom hung over the house, the same lassitude lay on the garden shaded by tall trees and split up by shrubs and secretive hedges. High surrounding walls topped by broken bottles set in concrete, though designed to protect rather than enclose, intensified the institutional atmosphere. And the very climate was one of depression, a city at sea level forty miles from the ocean. Ten-thousand-ton ships, riding high above the surrounding countryside between the river's dikes on the incoming tide, discharged grain cargoes into silos just beyond the bottom of our garden.

I soon realized my transfer had weakened my bargaining position substantially. The Superior of the house of studies had washed his hands of me. The Limerick Superior, one of Father Provincial's two official consultants and consequently fully briefed, had no intention of receiving me as a member of his community. In high school I had known him in the remote way a schoolboy knows his teachers. We liked him for his rare gift that classes passed quickly and casually as game periods, yet at year-end we made highest marks in the subjects he taught. Then we had thought him worldly, offhand about rules. Now I uncovered other less attractive characteristics. He fancied himself mightily as power politician and was typical power politician in his ability to persuade himself that the ends sought justified the means to hand. I had and have no idea what part he played in making the decision that had put me where I was, but I soon recognized he was leading the campaign to finish with the distasteful mess by having me ask a dispensation and take myself off about my business. I soon recognized, too, that in their own minds the superiors already regarded me in all but legal form outside the Congregation, no longer a brother to be helped, encouraged, aided, but an unhealthy growth on the body corporate to be removed by whatever means available. This realization was the supreme disillusionment, a far greater sorrow than the hurt suffered from the decision to refuse me ordination. That decision I believed mistaken, yet could not but recognize as the exercise of a discretion; and when I reflected soberly on it, I had to concede that whoever made it must be presumed to have decided, however mistakenly, after a conscientious weighing of the facts as presented.

But the concrete situation which I here faced was something quite different. These very same superiors had raised and nurtured me on a set of principles which now, on the day of the storm, they repudiated. They had told me the year's novitiate enabled each party to know the other without legal commitment, that when the Congregation accepted the vows of the novice, it created clear obligations on both sides, on his side to live according to the rule, on its side to take the place of parents and family and provide the material and spiritual facilities he would need to live up to his bargain. In only one way, they had said, could the Congregation end that arrangement, in accordance with the prescriptions of Canon Law if the individual contumaciously and repeatedly violated the rules. He had to be warned formally on three occasions, and final action could be taken only if he still persisted in his breach of the rules after those warnings. That was the theory. Now, I found myself written off without any of those circumstances developing. Moral pressure was being brought to bear to abandon my vocation by the people who yesterday told me the person who abandoned his vocation lost his soul. One friend, while we were discussing these developments, had bitterly paraphrased Robespierre. "O common good," he had said, "how many crimes are committed in your name!" His comment seemed to me just. The superiors had so glorified in their own minds a concept of the common good as they envisaged it that all rights seen as conflicting ceased to signify. They shut me out of their interests and out of their hearts. That, I had been told, happened in the outside world; those you thought your friends and those who assumed obligations toward you let you down in a crisis. That, I had been told, one escaped in the religious life, because one depended on people whose lives were guided by Christian principles.

I had plenty of time to think these bitter thoughts those first days in Limerick. Immediately on arrival I received first indication of what to expect. Instead of getting one of the rooms allocated to the members of the community, I was placed apart in a wing reserved for outside visitors. Politely the Superior told me to do as I pleased. For him I didn't belong there. He had no intention of letting me feel myself a member of his family. And I wanted nothing so much as to belong. I was determined to integrate myself all I could into the community, to let it be seen I desired no privileges or special treatment. But there wasn't much I could do beyond attending the common exercises in the oratory, the meals, and the recreations. The recreations in common were to be a perfect hell. The priests were for the most part complete strangers, and I soon discovered, briefed to mind their own business and deny aid and comfort to the enemy.

Most did as they were told. But fortunately for me, not all. A member of this community was my cousin. He was ten years my senior. We had never known each other well, but I had met him at different times and had corresponded with him during five years he had spent in the Philippine Islands, from where he had recently returned. As I learned later, the superiors had approached him as soon as they realized I wasn't going to give up without a struggle. Without revealing the motives that underlay their decision, they persuaded him he would do me a kindness if he would try to convince me nothing could be gained by my efforts to resist the inevitable. It had been arranged he would come to the house of studies under some pretext of business, but the subsequent developments made this unnecessary.

He began his assignment with what enthusiasm he could muster. That wasn't much, not only because he disliked the task, but because his term in the steaming heat of the tropics had taken every ounce of energy and physical strength out of him. But he was sincerely convinced the superiors hadn't made their decision lightly and that consequently I should accept it. Since neither he nor I knew the reasons that motivated them, we were like two blind men discussing colors. But we kept at it day after day. And he finally was the one who cracked. Once again I had an ally. And that made a terrific practical difference. For I was as innocent as a lamb of the tricks of diplomacy, unsuspecting of the subtle mental reservations with which apparently open and straightforward undertakings or promises were given.

It soon became apparent that nothing was to be hoped from negotiations with the Father Provincial or any of the subordinate superiors of the Irish Province. In the fall of each year the Provincial visited each house of the Province, and during the visitation every member of each house was received in private audience. My confessor and my old Master of Novices had been confident they could marshal enough influence at this time to persuade the Provincial to reconsider his attitude. But the report each carried back deepened the gloom. And so we had to see if something couldn't be done with Father General in Rome.

I was ready to try anything rather than give up membership in the Congregation. First I sought a reopening of the case, at least on the basis of postponing a final decision for one or more years which I might pass in teaching or other useful work. When that failed, my next proposal was for a transfer to some other province of the Congregation. Many provinces had more difficulty than Ireland in getting members. It was not unusual to transfer somebody who was not hitting it off too well at home to a province whose superiors were so hard up for workers that they were willing to take a chance. That also drew a blank. Very well, I then wrote Father General. I could but accept the decision. But I was determined to remain a member even if it meant becoming a lay brother.

Up to that time I hadn't given very much thought to the life of the lay brothers, and when I did look at it, it didn't strike me as one I'd have chosen in other circumstances. The lay brothers were the servants of the community, their function to do the cooking, cleaning, tailoring, gardening, and other manual tasks. The usual reason one decided in the first instance to become a lay brother was that one felt the call to the religious life but didn't have the education necessary to become a priest. Humanly speaking, this life offered little. Intellectual activities and interests were discouraged, and their subordinate status was constantly emphasized. Their recreation periods were even shorter than those of the other members of the community, and were spent by themselves. They had no part in shaping or enforcing policy. The monotony was never interrupted for them as for the priests, by going outside the monastery to give missions or retreats. No fame came to them as preachers or teachers, none of the social standing that followed the priesthood. I was certainly not enthusiastic. Such a life required an extreme degree of virtue. Yet it seemed a possible solution to my problem. They took the same vows as the other members of the Congregation and shared the same call to perfection. The obligations I had taken and by which I remained bound could be carried out as a lay brother. And besides, though this thought I didn't include in my letters to the Father General, there was the hope that if I could hold on long enough as a lay brother one day my case might be reopened and redecided. My own companions would one day be rectors and consultors and provincials. To leave the Congregation would close the matter irrevocably. But while I continued a member, there would always be hope. And in my heart I didn't doubt my companions would have decided, would decide differently. They knew me.

But Father General didn't want that either. And looking at it in cold blood, I couldn't feel he wasn't right. It would have meant living all my life with a group of people of different backgrounds, tastes, and interests, with no opportunity to use any of the intellectual skills I had developed. Chances for success would have been slight.

Each exchange of letters took a couple of weeks. Between times, the days hung heavy on my hands. The only person with whom I felt free to discuss my problems was my cousin, and I spent a considerable amount of time in his room. He had burned his boats. Not only did he report back to his superiors that he had failed in the mission entrusted to him, but he made no effort to hide his conviction that I had been treated unjustly. Yet, the hours I spent in his company first caused me to wonder if I was indeed wise in my resolve to keep struggling. For he was a good example of the colossal waste of good human material that resulted from the way the superiors ran the business of the Congregation. Within a short time of his arrival in the Philippine Islands his health had broken down. Ignoring the differences of climate and the more exacting work to be done in those islands where there were few priests, the superiors insisted that the men assigned there lead the same exacting life, almost to the last detail, as in Ireland. Even when, as in his case and that of many others, the result was a physical collapse, they insisted that the individual complete his tour of duty. Eating scarcely enough to stay alive, he had survived simply by withdrawing into himself in a kind of stoicism that let everything flow over and around him without making an impression. Never before had I seen or imagined the resulting state of suspended animation. I didn't understand how one could live so negatively, without desires or ambitions. Was it for this I was fighting so hard, I sometimes asked myself.

Only one other member of the community attempted to befriend me, and I had to avoid the appearance of having fallen under his influence. I never went near his room or otherwise showed any desire to talk with him. I knew little about him, and that only by rumor and innuendo, but it was all unsavory. His reputation was that of a trouble-maker. He had spent several years in the English Province of the Congregation. A transfer from one province to another was granted only for serious reasons, usually either because one didn't get on with one's superiors or had done something to arouse resentment or cause scandal among the laity that would most quickly be forgotten if the principal disappeared from the scene. But he hadn't settled down there either, and after a few years he returned to Ireland to a life of enforced idleness in a community in which he regarded himself and in which he was regarded by his confrères as a stranger.

Occasionally he invited me to take a walk with him in the afternoon, and I had no good reason for declining. Time hung heavy, and besides I knew and loved every inch of the countryside. During the five years I had spent at high school in Limerick, at least one afternoon a week we had sallied forth, three deep, on route marches that took us to every point of interest within walking distance. We would inspect the walls of the old city. In the seventeenth century the French general, Ruth, had pulled out his troops as the armies of William of Orange approached, saying those crumbling walls could be battered down with roasted apples. But the women of Limerick had stood in the breaches with their citizen husbands and thrown back the Dutch assaults week after week and month after month until William signed terms granting the thing for which they had fought, freedom of religion for the entire country, the famous Treaty of Limerick destined to be broken by an English Parliament "ere the ink wherewith 'twas writ was dry." We would go upstream along the top of the immense dike containing the Shannon within its artificial bed to the narrow metal bridge built to permit barge horses to cross over and follow the canal on the other side which brought the boats past the rapids. As boys, immersed in the Gallic wars, we had named it Caesar's bridge from some fancied resemblance to one Caesar had thrown across the Rhine. We would go out the Ennis Road past Cloheen to the crossroads where still stood in majestic permanence the expanse of trees from which each fall we had loaded our pockets with chestnuts to be seasoned and hardened for use in a game of childish rivalry from which we had derived infinite enjoyment. We would break across country to strike the river again at the falls of Doonass, where Sarsfield and his horsemen had forded it in a daring moonlight raid. We would descend the winding road in a cloud of limestone dust past the gaunt crag-perched ruins of Beauty Castle, which tradition said would fall on the first to pass that way more beautiful than the one beloved of its medieval builder.

We had little in common, this priest who regretted nothing more than that he had become one, and this student who wanted nothing more than to become a priest. And what we had of like experience, I had no intention of sharing. He, for his part, made no attempt to pump me. But one day, after the walks had continued a couple of months and he had satisfied himself I was worthy of trust, he amazed me by telling me that he had known my situation even before I had left the house of studies. Details he supplied, which could not have otherwise been known, confirmed his direct testimony as to the way the information had reached him, establishing a grave violation of secrecy by one of the superiors. This did not affect my substantial situation one way or the other but was nonetheless a serious shock, new evidence that no holds were barred on the other side.

I wasn't yet ready to recognize it, but the conviction was growing inside me that my position was hopeless. My cousin, now my only confidant, wouldn't admit it either, but he also knew. The correspondence with the Father General had gone on for months, and the tone of his letters—always final—was growing sharp. There was absolutely no use, he insisted, in my trying to find out the reasons or motives that had prompted the decision. He was under no obligation to give them and he wasn't going to. There was now no place for me in the Congregation and I should get out. He didn't pretend he could force or order me to leave, but one day he sprang a new one. It was true, he wrote me, Canon Law provided only one procedure under which a member could be expelled, and there was no question of applying that procedure, since I had neither violated any rule or disobeyed any order. But the Holy See could override Canon Law, and if I didn't quickly take the action he wanted me to take, he would apply to the Holy See for authority to expel me. I didn't nor don't believe he could get away with that, but that was what he wrote and it made perfectly clear to me nothing further could be hoped from appeals to him. We were near a stalemate, and in my heart I knew a stalemate was only a hair's breadth short of total defeat.

Many a time I discussed this contingency with my cousin. There was, absolutely speaking, no reason why I couldn't hold out the way I was for a whole lifetime, occupying myself as best I might. There was an excellent library in every monastery and as of now there was no restriction on my using it, though the possibility couldn't be excluded that even this might be placed out of bounds as a further inducement to leave. I might occupy myself indefinitely exploring endless avenues of knowledge, just as at the moment I was absorbing every last scrap of information I could find on the subject of immediate concern, the legal and moral rights and obligations of one in my situation. There was not and there certainly would not be any limitation on the time I might spend in prayer and meditation. In fact, no day went by I did not spend several hours on my knees in the oratory asking for divine help and guidance, for the light to see the path I should take and the strength to keep to it when I saw it, for the grace to overlook the human factors that tended more and more to confuse the objective rights and wrongs, and to decide on the merits. And the more I thought and prayed and discussed, the more it became a conviction—rather than a reasoned conclusion—that I was under no moral obligation to live a stalemate, that if I got nowhere with my efforts, I should do as my superiors were urging, not indeed because they so wanted (for they had no right to insist and must each in his own day make his explanation before a court knowing all the facts), but because they were making any other course morally impossible.

That point had not yet arrived. One further attempt I could still make, an appeal to the Holy See. There wasn't much to say. Fighting the unknown was beating the air. I could but set out in a memorandum to the appropriate ministry, the Congregation of Religious, the facts of record of my brief career and ask it inspect for itself the latest chapter. For a couple of months I had been making drafts, poring over Latin dictionaries and grammars the while, for I wanted my meaning to be clear and the language to be such that the purple-robed *monsignori* reading in their Renaissance palaces would not have too many laughs at the solecisms of the bog-trotting barbarian.

But it remained thin on content. Each time I reread, I saw that more clearly. And January was an unsympathetic month in Rome. I fancied myself in the place of a liverish civil servant shivering at his desk in a drafty underheated expanse of marble columns and faded tapestries. Wouldn't he sniff irritably and condense the entire matter to an annotation on the file for the approval of the higher-up that the superiors of X, after due deliberation and prayer, had decided they weren't satisfied he'd make a good priest, and they should know? That was the snag, that presumption. If only I had something concrete, something tangible to rebut it, something that would stir him into making his annotation read: "I think we should take a look for ourselves at the evidence."

Then Father Provincial made a suggestion that seemed to provide the chance for which I'd been waiting. A most unusual suggestion it was, one that in itself didn't appeal to me at all. It was that I spend Christmas in my parents' home. It shocked me. Normally a member of the Congregation visited his home only for the death of an immediate member of his family. As I listened to his proposal, I was thinking forward to how it would look if (as seemed too likely) a few months hence I should reach the end of the road. More than six years previously, still a boy, I had left the village where my family lived. The neighbors knew where I was, had kept informed of progress. In the Irish village a priest in the family was a distinction. But a "spoiled priest," one who had the chance and hadn't made the grade . . . Why should I rub salt in the wound by going home still wearing the religious habit, presenting myself as though only months separated me from ordination, if tomorrow or the following day the bubble was like to burst? It would be an unnecessary cruelty to myself as well as to my parents.

Nevertheless, I jumped at the offer. It seemed a disposition of Providence to get the additional material I needed to inject significance and authenticity into the appeal to the Holy See. A few months previously, a fellow student had left unexpectedly, unexpected not only in the ordinary sense of no advance notice but also in that nothing in his conduct or conversation provided a motive. Subsequently, word filtrated to me that he had been pushed out. He had had no power to resist. His period of temporary vows having run out, the superiors had refused to admit him to permanent vows. Such was their legal right. But if the exercise of that legal right had been arbitrary, as I understood, it might help rebut the presumption that it had not been equally arbitrary in my case. By availing myself of Father Provincial's offer, I could see him and establish the facts.

It was a humiliating experience. After a day of apparently aimless meandering from bleak station to bleak station, the train arrived a little after nightfall at the cluster of twenty houses where I had been born. A few stations back, the guard had passed along the tops of the three chubby coaches, carrying a flaming torch to light the single mantleless gas jet in each compartment. But the resulting brightness within was not so great nor the darkness without so dense that I could not distinguish, peering through the window, each landmark, bush, fence, and building. Everything was unchanged and still everything was different. The schoolhouse I had once thought the greatest triumph of architecture since the Pyramids was an oversized barn. The millstream, where once a battle squadron would have seemed not out of place, had so shrunk I could almost step from bank to bank. And that rush of water over the weir that used to make me marvel at the impetuosity of the salmon fighting upstream in October floods, now it seemed scarce to trickle around the gaping stones. The fields behind their low earthen fences topped with gawky, untrimmed whitethorn bushes seemed shrunken to the size of handkerchiefs; the once impenetrable fairy-inhabited forests, to shelter clumps of a dozen trees.

The sleepy train had crossed the country more quickly than my telegram, and I consequently announced my own arrival. My mother was sitting before the fire in the living room when I came in. Her face lighted in a welcome as she saw me, a smile that twisted into pain as she tried to rise. Normally active and agile, she had got a chill that as always had developed into sciatica. She did not speak as I stooped to kiss her, but time and again during the evening she wiped the tears from her eyes and sighed softly at her dreams dissolving in the turf embers. Only several hours later, when I could talk to her alone and tell her my story, did I realize what she had been thinking all the time—that I had come home to stay. What I had to tell her was little less comforting, but she was and is a woman of infinite courage. As a child I had seen her take a kettle of boiling water from the fire, advance upon and disarm a drunken soldier brandishing a revolver. She showed now the same spirit.

"There's not much I can tell you," she said, as she sat on the side of my bed (wincing once in a while from the intense physical pain she was experiencing) and ran her fingers comfortingly through my hair as she used to do when I was little. "You've grown too big for your mother to make decisions for you, even if she wanted to. You have reliable friends in the Congregation who know the facts, and your own conscience, to tell you what is right to do and what not."

Gently she chided me for letters I had written her showing too great disappointment at what had happened and too much anxiety to achieve the goal I had set myself. "Don't think me unsympathetic," she said in tones that left no room to doubt the reality of her sympathy, "but I can't help asking why such anguish. I have ceased to ask God favors. Instead, I say: 'Dear Lord, just give us what is for our salvation, not what we wish.'"

Then, practically, she brought the conversation round to what would have to be done should I finally leave the Congregation. I knew, she assured me, I'd always be welcome home. It mightn't be a bad idea to take a few months to readjust and to make plans. I, however, had already made up my mind on this point. If I hadn't had to make the present visit, I explained, I might perhaps have welcomed the invitation. Now it would cause unnecessary embarrassment to everyone, myself included. "I hope to get enough money to keep me afloat until I find work," I told her. "In the first instance I can go to the others [my brother and sister] in Dublin. It will be soon enough to come back here when I get on my feet."

To be home was good. Here were no tensions, no suspicions. I was among friends who trusted me, whom I could trust. With my family I needed to keep up no pretenses. But when once outside the door, or when aunts and uncles and cousins and friends called, the mask was assumed again. I lived a double life, behaving as was expected of one chosen from thousands for the privilege of the religious life and of the priesthood soon to be conferred, thinking the while of the reality behind the pretense, a reality soon to be published to my confusion and my family's.

Still it was a necessary means to an end. And the end I accomplished a couple of days after Christmas. My sister drove me fifty miles to the meeting place. What I there saw and heard I'll never forget. On a drab, overcast, dark winter afternoon we reached the small gas station on the outskirts of a village a few miles from my former fellow student's home. He was waiting beside the borrowed bicycle, dressed in a shabby suit of clothes and a thin overcoat that half protected him from the bitter wind. A dozen pictures passed flashing through my mind. I saw him a boy on the football field weaving his confident way toward the goal, the ball dancing with his toe, scattering opponents right and left with that inimitable trick of leverage it took me years to learn to counter. I saw him the day he reached the house of studies from the novitiate, neat in his new habit, clean-cut, collected, eager to get down to studies he didn't relish yet never shirked. I saw him dominating the stage, tall and gaunt in his witch's attire, as the curtain went up on *Macbeth* to the question that would now be hard to answer: "When shall we three meet again?" I saw him that last night at recreation before his unexplained disappearance. Then, as always, he had radiated good feeling, good humor, goodness. Only three months ago. And now he had collapsed! It was a pity to look at him, a spiritless parody of himself.

We walked along the road together. He was less bitter

than bewildered, a man clutching animal-like at the slithering walls after the bottom had fallen out of his world. His story was brief. As a first-year student, he had found things a bit tough. The glamour of the novitiate wore off, and philosophy didn't make much sense. He began to ask himself was this for him; and being of frank disposition, explained his doubts to his immediate superior and the Father Provincial, as he understood was his duty. They told him forget it, and so soon he did. But the incident went on the record, and the new Superior of students appointed two years later insisted on probing for himself. My friend could help him little. Vague the first day, two years later his fears were formless and indefinable. The Superior was annoyed, told him he was a difficult type, pig-headed, lacking in frankness. So the matter stood until eleven days before they were due to expire he learned by letter his temporary vows would not be renewed. Father Provincial wouldn't entertain his request for a short extension to give him a chance to show this thing was a misunderstanding. He did, however, promise a good reference should he decide to go on for the priesthood elsewhere. That was his intention, and on leaving he immediately set out to find a religious order or mission society that would take him. He tried three. Each in turn was extremely interested, subject naturally to a satisfactory reference from the previous superiors; and each in turn had dropped him like a hot brick on hearing from Father Provincial.

I left him with a heavy heart and with a heavy heart went back to my monastery. It seemed just what I wanted, independent confirmation of a state of affairs and a manner of acting calculated to rebut the presumption that decisions were being made properly and with impartial justice. But it frightened me. As never before, I realized I was dealing with men whose zeal had blinded them. It was idle to hope any influence short of a directive from the Holy See would budge them from a position publicly adopted. And in my heart I knew a miracle more likely than such a directive.

My petition went, and nothing remained but to wait. I wasn't so ingenuous as not to know it was a chance in a million. I even knew that the decision was most likely to be the avoidance of a decision. Centuries of experience had taught the Roman *Curia* that few judgments equaled those of time, and it had learned that lesson well. I also knew what action I'd take if I proved right in this forecast. I should surrender.

It wasn't pleasant so to decide. I thought about it incessantly. I thought about it as I walked alone in the garden listening to the shouts of the high school boys playing handball on their side of the fence. I thought about it as I lay awake deep into the night. I thought about it as I knelt in the oratory praying for guidance and forcing myself to keep on understanding that the injustice or inadequacy of individuals did not destroy the validity of the principles they proclaimed and didn't practice, nor lessen my obligation to keep on observing those principles so long as I believed them to be right.

It didn't become more attractive by thinking about it. But it became more familiar. And it gave me something to occupy my time. For having decided that in certain circumstances I would leave, I naturally jumped ahead to what next. That question I was badly placed to answer. Of life outside the monastery I knew substantially nothing, other than that the world was wicked and full of the occasions of sin, particularly the big cities. One point, nevertheless, was clear in my mind. Having seen that December evening my former companion going to pieces in a country village in his illusions and disillusionments, I was determined to escape that fate. In the big city I would make myself or lose myself.

I had no precise idea what I might do. Nearly seven years had passed since I entered the novitiate. In all that time I had had scarcely a brushing contact with world events. I had heard about millionaires who had lost fortunes overnight and jumped to death from Wall Street skyscrapers. But that was years ago, and it never occurred to me it was tied in with the job-hunting I might soon start in Dublin. I had never seen the word depression written with a capital nor spoken as I knew frightened men had mentioned the Black Death in the Middle Ages. But I had grown up in Ireland, a country with a perennial excess of intellectual workers and an old-world inelasticity in its job-filling mores. I knew I was too old for the kind of job that required a high school certificate, the only paper qualification I held, and that the civil service was accordingly closed to me. I'd need money to get a university degree or take a law course. If I ever did that, it would be with money I myself earned. My father had for years been denying himself the necessities of life to educate nine children, three of them still in college. At my age, I wasn't going to be a further burden.

There remained the refuge of the desperate, writing. Even I had some notion of the esteem in which that tribe was held. But it had the advantage that it required neither training nor qualifications. And even if it provided little money, it would supply a convenient description until something reputable, a safe ten-dollar-a-week job as a store clerk or commercial schoolteacher should develop. And it was something I could start on right away. Thus began the great novel, of which happily all that survives is the title: *Wet Clay*. It started on the train, the train I should take to Dublin if and when the worst I was anticipating as I wrote happened. From there it led through cheap lodging houses peopled with irreligious, self-centered people interested only in high living and low money-making schemes, to sordid slums where drunkards and dopesters stumbled in the dark of their own rottenness and that of their surroundings. It wandered through gin orgies and dance halls and a dozen other evidences of decadent civilization. It might eventually, if events hadn't been geed up by an American archbishop, have found its way to some subbasement of despair. This American archbishop was papal nuncio to Ireland. He was reputed to conduct nunciature affairs with a dispatch and directness that had not always endeared him to higher-ups among the Irish clergy. I was getting desperate. Seven weeks had crawled by since I mailed my first letter to his Most Reverend Eminence, the Lord Cardinal Prefect of the Sacred Congregation of Religious, and no word had emerged from the marble halls of the Palace of the Apostolic Chancellery, not even an acknowledgment of receipt either of my first missive or the three that had followed with additional data, commentaries, and arguments in compiling which I had occupied the empty days. And they were empty, empty and long. I was free to do whatever I pleased. On the basis of the fiction that my health required it, though the unexplained pains which had provided the excuse for moving me from the house of studies had disappeared within a matter of weeks of my arrival in Limerick, the superior had authorized me to get up when I liked, to go to bed when I liked, to go for walks as often as I could find a companion free and willing to come, to read books from the library at discretion.

I did what I could to occupy the hours. I studied every line of Kate O'Brien's *Without My Cloak*. Kate had taught in a convent only a couple of hundred yards up the road. Her book had disguised ever so slightly place names and houses and people in and about the city. It gave a point to an afternoon's walk to try to track down a particular scene. At hours when the habitual silence within the monastery was suspended, if I found the common room unoccupied, I would play on the phonograph the few items I liked of the small collection of records, over and over again to the point that to this day I can't hear the "Miserere" from *Il Trovatore* or "Liebeslied" without an accompanying picture of that narrow, dark room with straight-backed wooden chairs grouped around a long table, a bare waxed floor, and cheap religious prints on the walls, of the door opening and the intruding face hastily withdrawn on realizing who was inside. That was the worst thing of all. With few exceptions, every face asked the same question I was asking myself, how long more. Every safe-playing free-wheeler in the community kept as far away from me as he self-consciously could. It couldn't go on. I had to find out. And so one day I sat down and wrote the papal nuncio. Briefly I told him who I was, where I was, how I was. But one thing I asked of him, to find out and tell me what was going on. He wasted no time. Within a matter of days, his reply was in my hands. It contained the decision of the Sacred Congregation, the precise decision I had anticipated and feared. Three simple words: "*Parendum superioribus suis*"—"Let him obey his superiors." It settled nothing, for my superiors had given no order I had not obeyed without protest, and the pythian drafter knew that. But it settled everything, and no doubt he also knew that. I was finished. It remained only to gather up what fragments I might.

The fragments were to be few. Many times I had discussed at length with Father Provincial the help I might expect from him to start my life as an independent unit of society. He was as uncooperative as one could be. There was a well-established tradition and all his traditions were written on tablets of stone. The miserable one who left the Congregation was fitted out with clothes and given a rail ticket. The thought of making my living frightened me. True my tastes were simple, but that did not lessen the impact of my first experience of the notion of insecurity. I was habituated to, and constantly reminded of, the security from fear and want provided members of the Congregation from profession to grave. But neither Father Provincial nor Father General would be persuaded to share my concern at the possibility that it would take time to become self-supporting. You have nothing to worry about, Father General wrote. And besides, he added, with what may have been meant as a protection against an implied obligation in that expression of reassurance but to me read as callous indifference, "that is your affair."

Nevertheless, I did still have some nuisance value. They wanted me to go quietly and so we struck a bargain, twenty-five pounds—then the equivalent of one hundred dollars—to stock my wardrobe, and twice that amount as working capital. Father Provincial also gave a firm but verbal undertaking, which later he cynically repudiated, to contribute part of the cost of law school should I raise the balance.

CHAPTER 12

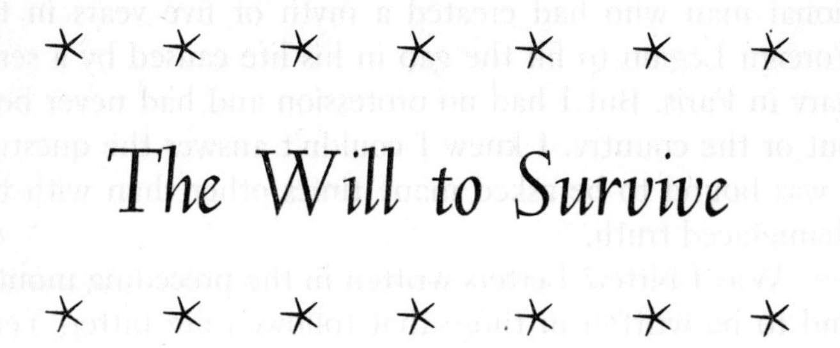

The Will to Survive

At a distance of eighteen or twenty years, it is easy to adopt any one of a half-dozen attitudes in re-creating the emotions experienced while riding to the railway station on the jaunting car that in Limerick had not yet yielded to the taxi. It's not so easy to re-create the shadings of the reality. Superficially, I was full of shame, of the shame of failure and its accompanying stigma in the tight-knit, homogeneous, single-track, Irish social structure. The driver who sat over opposite me, balancing the small suitcase that held the entire of my possessions, and touched his cap as we passed in front of the public church on the way out from the heavy door that had clanged shut behind me forever—he was a member of the eight-thousand-man confraternity attached to the church—would have despised me if he had known the material facts. But he didn't know. I was still wearing the clerical collar and knee-length black jacket we substituted for the habit when traveling. Others, however, must soon know. I had heard of one prominent Dublin professional man who had created a myth of five years in the Foreign Legion to fill the gap in his life caused by a seminary in Paris. But I had no profession and had never been out of the country. I knew I couldn't answer the question I was bound to be asked many times other than with the shamefaced truth.

Was I bitter? Letters written in the preceding months and to be written in those that followed are bitter. Yet I think that, too, was superficial. I was not bitter at the decision that had been made so much as at the way it had been implemented, at the discovery that so many who had professed themselves brothers had, when I needed the understanding and backing and comradeship of a brother, thought only of their own reputation or convenience or vested interest. I was most bitter at the senseless social atmosphere traditional in Ireland both within the Congregation and in the entire community which branded as rejects if not as reprobates all who, in such ways as I, had experienced such things as I. The philosopher endures his neighbor's toothache patiently, but each knows where his own shoe pinches. A few months ago the universal social attitude had been my attitude. Now I saw it for the first time consciously, and, looking at it, saw it as cruel and cruelly unjust.

Both then and in the following months I had many an occasion to be reminded of it, until finally the absurdity of the whole business forced itself on me. For the extraordinary thing was and is that for centuries this single institution of the "spoiled priest" has animated and perpetuated the Irish society which abhors it. One of the many curious features of Irish society is that since the sixteenth century it has had no hereditary ruling class. Generations of English had passed from Harrow and Eton through Oxford and Cambridge to leadership in commerce, politics, and diplomacy. Graduation from these was one's passport not only to success but to belonging. In Ireland, from the day Queen Elizabeth founded Trinity College to perpetuate an alien ruling class designed to maintain its privilege at the point of foreign bayonets, the leaders of the Irish had come the way that I had. For two centuries the only universities the "mere" Irish might attend were the seminaries in exile in Paris and Prague, in Salamanca and Valladolid, in Lisbon and Rome. Leadership was a by-product of these institutions designed to train priests but casting off along the way a full half of the candidates who started on a career to which many were called but few chosen, a leadership that netted the best brains of every economic group in a way impossible in the class preserves of Oxford or Harvard, and that deserved the gratitude of the Irish in that it spiked the Elizabethan plan to repeat in Ireland the system of class privilege the Normans maintained in England over the Anglo-Saxons for a thousand years. For two centuries this leadership held the Irish together underground until by the nineteenth they had recovered enough strength to raise their heads again a little and re-create at home a system of higher education built from the same blueprints. So it has continued, this seminary system, as the basis of Ireland's education and the mechanism to select replacements for industry, commerce, education, and politics. And, nevertheless, with a perversity compound of many complexes, the Irish people expressed in each instance their distaste for the individual they had chosen in this unique way to join their elite.

The coaches had enclosed compartments with seats for ten, five and five facing, and a corridor running down one side of the coach, separated from the compartments by sliding doors. Having arrived early at the station, I found an empty compartment and tried to hide myself in a corner behind a newspaper. But it was not easy to hide me. That strip of celluloid about an inch and a half deep, cracked at several points and discolored from wear, which encircled my neck and was fastened at the back, marked me out. As the train began to fill up, each arrival saw the clerical collar and saluted me respectfully. Cautiously I watched them take their seats, peeping over the edge of the newspaper I pretended to read. They seemed tame, innocuous people, a tight-lipped stockbroker type with brief case, an overweight woman carrying a child in her arms, another woman more smartly dressed who seemed to fit into the horses-and-dogs society of Kate O'Brien's novel, a couple of salesmen who promptly began to swap records of their successes and failures with Limerick buyers. One thing I disliked or at least envied about them all. They were at ease; I wasn't. They belonged; I didn't.

By the time the train began to pull from the station, not only were all the seats full but people were standing outside in the corridor. That was a complication to my plans I hadn't anticipated. I had counted on empty seats in other compartments, must now revise my arrangements. But there was no immediate urgency. To give time to study the next step, I took out a large black-covered notebook and busied myself making an inventory of my worldly possessions. I smiled grimly as I made my notes. Never in the twenty-five years of my existence had I owned so much, and still what I was not wearing went easily in the overnighter, little bigger than a brief case, at my feet. It contained three woolen shirts, a couple of pairs of pajamas of similar material, one pair of shoes, handkerchiefs, underclothing, a pair of cutthroat razors, the inescapable toothbrush. It also held a dozen notebooks like the one in which I was writing, all of them crammed with notes in Irish, English, and Latin written in my not overlegible hand. The black suit I had on had fitted me much better when I bought it seven years earlier, as had the overcoat of clerical gray of the same vintage. In my pocket were twenty-five pounds in cash and documents showing title to fifty more.

The inventory was easy to make and totally unnecessary because my memory held a perfect picture of each worthless item. But the making it helped me steady myself a little. I was hopelessly self-conscious, fancied all eyes followed my every movement, waited for some slip that would betray my sordid secret. But the others loosened up and adjusted themselves for the long journey. The ticket checker made his rounds. One of the men went out and shortly came back. Finally I forced myself to get up and go outside. Unobtrusively I peeped into each compartment. As was to be expected from the people standing or sitting on their bags in the corridor, not a seat was unoccupied. In the next coach, the same situation. Then I reached a Pullman and glanced rapidly inside. It was nearly half empty. That was all I wanted.

I went back to my seat and for a further half-hour occupied myself glancing sightlessly at the newspaper's pages. Then once more, awkwardly and self-consciously, I stood up, this time clutching overnighter in hand, and headed in the direction of the Pullman. As on the previous occasion, as I moved between the seats and walked along the corridor, each man who was wearing a hat raised it briefly. It was a courtesy to which I was accustomed, a courtesy that till then I had felt normal and natural. But now I was humiliated, shattered by each repetition. It was the searing of a red-hot branding iron on my soul, the rubbing of salt in the open sores of my spirit. I wanted to shout to them for God's sake to stop. I wanted to turn and rush back to my seat. I wanted to collapse in tears just where I was. But I did none of these things. The training in self-possession stood me well. I continued on with exterior calm, casually acknowledging each casual salute.

On the way to the Pullman was a toilet, and there while the train sped across the bare February plains of Tipperary, I ripped off my clerical collar. The toilet window was hard to open, but I levered it down a couple of inches, enough to push the yellow-stained celluloid collar and the green-faded black stock through. It was six and a half years since I had knotted a tie, but I managed it. I slipped the bolt, carried my suitcase through to the Pullman, paid the excess, and settled into a seat. I was aghast at my extravagance in thus digging into my slim capital. But there had been no choice. And besides, a grand gesture was in order to mark the end and the beginning.

For, in spite of everything, my mood was not as negative as I had thought it was going to be. There was sadness, there was bewilderment, there was fear of the unknown, but there was also anticipation. My visit two months earlier to my former companion had not helped me in the way I had hoped when I made it. But it had fruited my thinking. I saw what looking in the past had done for him and knew the only way to look was into the future.

Near midnight the train reached Dublin. My sister, a

civil servant, and my brother, a pharmacy student with a part-time job, met me and took me to the apartment they shared. I had so long been used to having my decisions made for me that I found no difficulty in letting them take over. They did it intelligently, with considerable thought for my susceptibilities but with a clear line of policy that revealed itself to me only when already in full effect. The first step was to make me look the way I should. In the morning my clothes had disappeared. In their place were some old ones belonging to my brother, to be worn until I could fit myself out. As for a place to live, they invited me to stay with them as long as I might care, paying my proportionate share of the living costs while I had money.

Everything that followed in this and the following weeks seemed to me perfectly aimless. I was encased utterly within myself, inhibited by my conditioning from expressing to myself and still less to others what I thought or felt or wanted. I had no experience in common with the people I met. Try as they might, they could not establish communication. When friends of my brother or sister dropped in, I didn't know what to say to them. I knew nothing about how their world ticked, didn't even realize at first that it had characteristics, still less that it was important to know about them. What I did see didn't enthuse me. I remember the first time I went to a talking picture. My sister had picked it, I later suspected when I had seen more of the crop of that period, with considerable care. It was *The Private Lives of Henry VIII*, and it simply revolted me. I can still see Charles Laughton rending roast chickens like a ravenous golden eagle, the while scowling amorously at overeager and underdressed wenches. Other movies were still more horrible. The bad taste of the public osculatory clinches, though they had been individually stop-clocked by the censorship, left me tingling with disgust. And with the eye-rolling profligate of *Roman Scandals* I decided I had seen everything and didn't think much of it.

What I couldn't reconcile with this flagrant evidence of social decadence was the way young people I was getting to know seemed to live and think. For in spite of my own shrinking away, I was being infiltrated. There was one young fellow nearly my own age in the shorthand and typing night classes I began to attend immediately in the nearest technical school. For I was going ahead with the idea of writing until something better turned up, and almost the only thing I knew about starting was that shorthand and typing were indispensable for any kind of newspaper job. We were a few years older than the others in the class, and he took the initiative in introducing himself to me. It would never have occurred to me to talk to a stranger, and even when he spoke to me, I gave little encouragement. But he persisted, and soon we would walk up the street together after class was out at nine-thirty. Gradually realization forced itself on me that he had no ulterior object in trying to establish acquaintanceship. He was a revelation to me. He lived in precarious poverty, as did mostly everybody in those Depression years. He earned a few shillings as part-time secretary and researcher for a medical doctor who had literary aspirations. He wasn't particularly ambitious, still less brilliant. But he belonged and was happy about it. He could talk unobtrusively about himself, even succeeded in getting me to tell him a little about the invisible wall that stood between me and the world into which I had been cast. Our ways soon parted. I don't think he ever came to much, but he did help me find myself.

I was still a long way from having established a new equilibrium. My immediate objective was economic independence, and on the spot that seemed even more hopeless than it had from a distance. Several of the priests who had stood by me in the Congregation wrote recommendations to political and business acquaintances. A few interviews followed. But what had I to offer? No skills, no experience quotable in the market place. Yet I had to keep occupied. I had spent so many years of unceasing activity that it was unthinkable just to sit around. I consequently wrote unceasingly. It was unbelievably distasteful, but I forced myself to keep at it. The routine I established called for a thousand words a day, seven days a week, and I stuck to it like that for an entire year, making up the following day if on the previous one I fell short of target. I had no guidance, for I didn't know a single professional writer; and even if I had, I doubt if I'd have plucked up courage to put myself in his hands and be dissected in my nakedness. In fact, I was so anxious to cover up my writing identity that I played myself a curious trick. Ireland is an officially bilingual country. One may use freely either the Irish or the English form of one's family name, and these two forms are usually entirely different. As up to that time I had habitually used the English form, the Irish seemed to provide a suitable disguise for publication. Which made no immediate difference while I accumulated rejection slips but in the long run made me known to so many by the Irish form that I followed the line of least resistance and learned to know myself by it.

And the rejection slips began to accumulate at the rate of three or four a week; in fact, in exactly the same number as the offerings to editors. In retrospect, there was nothing surprising about this. I didn't even know what I have come to recognize as the first rule of writing for periodical publication, to tell people about things within their sphere of interests and the writer's personal experience; and even if I had, it would have helped little since I knew next to nothing about my potential readers' interests and my limited experiences belonged in a world of their own. I had never heard the magic words, "Study your market," consequently didn't know that an article of seven hundred and fifty words or of twenty-five hundred came back unread by the editor who wanted only from one thousand to fifteen hundred. But my ignorance didn't stop me trying. I rehashed articles from all kinds of sources, encyclopedias, reference books, travel books, old magazines, whatever I could root out in the public library. I tried my hand at short stories. I even wrote several chapters of a pulp novel, a spy adventure set in Poland during the first World War.

There was no pleasure in it. Every line was written in blood. I was obsessed with the notion which teachers of composition at school used, and for all I know, continue to propagate, that the writer must have style. When I got a sentence down, it looked jerky, horrible. It didn't flow, didn't hide the absence of thought. I would take a book and search page after page until I'd find a sentence I could plagiarize or bowdlerize, and thus build up my day's quota of a thousand words, using as few as possible of my own. It was certainly the hard way. Far easier, as I concluded much later, to have something to say, say it, and stop.

But even this hit-and-miss method didn't always miss. Never shall I forget that morning. There was not then, nor for long to come, place in my budget for such luxuries as a penny for a newspaper, and so each morning I walked to the library to glance through the papers in the reading room. It was sort of depressing in the early morning. It hadn't taken me long to realize who were the kind of people to frequent the reading room at that hour. A few were regulars, vagrants, or unemployables, interested in passing the time. Most of the others were job-hunters, pinched, worried, shabbily dressed, furtively scanning the Help Wanted columns before starting another day of footsore door-knocking. I, too, went methodically through the Help Wanted, though without serious hope of finding anything that way, but I also turned the pages to see what was doing in the contributed features. It was gradually dawning on me that ideas for articles might be suggested by articles published. Besides, I had to keep on hoping that one would finally not win a rejection slip. And there it was, across three columns on the editorial page of one of Dublin's morning papers, an article on the Holy Year that had been extended to the world.

My first reaction was one of disappointment. Somebody had succeeded where I had tried and failed. Perhaps it was a friend of the editor, or perhaps just somebody who knew more about the subject or wrote better than I did. Then I began to read. It was familiar, but that wasn't surprising, for after all it was the same topic. No, it was more than that, those were the phrases I had written. How could it be? Was it possible somebody in that office shamelessly appropriated other people's ideas? Only then did my eye light on what was standing out on the page, in a box in heavy type in the middle of the article. By me. My by-line, even if I then didn't know the word. My knees suddenly didn't seem to want to hold. That sensation had come over me once before, at Mass the first morning in the novitiate. Eddies of fog had begun to swirl around the candles on the altar. I closed my eyes and when I opened them I was lying on top of a wide chest of drawers in the sacristy and the priest, still in his vestments, was dashing little sips of cold water from a glass into my face. Now the fog was swirling again. It had caught up my name from where it stood out in the middle of the page on the high reading stand and was swinging it up and down as an altar boy jerks a thurible to keep the charcoal alight. I gripped the stand with all my might and refused to let my eyes shut. I could hear a clock tick, each tick a lifetime. And after several lifetimes, the fog began to dissipate and the name finally settled again in one plane on the page.

Cautiously, with the elaborate carefulness of one who is drunk and knows it, I picked my steps to the other room where there were seats and desks for students. I was elated, and frightened. Elated for obvious reasons. Frightened at the irrevocability of publication, at the thought of thousands of readers, thousands of critics, dissecting each word, at the possibility of someone discovering that huge chunks had been extracted verbatim from encyclopedias, at the public disclosure that I had perpetrated a huge hoax, knew nothing whatever about the subject.

But the die was cast. If I had doubts previously about my career, I knew that morning they had ceased. I might have to take other jobs. I did have to take other jobs. When the check arrived in payment, the vast, unbelievable amount of one guinea, I went straight out and put the entire sum as a down payment on a typewriter.

The city recovered from the experience, and even I finally got my feet on the earth again. There were neither telegrams of congratulation nor letters of denunciation. In fact, when it all boiled down, the only practical difference was that I had a new portable Underwood and the obligation to pay a guinea a month for twelve more months.

That was the time I got my first steady job. The job was teaching and in three weeks I was fired. It was an amazing institution which confirmed absolutely my convictions that the world was crazy. They coached teen-agers, mostly those who had flunked or hadn't done as well as darling parents thought they should have done in third- and fourth-year high school, giving quick preparation courses for university entrance, railway, civil service, and similar examinations. In Ireland nobody accepts anybody else's examinations, which makes a lot of business for coaches. My job was part-time, twenty-four hours a week, and paid fifteen pence an hour, which—if one was tempted—would have given six dollars a week, not counting the banker's commission.

It was supposed to be a very slick operation, each course geared to a specific need. Actually, the place was like a madhouse. The teachers on the day shift—there were seven or eight of us—met each morning a few minutes before nine in a little foyer scarcely bigger than a closet and decided which classes each would take. As far as I could discover, nobody was in charge, and the nearest thing to a principle in the allocation of the classes was that nobody taught the same subject twice running. That suited the students perfectly. Mr. So-and-so, who took whatever class yesterday, had forgotten always to prescribe home lessons. They were a hard-bitten crowd, those city slickers, and it didn't take them long to discover that they were three jumps ahead of me. I knew nothing of them, their ways, or their problems. The crisis came when a fish of substantial dimensions, which one of the bright boys had decided would enliven the dullness of class, was fumbled by a catcher, shot through the window, and found a reputable citizen between it and the street four floors below. The proprietor of the school in the ensuing inquiry found me guilty of a grave dereliction of duty. I was slightly outraged, not realizing that the ability to be at a given window ahead of a flying dead fish is no less a part of the successful professor than a familiarity with Latin supines. But I was conditioned to taking correction in silence, didn't even dare ask for the week's pay I had earned.

Only gradually did I begin to realize something of the enormity of losing one's first job inside three weeks. I hadn't been long enough at the school to establish more than superficial acquaintanceship with any of the professors, but several people—friends of members of my family, relatives—concerned with my progress didn't succeed in hiding their reactions entirely. One, a friend of my sister and a lady sufficiently my senior to be heard with respect, didn't mince her words.

"It's a great pity," she said severely but not unfriendlily, "that this thing didn't work out. I know you were paid practically nothing, but it was a toe-hold. If you made a success, in a couple of years it would lead to something better. Teaching is the one thing you are equipped to do, and this was the way in."

For my part, teaching was the last career I wanted. Besides, my attitude toward the entire episode was one of defiance rather than penitence. Nevertheless, I preferred to deflect rather than bear against the thrust. I was working on something much more important, I told her, the first of a series of cultural and uplift booklets for which I had got a contingent commission. If I could deliver the goods, I should be paid four pounds apiece for ten-thousand-word pamphlets. "Even if each takes two weeks, I'll still come out better financially," I concluded in triumph.

She shook her head. "There's no future in it," she said decisively. "One month, two months, you may do well. But that kind of life is too insecure. How can you ever hope to make a home, get married, raise a family? One of my closest friends tries to do that—he's on Fleet Street now. One year they are in clover, the next penniless."

But I wouldn't be convinced. I lived in a world of my own, very concerned indeed with the need to pay my way but lacking the practical experience of the workings of economic laws which made those around me shudder at my cavalier disregard for security. I had set myself up a budget on which I found I could live, twenty-seven shillings and sixpence a week as my share of the apartment and food, a further ten shillings for outside meals, a few cigarettes, or an ounce of tobacco. For transport I was able to borrow a bicycle as needed. Of my original seventy-five pounds, twenty had gone on clothes. The balance would keep me twenty-nine weeks on my budget. I had grossed three pounds from my teaching and a few more from articles published. The booklets project, though still in its infancy, promised a further important contribution. I was convinced that one way or another it would be a year before the savings account would be empty. And so I bade farewell without regret to the ferule.

The reactions of my friends were, I suspected, motivated in large degree by the fear I'd end up a drifter unless I soon found an anchorhold. I couldn't entirely blame them for adopting that attitude because I was myself conscious the danger existed. But I was convinced that the process of mental adjustment would have far less chance of reaching a satisfactory conclusion if I let myself be maneuvered into a mediocre security that failed to offer goals commensurate with my aspirations. I was in fact beginning to become aware, concurrently with the slim improvement in my material fortunes, of the pressing need to restore interior harmony. It was starting to concern me that I was so completely turned in on myself, not indeed hankering after a past I knew was gone, but unable to enthuse over a future that displayed no inducements calculated to make me go eagerly in search of it.

A former companion helped me bring this problem into focus. He had left the Congregation about a year before I did and had accordingly been a longer time thinking it over.

"Did you ever hear the story of the Arab chieftain who was approached by a spokesman for an American oil syndicate," he asked one day. "The American sketched a good selling picture of the comfort and luxury he could substitute for the barrenness of his splendid isolation. It called for no effort on his part. He had only to give the go-ahead and the royalty dollars would gush into his lap."

"And the Arab's decision?"

"He thought it over for several weeks. Then he told the intermediary to tell his principals he was sorry he could have no part in such a project. He didn't like the idea of votes for women."

"That's very subtle," I said, "a little too subtle for me." I had been expressing my disapproval of the jazz craze and suggesting it was the duty of the public authorities to stamp it out. I couldn't see what an isolationist Arab chieftain passing Sphinx-like judgments as he sat in the shade of his fig tree had to do with the matter.

"It's not subtle at all," my friend replied testily. "You and I have simply got to face the fact that a society is all of one piece. Even the apparently most irrelevant excrescences on its body are a part of it. To eliminate one of them starts a chain reaction that may end by destroying the entire body or at least changing its nature."

I wasn't yet prepared to admit that my friend's allegory was applicable. But it stuck in my mind and helped me gradually to a realization that I was now cast in a milieu that required for its domination a set of physical and mental habits, of ways of thinking and objects of thought, of scales of values and attitudes different—if not in kind at least in substantial degree—from those proper to the cloistered, noncompetitive organization of the monk. It was understandable, probably inevitable, that I should at first have approached my survival problem with something of the pragmatic selectivism proposed by the American businessman to the Arab. Entrenched in the fortress of my intellectual hauteur, I would dictate my own terms, accept and reject as I thought fit. But the Arab's summing-up of human nature was more accurate. He undoubtedly believed himself capable of the *tour de force* of riding from oasis to oasis in a Model T Ford, perhaps even of keeping a coke in the icebox, while refusing to take in the morning paper. But he knew the resultant freak would be as sterile as hybrids are wont to be.

The companion with whom I had this illuminating exchange was one of four or five who had left the Congregation during the year preceding my leaving and who had gravitated like me to Dublin. They had spent varying periods in the monastery and each faced in varying degree the task of readjustment. None of them had at this time had any notable success either in finding a job or in establishing a new emotional equilibrium. Those whose parents could afford to put them through university or professional school had usually the easiest passage. The three or four years of studies with people younger than themselves gave a chance to resume growth where they had left off, and reach a reasonably normal social attitude by the time they had to make a living. They then also found themselves in a cultural group more on a level with their monastic experience. The others, for all their liberal learning, had nothing to offer in the labor market. Three of my immediate friends, after groping around Dublin at random for months, trying to absorb a smattering of some trade or skill by means of a canned course, crossed to London where they found jobs in saloons. And a headful of Saint Thomas is a poor preparation to integrate one into the stratum where one belongs as a bartender in England's rigidly compartmented society. They'd have been better off, and made more money too, in similar jobs in Dublin. But that was out of the question. Trades unions are much stronger in Ireland; and try as they might, none of them could pull strings to wangle a card.

While they were still in Dublin, we spent much time together, in libraries or other places where we could talk without spending the money we didn't have. As a rule we hadn't much to say to each other, but we shared the same frames of reference and understood each other's silences as others didn't. With the daring that comes of numbers, we even ventured out occasionally to explore the jungle. We discovered it was possible by standing an hour or two in line to get into the back gallery of the Gaiety, the famous "gods" where you quickly got used to feet in your back. It cost only ninepence, tenpence if there was a specially elaborate musical comedy with full London cast. White Horse Inn, with its revolving stage and syrupy sentimental songs so enthralled me that I went back a second time, an extravagance paid by passing up lunch.

But I don't think I could have recognized and consequently enjoyed White Horse Inn for the piece of unsophisticated escapism that it was, if it hadn't been for a lecture on social behavior patterns to which one of the group of my ex-companions had subjected me. One of the rare treats in which we indulged was a visit to the deep-carpeted luxury of the Savoy Restaurant where, for a charge of ninepence apiece for a pot of coffee and cookies, we might spend a couple of rubber-necking hours. We were spectators, not true members of the cross-section of the public that came and went, buying their few moments of illusion at the price of stinting themselves for the rest of the week of things statistically far more necessary. We hadn't established communication with them or their motives, though externally we sought to ape them, to behave as though we did. But at least we were making some progress in thought exchange. Among ourselves we were learning to express our ideas with a freedom unthinkable while bound by the conventions of our former life.

"You know, I never thought it was going to be anything like this," I said with an apologetic half-laugh. There had been a moment of awkward silence following scattered applause at the end of a session of the small orchestra led by a bony-armed woman who made her violin sob and gasp and laugh mischievously as she bowed with tempestuous angular grace. "I mean to say—oh, I don't know what I mean—but you know all the things we used to hear about the temptations of the world and that sort of thing."

My companion—we were but two on this occasion—was a soul-searching, solitary, neurotic type, who had read more psychology than I thought was good for him. I had known him intimately for twelve years, yet never was sure how he'd react to any given remark. "For Christ's sake, shut up," he had said savagely one day when he saw I was trying to make polite conversation. Now he seemed not to have heard my remark. He stared moodily ahead of him for a considerable time. Then he spoke.

"I'm going to shock you with what I'm going to say. Or at least I hope I am, because the way I've been seeing things lately, we all could do with a good shocking to wake us up to the facts of life.

"You probably imagine that you divide the world into two kinds of people, the good people who live in monasteries, and the wicked people who cheat and steal and fornicate and batten on the misery of their kind. But you don't really. You divide them into three kinds. You are overlooking the people you know well either directly or by association. They don't fit into your prefabricated categories. The people you know well—your relatives, my relatives, the people you are living with—you know they are not bad people, as your myth would have it. They live good lives. They have good instincts."

He seemed to be persuading himself rather than me. And as he spoke, he drew lines on the tablecloth with the blade of a knife, many parallel lines close together to help him keep his thinking from slipping to one side or the other. "Now I begin to see what's wrong with the lot of us," he continued with a deliberation that seemed to be oratorical but more likely was caused by a determination to get it just right. "We're too damn superior. We don't want to be like the rest of men. We want to maintain for ourselves an illusion. But if you break down that faceless monster you have invented into its component human individuals, you will find each of them very much like yourself or the people you know. Each makes an effort to lead a decent life. Each has good instincts."

"Is that the whole story," I asked. He seemed to have come to a full stop.

"That's about enough for one quick lesson. What more do you want?"

"And the shocking part?"

"Aren't you shocked enough?"

"No," I said, "I'm really not. You see the funniest thing happened to me the other night. You know the D'Oyly Carte company that was playing here last week. Well, they were staying—not the stars, but the rank and file—up in McCarthy's in Charlemont Street. My brother had a room there one time, and he dragged me along to a party after the show finished.

"And there they went on till four in the morning, singing the choruses from the operettas and drinking the odd bottle of stout and trying to initiate us into the mysteries of the old English game of shove-halfpenny. Everyone was having a wonderful time, but what I was thinking all the time was what you have put in words. I mean to say, they were people of no consequence, when you boil it down. But they were all right. They've got something. It takes people, an awful lot of people like that to keep the world going."

"Now you're getting somewhere," he said. And dropped the subject.

We often got to talking, sometimes sarcastically, sometimes bitterly, sometimes seriously as on this occasion, about the misleading impression that had been instilled in us about these people who made up the mass of humanity. In the emphasis on the perfection of the religious state, lauded and developed—naturally enough—in order to encourage those who had undertaken it to continue in it, the picture had been simplified to the specifications for an advertising poster or the propaganda blasts of a great power preparing aggression, presenting all within the monastery as white and all outside as black.

I think we were perhaps even a bit disappointed at the beginning at the inaccuracy of the picture. Some of the spectacular villainy we had been expecting would surely have been worth seeing. And it would have been relatively easy to retain a moral attitude of outright opposition and rejection, to live in the world but not of the world, behind virtuous stockades like settlers in Indian territory, if the world had been simply wicked. Instead, it was appearing, more and more, complicatedly dull. These people we were getting to know by rubbing shoulders with them in rooming houses, on the street, in libraries and restaurants, led lives that were spectacular only in their monotony. They could expect, and seemed to ask for, little of pleasure or excitement. If some of them were spectacularly wicked, they hid it quite successfully. That some were spectacularly good was more evident, particularly if one took the trouble to follow the crowds of able-bodied unemployed who hurried through their morning ritual of signing at the euphemistically titled Labor Exchange to be in time for the last Mass at the Pro-Cathedral.

As my friend's analysis of the situation indicated, all this discussion and criticism was no carry-over of hair splitting on our part. Though we were but vaguely conscious of it, this was for each a matter of vital concern. We were experiencing a crisis of spiritual readjustment, and on the success of that process, the ability of each to fix himself workable norms and satisfying goals, was to depend the entire subsequent attitude, to himself, to life, and to the world.

Two questions called for decision, the external and the internal. We had been habituated to a set of devotional practices occupying several hours daily, plus the additional tuning up of a monthly day of recollection and two similar five-day periods each year, all set into the broad framework of a life devoted expressly to the service of God. In our first weeks we tried, each in his own circumstances, to keep what we could of this pattern. But it couldn't be done. The needs of the body were too immediate. The hours made free for spiritual contemplation by the monastic organization had now to be devoted to the activities required for keeping alive and looking after our affairs as independent units of society.

But there was more to it than that. There was the growing realization that we had the choice to live in a vacuum, unable to contribute to the community in which we were destined to live, or make ourselves a part of it if we were to influence it. That is why I accepted tranquilly and indeed gratefully the remarks of my companion when he told me stop thinking of myself as on a pinnacle of superiority above the people around me. I wanted to contribute. The sense of vocation which had carried me into a monastery and had made me fight to the end to stay there was not to be gainsaid. And if it was necessary to stop classifying myself as an out-of-scrics unit of an elite in which I was no longer numbered, then I would identify myself wholeheartedly with the mass while not abandoning hope that in some way I couldn't see this lump should prove a leaven.

External events were conspiring to enable me to apply my new theory to the test of practice. About this time I made contact with a man who was to help create the situation that would establish me as a reporter. Such a development was far from my mind when I first came to know him. He was not many years my senior, devotee of one of the least commercialized of the theoretical sciences. He was a folklorist. Having studied modern techniques of collection and classification in Sweden, he had set out with the one-track enthusiasm of the zealot to create in Ireland an organization to gather up the fragments surviving in the rapidly shrinking islands of the old culture still to be found in most parts of the country but mainly in such mountain-locked valleys near the coast as I had known during my student vacations. After years of derision, he was beginning to get somewhere. The university had agreed to provide office space, the government to set up a Folklore Commission and provide funds for a small field organization. While the wheels of state ground creakingly, he was lining up personnel. At the instance of a mutual friend he agreed to look me over. I liked him from the first moment, his single-purposedness, disinterestedness, enthusiasm, and a sense of humor and anecdotal skill which prevented his conversation—always on his affection—from becoming professorial monotony.

Though he shied instinctively from commercialization of his specialty, he was alive to the existence of commercial angles; and when he learned of my interest in popular writing, he didn't hesitate to encourage me to cash in on curiosities he had come across in field investigations. We batted the project back and forth. It would be months in any case before the Folklore Commission would come officially into existence, and the research I'd have to do would be good preparation for the job as folklore collector I might then get.

He knew more about my business than I did myself, discarding a dozen subjects he'd have preferred to see publicized in favor of an idea he thought salable to one of the English Sunday papers. Many of them then printed editions slanted at Irish readers and had the same penchant for the quaint and bizarre as has *Time* in its coverage of the rest of the world. The subject, traditional crafts, in fact a fascinating study. I sent out a letter to a half-dozen news editors, got back a cautiously favorable reply from the *Daily Express* which would pay two guineas an article for any it liked, an enthusiastic one from the *Sunday Graphic* anxious to sign a series at five guineas apiece.

It was a fantastic amount of money, five guineas, enough to keep me alive three weeks on my budget. What I didn't realize till later was that the payment was the least part of the benefit. I was in. The articles were a lot of fun, each an interview with a leading exponent of a folk craft and a description based on on-the-spot observation of his skills. The most exciting was a moonless night spent crouching under a turf bank in a remote wilderness of peat bog, reassuring bird calls coming in at intervals from sentries posted at the four points of the compass, while the hot *poitín* (moonshine whisky) dripped from the worm of a home-made still.

These articles brought me into contact with a great many people, and I was simultaneously expanding my circle of acquaintances as a result of other assignments I had obtained as well as through my continuing search for a regular job. But the contacts with people were still to a large extent formal and superficial. Though I had begun to realize the importance of personal relations, I still didn't know how to translate this new theory into practice. The truth was I had little appreciation of people as people. The rigid division of mankind into we and they was not easily dislodged. They of the outside world had concerned us in the monastery to a considerable extent, especially in our moral theology studies, but as his specimens a butterfly collector. We of the monastery had been trained to live and think as independent units, to maintain relations on the intellectual level and repress emotional reactions. Only gradually did it come home to me that this kind of mental discipline was not the norm, and until it did, I approached the people I met on the assumption that they made their decisions like intellectual automata. I had little concept of the complicity of motives and emotions involved in the daily dealings of business life, of the powerful bonds that join even those who as competitors form the units of any given trade or industry or other activity carried on in a given society. I thought of the energy of the community as the physicists used to think of the energy of the universe, a fixed amount which changed its forms according to unchangeable laws without changing its total quantity. The intangibles scarcely entered my calculations. I little realized that my wares would be more easily salable if I made friends with those who might have occasion to buy them, still less that I could have in many cases secured the help and support of my competitors simply by asking for it. The naïve belief was firmly established that making one's living was like the hunting of wild animals for food in the jungle, that what each ate was snatched from the snarling teeth of others. It was a naïve belief but it caused me much unnecessary unhappiness.

But even if it was naïve, its existence was not surprising. I had been rejected by the only society in which I had put down roots. My integration into that society had begun at an age so early that I had not yet reached the stage of growing up in which I was conscious of belonging. I had consequently no place to which to return emotionally, was in fact so uprooted that it was only gradually dawning on me that I was missing a great deal. And in addition there was the subconscious fear, arising out of the previous rejection, that if I offered the hand of friendship, I might be rejected again. The initiative for my integration into society could not come from me. Outsiders had to crash their way in and had to do so not only tactfully but in circumstances in which my suspicious mind could impute to them no selfish motives.

Probably my experience would have been similar if I had wormed my way into some other group, but the actual group into which I did worm my way, remote and suspicious, was that of Dublin's newspapermen. The same daily newspaper in which I had my first success published three or four more articles in the following nine months, was additionally impressed by the stream of those its editors read and rejected. The start of the series in the London Sunday paper clinched the argument. Just over a year after my unenthusiastic arrival in Dublin I was a staff reporter on a metropolitan daily.

I was still so far from knowing what it was all about that I was scarcely even surprised at my good fortune. But what did surprise me was my reception when I went on my first assignments, I mean my reception by my colleagues from the other dailies. As an outsider, I had known that bitter rivalry existed between the dailies, and with my notions of what went on in the jungle of competitive business, I anticipated less than civility from my competitors. I could scarce believe my ears, accordingly, when a stranger introduced himself at the press table as a reporter from our bitterest rival. I remember he addressed me in Irish, for the event was the annual convention of a cultural society, and the proceedings were entirely in that language.

"You're the new man on the *Irish Press*," he said with an affable handshake. "They told me about you when I called up to find who was covering this. There is nothing to it, the usual wind storm, worth three quarters of a column. I have the names and texts of the speeches. There's a room outside where we can type. Just ask me if you meet up with a problem."

I was suspicious. I had run into a crackpot, or perhaps there was a trick and a lot of phony stuff was being palmed off on me. I checked each detail. There was no trick.

On each succeeding assignment the same treatment. Strangers introduced themselves. "You're the new man? You stick with me. I'll show you the ropes." In the Dáil (Parliament) they explained how to get rush copies of the official note-takers' verbatims. In the courts they gave me "blacks" of their summaries of tricky cases.

This experience was a most valuable one in restoring my faith in mankind, providing a practical demonstration that the world didn't live on self-interest alone. Gradually, unbelievingly, I was initiated into an elaborate system of camaraderie that protected violently conflicting interests through a code depending on decency and good faith. Unwritten law divided assignments into special and routine.

The special consisted of stories originating either in the fertile imagination of the news editor or the ingenuity of the reporter. Here each was on his own. There was neither collusion nor collaboration. But these were the exceptions. Most day-to-day work was routine stuff, coverage of events in the public domain, law courts, political gatherings, conventions, city council, annual meetings. Here each helped all get the facts. If one could make a better story with the facts, good luck to him. But getting them was a joint operation. The principle was carried to the extreme that if nobody turned up at an assignment from one newspaper, it became the duty of his competitors to find through the grapevine why he hadn't. If it emerged that the paper had overlooked the assignment, the matter dropped. Nobody helped a rival newspaper. But if a man had been assigned and hadn't made it, even if he had gone fishing or was sleeping off an overdose of liquor, he got a "black." One didn't let a colleague down.

I suppose all of this scarcely meant a thing to my fellow newsmen. They took it as normal. They had sailed the trade routes to port in well-manned ships, their papers validated. I was making a desperate landfall, clinging to the battered branches of my uprooted tree. It had been a lonely voyage of the rejected soul since the day it was driven from the garden in which it had expected always to live in enjoyment of the fruits of brotherhood. And now, unexpecting, unbelieving, I was having heaped on my head burning proofs that people still existed ready to share their privileges, to look on me, accept me as one of them. I did not suddenly become an undifferentiated part of the social mass, nor did my atypical intellectual and moral conditioning cease to affect my ways of thinking and acting. But the willful apartness was over, the rest a gradual settling process that would ultimately enable me to look without bitterness on the unnecessary unpleasantnesses, to reach the stage of detachment where I could sit long by the pool of memory, casting casual pebbles in its depths and recording the broken reflections that rippled outward each time the surface of the waters was moved.

But valuable as was the feeling of being wanted, still another element was needed for peace of mind, the sense of having a contribution to make, an object worthy of one's efforts and capabilities. The experiences through which I had passed had not obscured for me the spiritual interpretation of life or the need for social and spiritual as well as economic goals. And I had the fortune in my early newspaper days to establish friendship with a fellow newsman who straightened me out on this point. He didn't impress me the first time. He was low-sized, inconsequential-looking, and considerably older than me. His clothes hung loose. A few pathetic hairs clung to the top of his head.

But for reasons best known to himself, he took the trouble to penetrate my reserve. Soon I was a regular caller at his home. He seemed to have an intuitive understanding of my mental state and of how to get my thinking into perspective. By normal standards, he hadn't been particularly successful, but it didn't take me long to realize that the reason was that he hadn't particularly wanted to. His interests lay elsewhere. Like many Irishmen of his generation, he had spent years in and out of jails and internment camps, traveling under aliases with a price on his head. At least twice he had survived hunger strikes of several weeks. I always suspected that part of the wisdom derived from those experiences was his unconcern with success. But he understood the principle of cause and effect and took pleasure in explaining for me the steps one had to take to achieve a particular purpose.

"You should go into politics," he urged me one day. "It doesn't matter much which party. Join a political club. Go to the meetings. Make yourself useful. It takes little to stand out in the average group. Get on delegations. Get to know the top people."

I didn't take that particular advice literally. But I remembered it and appreciated more the speaker for having given it to me. Though it revealed no particular profundity of wisdom in him, it did reveal an appreciation of my needs. The principle was valid for many circumstances.

He had a perspective of history and of the influence of the self-possessed individual on the course of events that was valuable to me in that it stressed again, at a moment when I seemed overwhelmed by the weight of circumstances, the fact of which I first became conscious when I had read Jörgensen's autobiography, that one can find the means to do the things one really wants to do. Though in many respects unorthodox in his political and religious views, he didn't stand for the idea of man as the prisoner of blind, uncontrollable forces. For him, man was the sculptor and the world his marble. Nothing was sacred merely because it happened to be the way it was. His mind constantly rearranged the people and things with which he came in contact, estimating the while with a mental agility that approached intuition the economic, social, and political stresses, checks, and balances that would result from each rearrangement of physical and mental forces.

One day we were in the country together, we climbed a hill to view the countryside. It was a low hill a few hundred feet above fertile lands rich with corn, potatoes, sugar beet, and rolling meadows, to south and east and north. But westward the view was different. It was typical of the middle and west of Ireland, an expanse to the horizon of dark, forbidding peat bog covered only by clumps of heather, bushy plants consisting mainly of thin, wiry dark-brown branches and topped with tiny clusters of new foliage and flowers, green, gray, and purple. Between black, open banks, where peat had been cut away for fuel, lay pools of dark-brown sluggish water.

"Cromwell knew what he was doing," I remarked as I studied the bleak landscape.

"Yes," agreed my friend. "It was Hobson's choice, wasn't it: 'To hell or to Connaught!' "

He sat on a stone, took an envelope from his pocket, and drew on it a rough outline map of Ireland. "But the funny part," he said as he sketched, "is that it would be dead easy to get rid of all those swamps and double the country's land resources.

"This is how Ireland looks, an oval saucer, mountains ringing a vast plain. See how much of the plain is drained by one river, the Shannon, which starts in the north and runs due south, falling steadily all the way. To lower the mean level of the entire watershed ten feet would be the simplest thing in the world. There are few barriers to excavate. Most of the drains and canals would run through soft earth. The levels are right. Primitive peoples have perfected more elaborate drainage systems. Think how small the effort with today's machines . . ."

"And the effect," I asked.

"The effect?" He plucked a stem of wild rye grass and

began to chew it meditatively. He wasn't pausing to collect his thoughts. He knew exactly what he was getting at. But he wanted to make sure it would sink in. "The effect would be the elimination of all that barrenness. Once you get the water out, it's a simple thing to reduce acidity of the peat and condition it so that the soil's micro-organisms will thrive. Look back behind you. Look north or south. It could all be like that—rich, arable land."

"I know," I said. "But I didn't quite mean that. I can see perfectly well that a scheme like this would change the lives of all the people who live among the bogs. I suppose it would make them comparatively rich. But would it make them better off? I mean to say—"

He checked me with a gesture as though to say he understood exactly what I was driving at. But he knew something more. He knew the deeper motivations that underlay the attitude I was expressing. And that was why what he had to say carried so great an impact. He never spoke directly about my past. But I knew that he had in his own way learned a good deal about it, and when we talked, we assumed this past as part of our common knowledge.

"You've read travel books about Ireland," he now said. "You know what every outsider who looks at us says, that we are so immersed in the life to come as to be indifferent about the present one."

He looked at me with a quizzical smile. "I think the criticism is valid of a lot of us, but I didn't think I'd catch you in that particular heresy. It is a heresy, you know. It's not only Aristotle who showed you must be able to combine moderate comfort and moderate leisure to become a philosopher. The theologians know that the poverty-stricken have a tough job leading a Christian life. You know that grace builds on nature. A high level of prosperity and culture is no hindrance but a singular help to virtue."

Chagrined at having the tables completely turned on me, I made a desperate effort to recover. "From what I hear," I said, "the experience with the people moved by Dublin Corporation from the slums into new apartments hardly bears you out."

He just laughed at me, a friendly laugh without sting. That was typical of him. When he won an argument, he never exploited his advantage. "Let's go," he said, hopping effortlessly to his feet. "But you think that over."

I thought it over and it made good sense. From boyhood I had always thought that Alexander the Great must have been something of a half-wit if—as the story goes—he wept on reaching the conviction there were no more worlds to conquer. It seemed beyond comprehension that an intelligent man could fail to see that more was calling to be done than the little already accomplished.

Now I began to see that I was behaving as petulantly as Alexander and with as little reason. Just because the specific social and spiritual goal to which I had aspired had been denied me, it did not follow that within the limitations imposed by the need to make a living I could not and should not pursue social and spiritual as well as economic goals. I knew without hesitation that material success for its own sake did not constitute a satisfying and adequate human ambition. The gravitational pull of the spirit to selfless activity was a fact of existence too obvious to be denied. Only by deliberately and determinedly refusing to think about it, the rejection of grace in the language of theology, can a man fail to set himself a spiritual purpose. What the insinuations of my friend did was to make me understand that the particular work to which one has to devote the greater part of one's time and energies in order to live is not an enemy of one's social and spiritual ambitions. So long as it helps to advance the common good at any level and one performs it as best one can and with the proper motives, that is enough.

And so I gradually came to see my place in the economy of the universe, to take the situations in which a force greater than I placed me and mold them in the directions in which my conscience told me it was desirable they should be molded, to the extent of my ability. It was long a disappointment to be unable to put to more than casual use the specialized training to which many years had been devoted. But I forced myself to recognize that was unimportant. And besides I never felt my years had been wasted. In addition to the opportunity to know intimately so many unusual people, in addition to the rare moral and spiritual experience, there was the amassment of knowledge. And knowledge delights the mind. Even when unpriced in the market place, it is good to hold for its own sake, enjoyable though nothing accrues of consequence beyond the using.

This wisdom was not born overnight. New tissue no more grows on the torn soul than on the mangled body in an hour. And even grown, the scar long disfigures. But the success of the graft was assured once I was able to see again that there was goodness in people as well as selfishness and pettiness, that though I didn't understand the reason for the things that happened to me, they had a meaning. I no longer clutched at a past that was gone, since there was still a future to which to aspire. Unreluctantly I closed a chapter, knowing it was in my hand to turn the page and begin another. Life was again worth living. It had not ceased to be a mystery, a mystery that was glad and sad, wretched and glorious. But it still made sense, if not in the bits and pieces, the broken pictures of people and scenes and events, the Pyrrhic victories over circumstances and the bitter defeats at their hands, at least in the deeper triumphs of the soul that with the aid of faith's illumination recognizes harmony in the noise, design in the doodling, beauty in the splashed pigments.